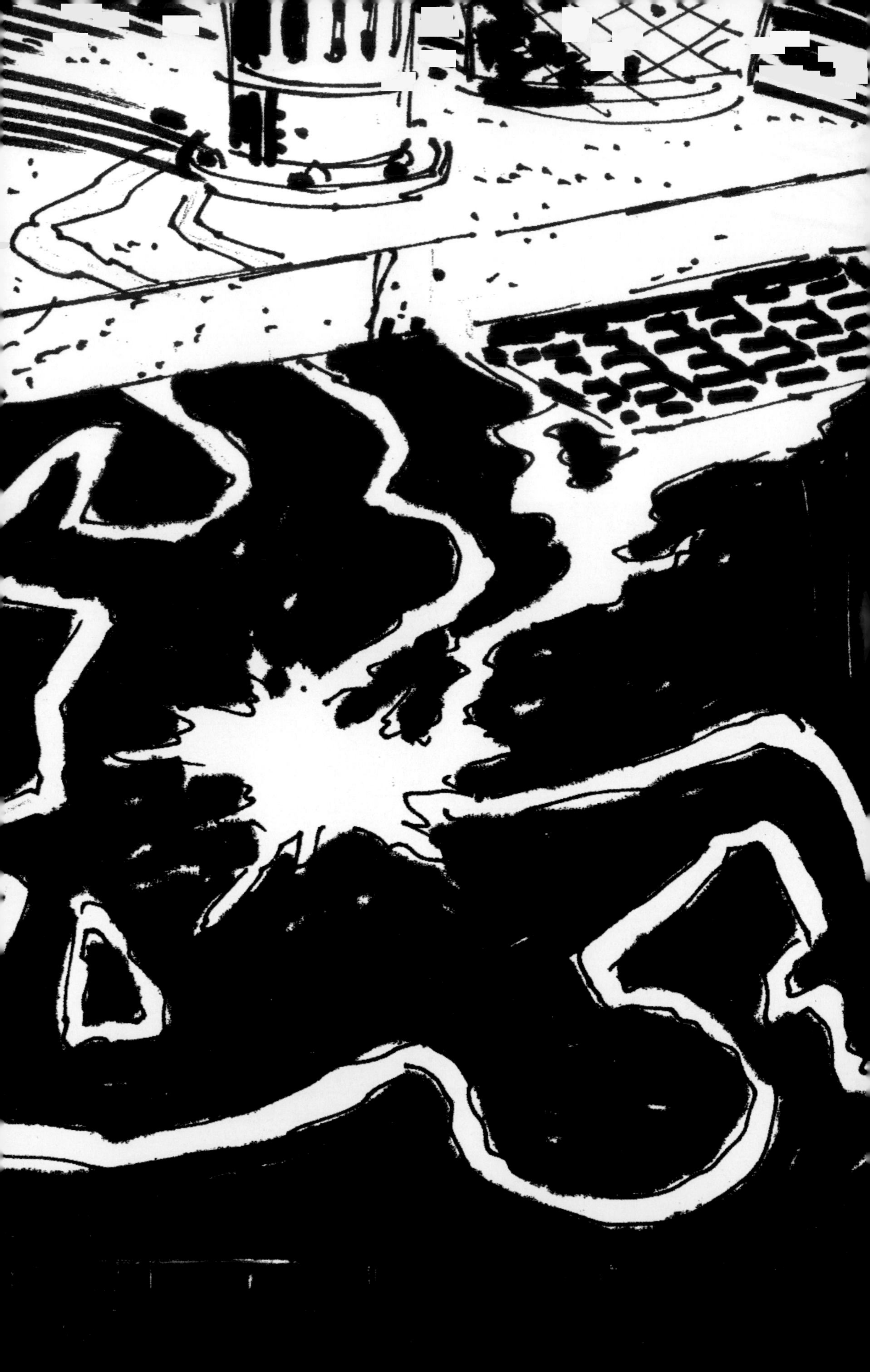

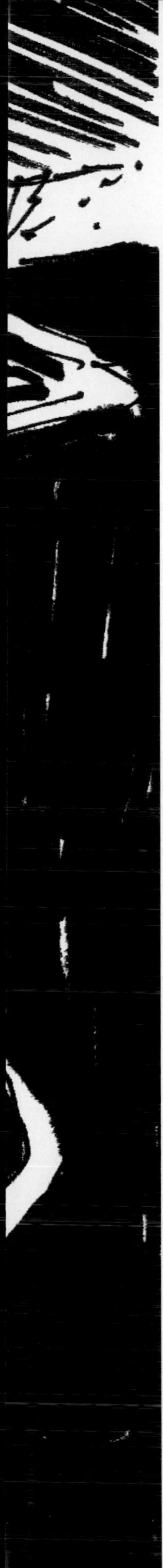

WRITTEN BY
STEVEN GRANT

ART BY
MIKE ZECK

INKS BY
DENIS RODIER

COLORS BY
KURT GOLDZUNG

ORIGINAL SERIES EDITOR
JONATHAN PETERSON

BOOM! STUDIOS EDITION:

LETTERS BY
ED DUKESHIRE

TRADE DESIGN
MIKE LOPEZ

EDITORIAL ASSISTANT
SEAN BURNS

ASSISTANT EDITOR
ALEX GALER

EDITOR
DAFNA PLEBAN

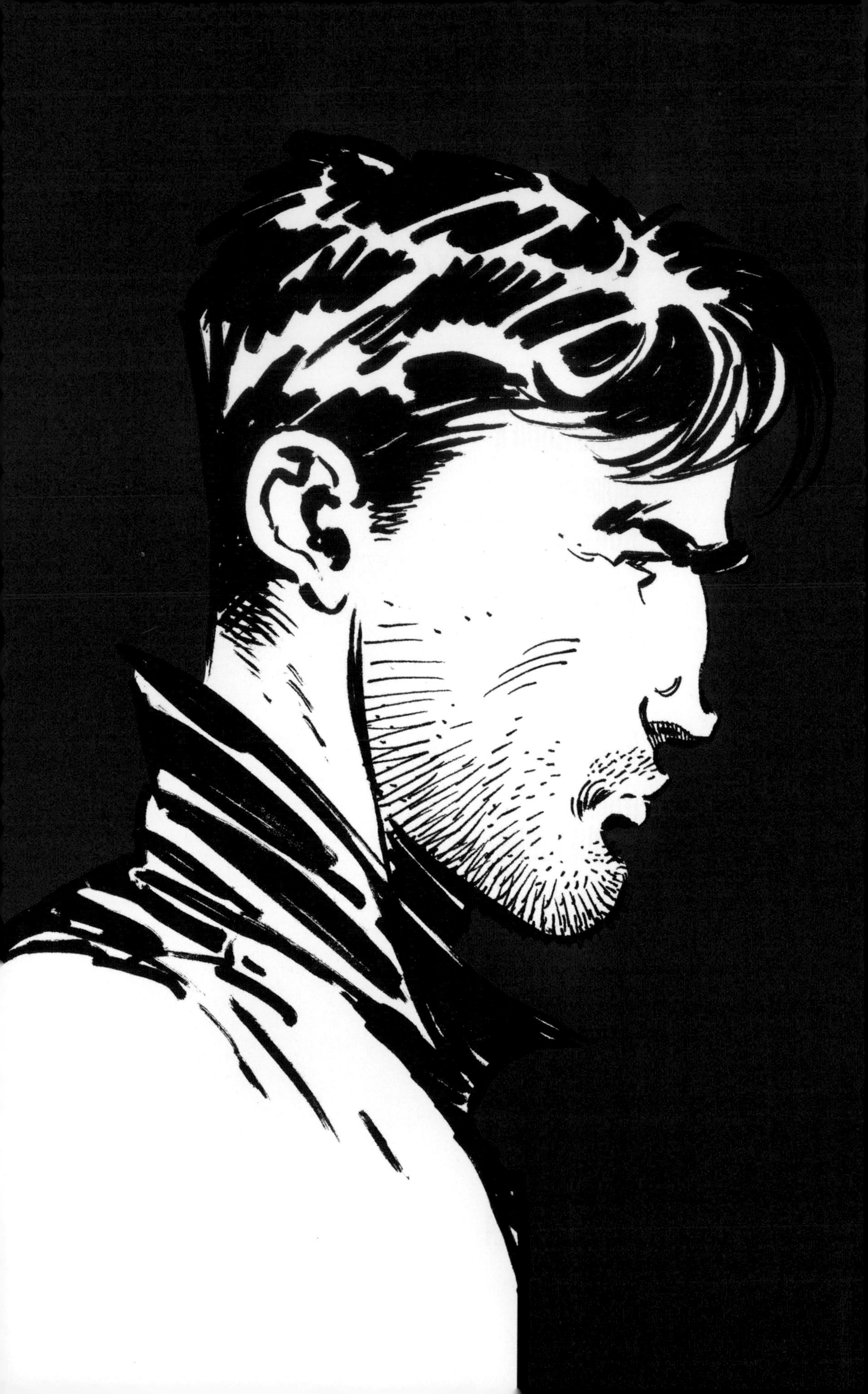

FOREWORD

For years following the success of our PUNISHER work, which we did our best to separate thematically and stylistically from the superhero comics surrounding it, Mike Zeck and I wanted to do a pure crime comic. For years we couldn't. Superhero comics had exploded into a bubble that subsequently collapsed into a black hole so dark publishers were terrified of anything that might alienate the tatters that remained of the superhero fans. Except horror comics that were mostly indistinguishable from superhero comics.

Then Jim Lee and Jonathan Peterson at Wildstorm introduced a creator-owned line, Homage, where talent could produce exactly what they wanted. Jonathan had worked with both Mike and me at DC, and asked us what we'd do given free rein.

Most of what you hold in your hands was our answer. To their credit, they didn't bat an eye. At anything. The story premise is simple: a convict makes a promise to a dying cellmate, and once out strives to keep it despite everyone he encounters making other assumptions about his motives. The whole story evolves from that. Mike wanted to try out a looser, more European art style, and he wanted to do it all digitally, on computer; DAMNED is arguably the first comic for a major American publisher produced entirely without paper, at least until publication. It's also the best expression of what Mike and I would've done all these years if left to ourselves, and we'd like to thank Jim, Jonathan, and everyone else at Wildstorm for that chance, and everyone at BOOM! for putting it back into print. DAMNED is what we'd like crime comics to be: a literature of flawed people struggling to make sense of their lives. Of course I'm biased, but I feel we got it exactly right. Please enjoy it.

STEVEN GRANT, 2013

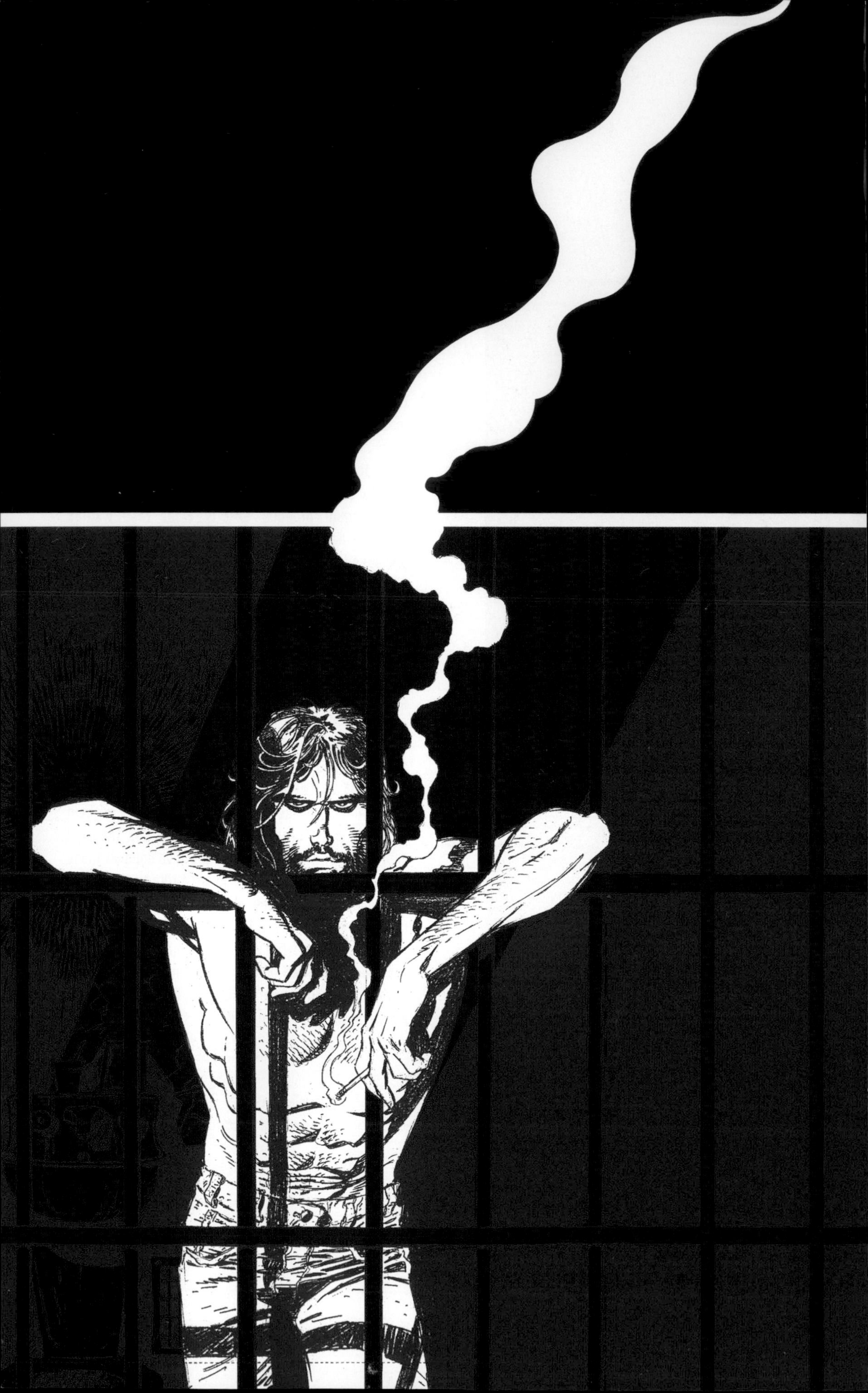

"ONLY THREE YEARS, MICK,
SHOULDN'T FEEL LIKE MUCH MORE THAN SIXTY."

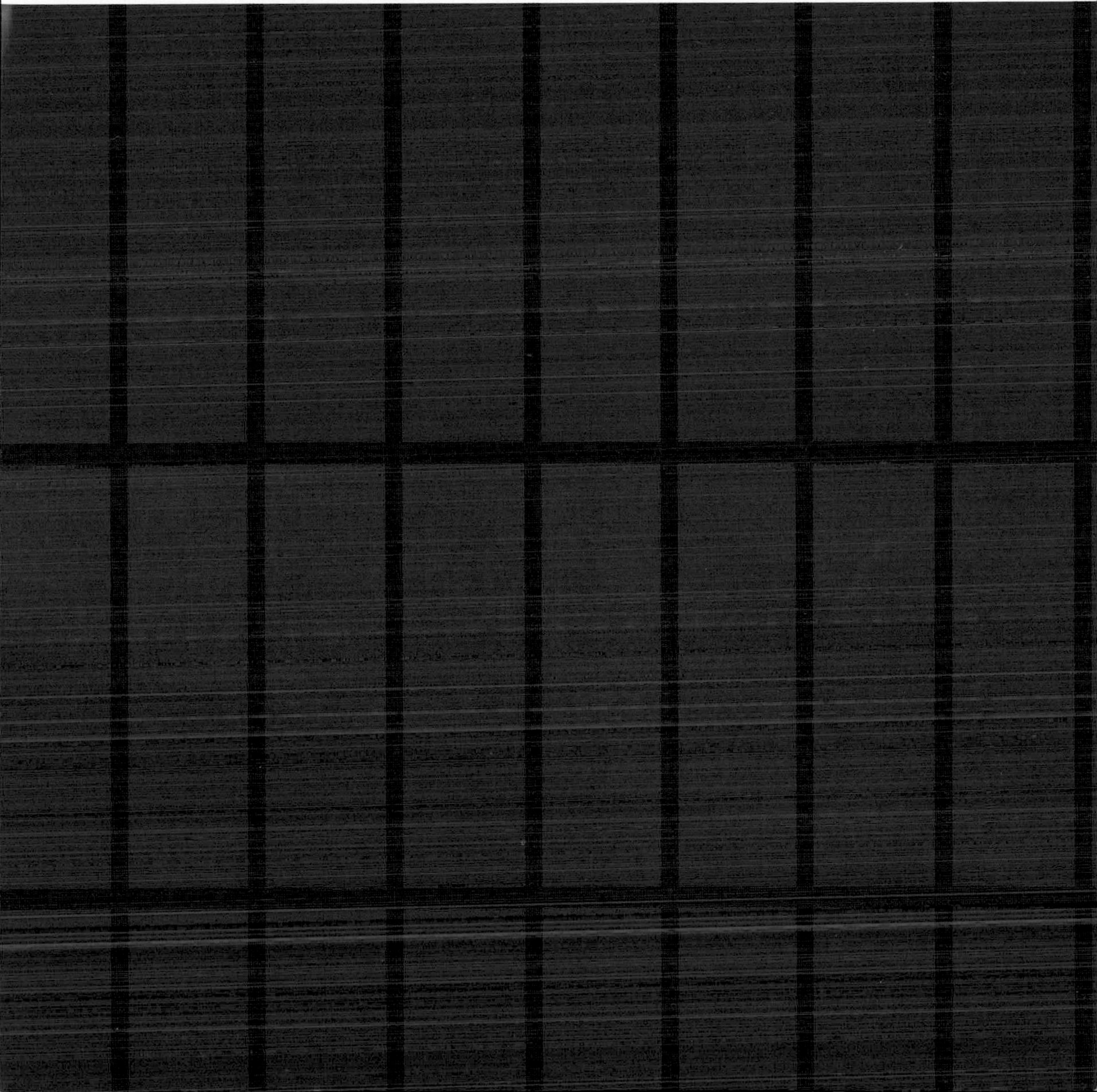

CHAPTER ONE

MICK THORNE / DAY 1447

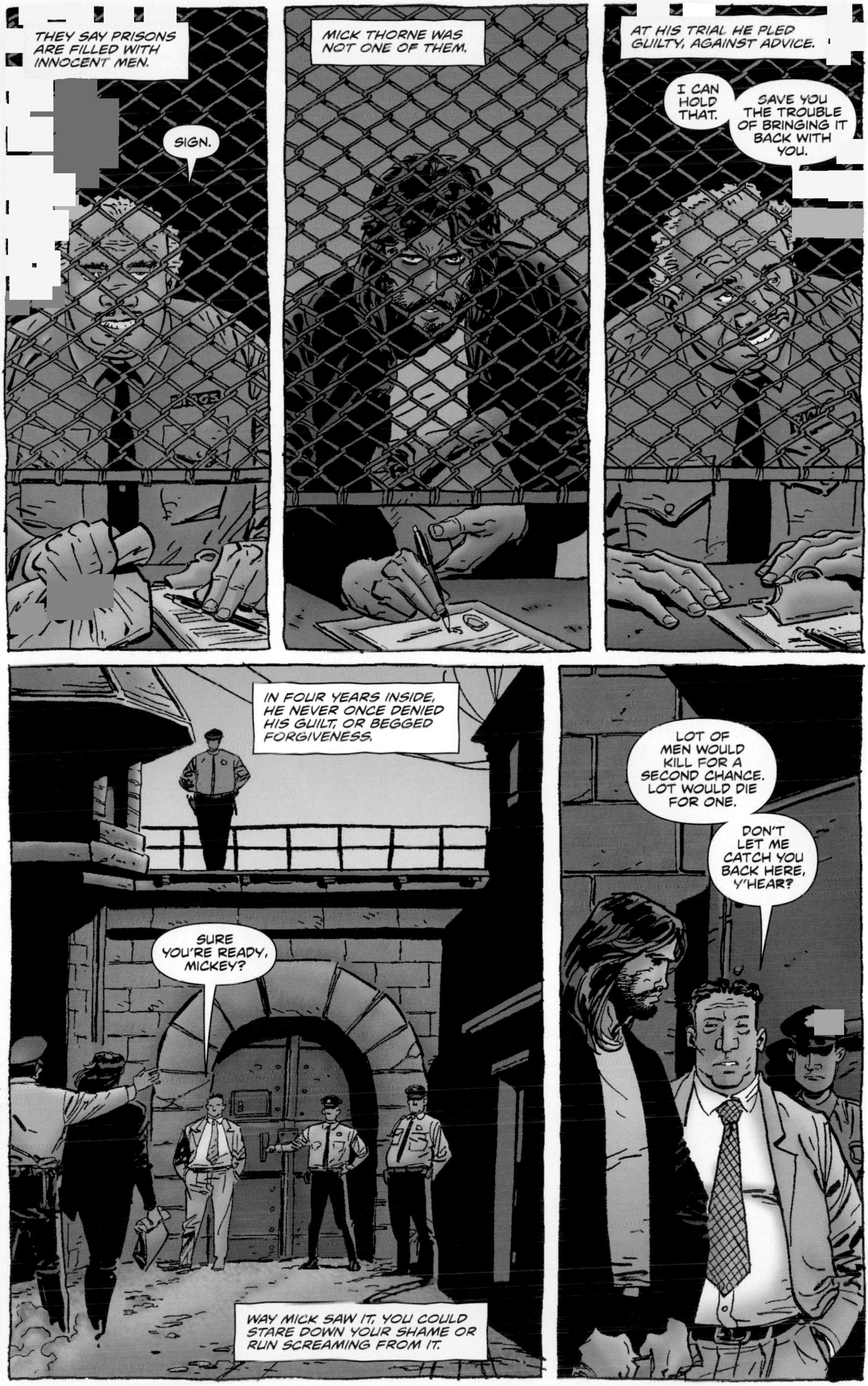
THEY SAY PRISONS ARE FILLED WITH INNOCENT MEN.
SIGN.
MICK THORNE WAS NOT ONE OF THEM.
AT HIS TRIAL HE PLED GUILTY, AGAINST ADVICE.
I CAN HOLD THAT.
SAVE YOU THE TROUBLE OF BRINGING IT BACK WITH YOU.
IN FOUR YEARS INSIDE, HE NEVER ONCE DENIED HIS GUILT, OR BEGGED FORGIVENESS.
SURE YOU'RE READY, MICKEY?
WAY MICK SAW IT, YOU COULD STARE DOWN YOUR SHAME OR RUN SCREAMING FROM IT.
LOT OF MEN WOULD KILL FOR A SECOND CHANCE. LOT WOULD DIE FOR ONE.
DON'T LET ME CATCH YOU BACK HERE, Y'HEAR?

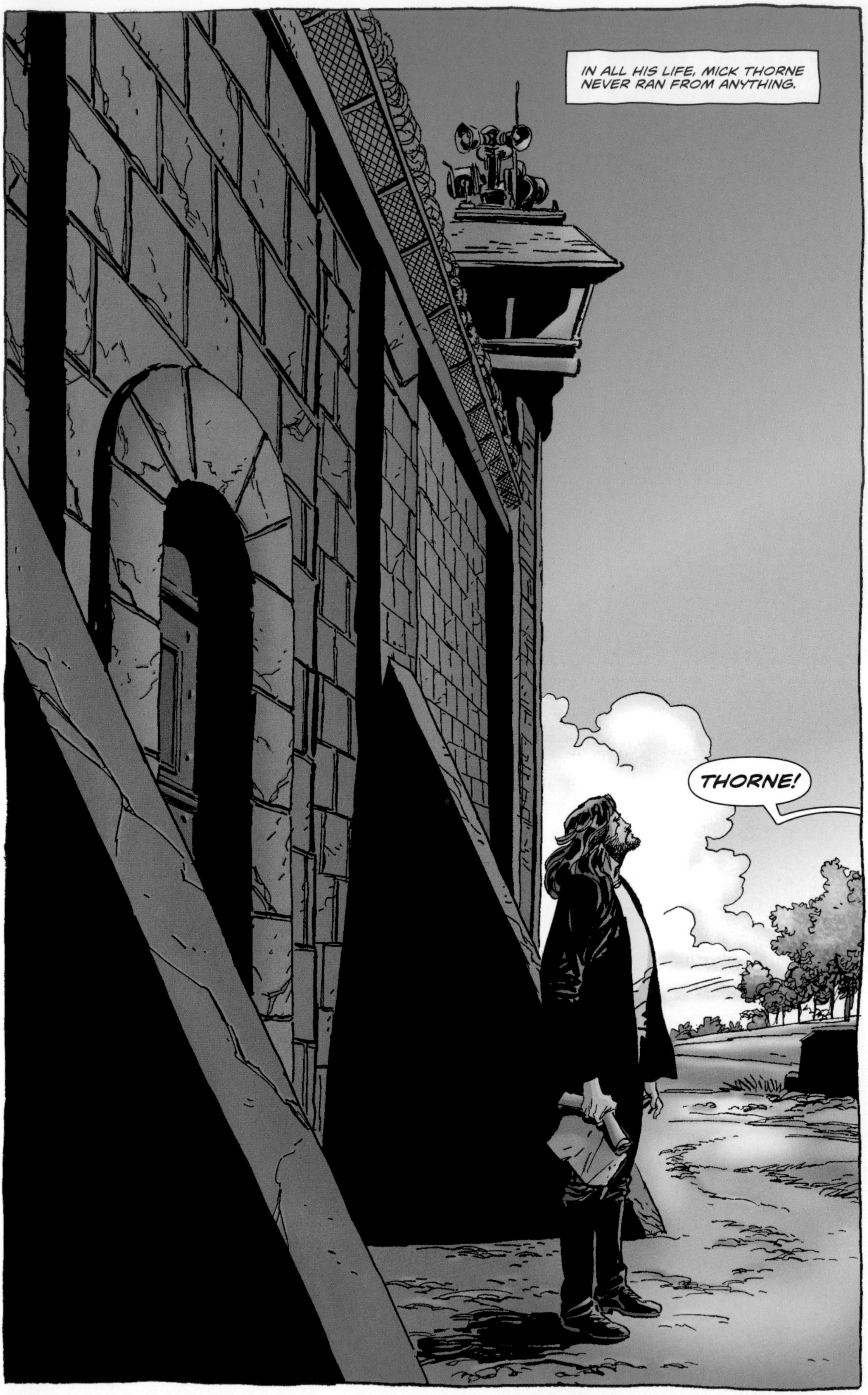
IN ALL HIS LIFE, MICK THORNE
NEVER RAN FROM ANYTHING.
THORNE!

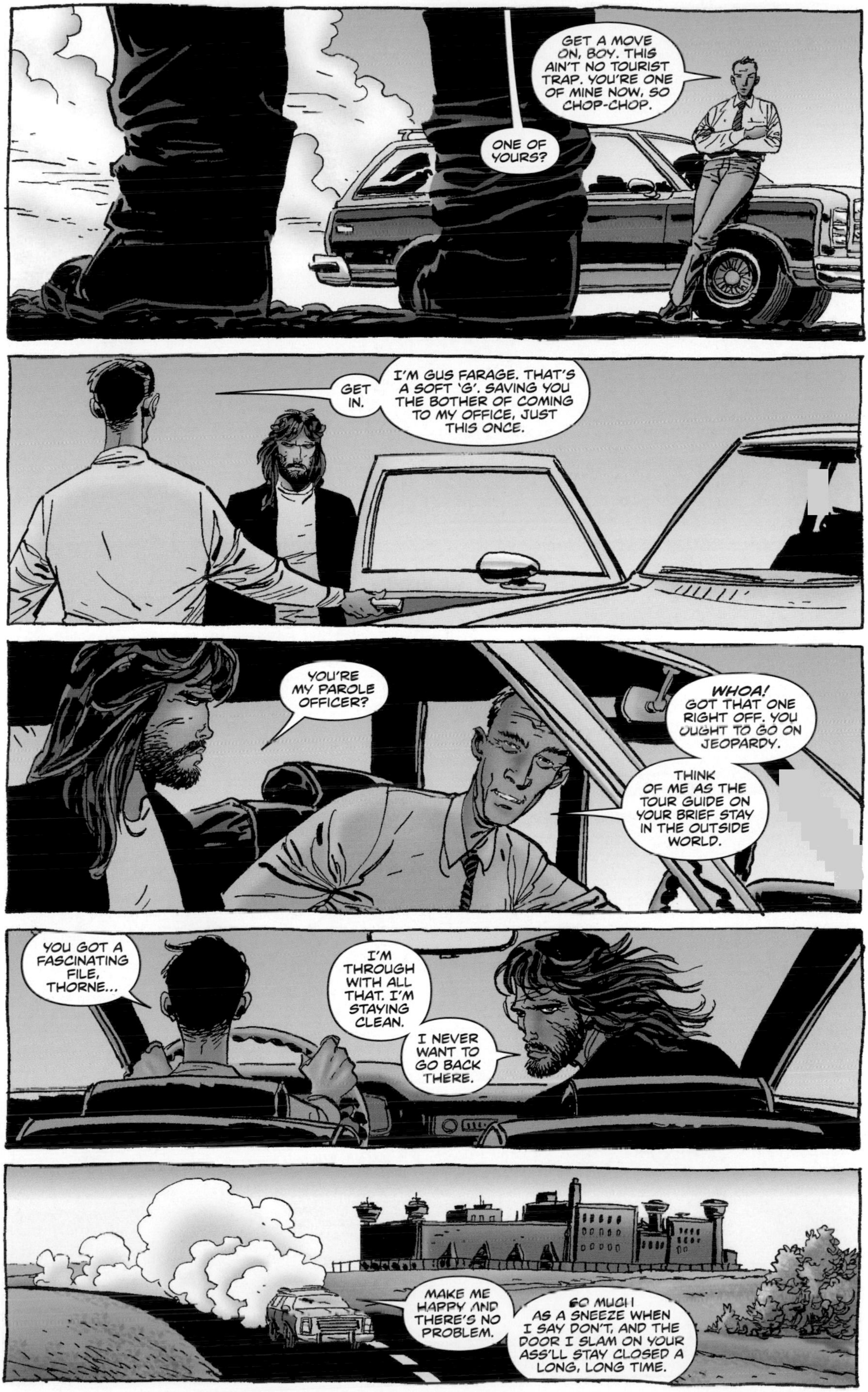
GET A MOVE ON, BOY. THIS AIN'T NO TOURIST TRAP. YOU'RE ONE OF MINE NOW, SO CHOP-CHOP.
ONE OF YOURS?
GET IN.
I'M GUS FARAGE. THAT'S A SOFT 'G'. SAVING YOU THE BOTHER OF COMING TO MY OFFICE, JUST THIS ONCE.
YOU'RE MY PAROLE OFFICER?
WHOA! GOT THAT ONE RIGHT OFF. YOU OUGHT TO GO ON JEOPARDY.
THINK OF ME AS THE TOUR GUIDE ON YOUR BRIEF STAY IN THE OUTSIDE WORLD.
YOU GOT A FASCINATING FILE, THORNE...
I'M THROUGH WITH ALL THAT. I'M STAYING CLEAN.
I NEVER WANT TO GO BACK THERE.
MAKE ME HAPPY AND THERE'S NO PROBLEM.
SO MUCH AS A SNEEZE WHEN I SAY DON'T, AND THE DOOR I SLAM ON YOUR ASS'LL STAY CLOSED A LONG, LONG TIME.

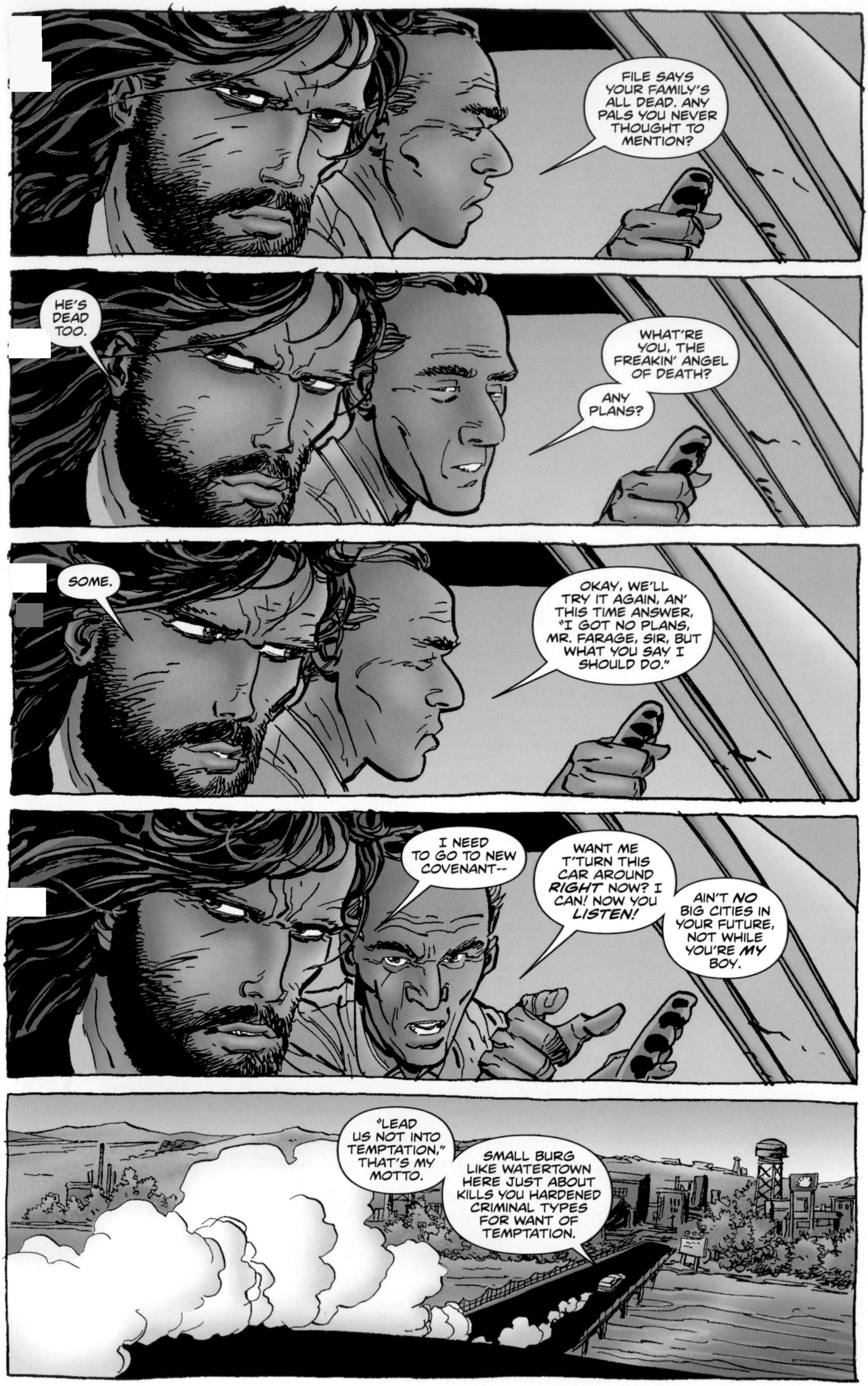
FILE SAYS YOUR FAMILY'S ALL DEAD. ANY PALS YOU NEVER THOUGHT TO MENTION?
HE'S DEAD TOO.
WHAT'RE YOU, THE FREAKIN' ANGEL OF DEATH?
ANY PLANS?
SOME.
OKAY, WE'LL TRY IT AGAIN, AN' THIS TIME ANSWER, "I GOT NO PLANS, MR. FARAGE, SIR, BUT WHAT YOU SAY I SHOULD DO."
I NEED TO GO TO NEW COVENANT--
WANT ME T'TURN THIS CAR AROUND RIGHT NOW? I CAN! NOW YOU LISTEN!
AIN'T NO BIG CITIES IN YOUR FUTURE, NOT WHILE YOU'RE MY BOY.
"LEAD US NOT INTO TEMPTATION," THAT'S MY MOTTO.
SMALL BURG LIKE WATERTOWN HERE JUST ABOUT KILLS YOU HARDENED CRIMINAL TYPES FOR WANT OF TEMPTATION.

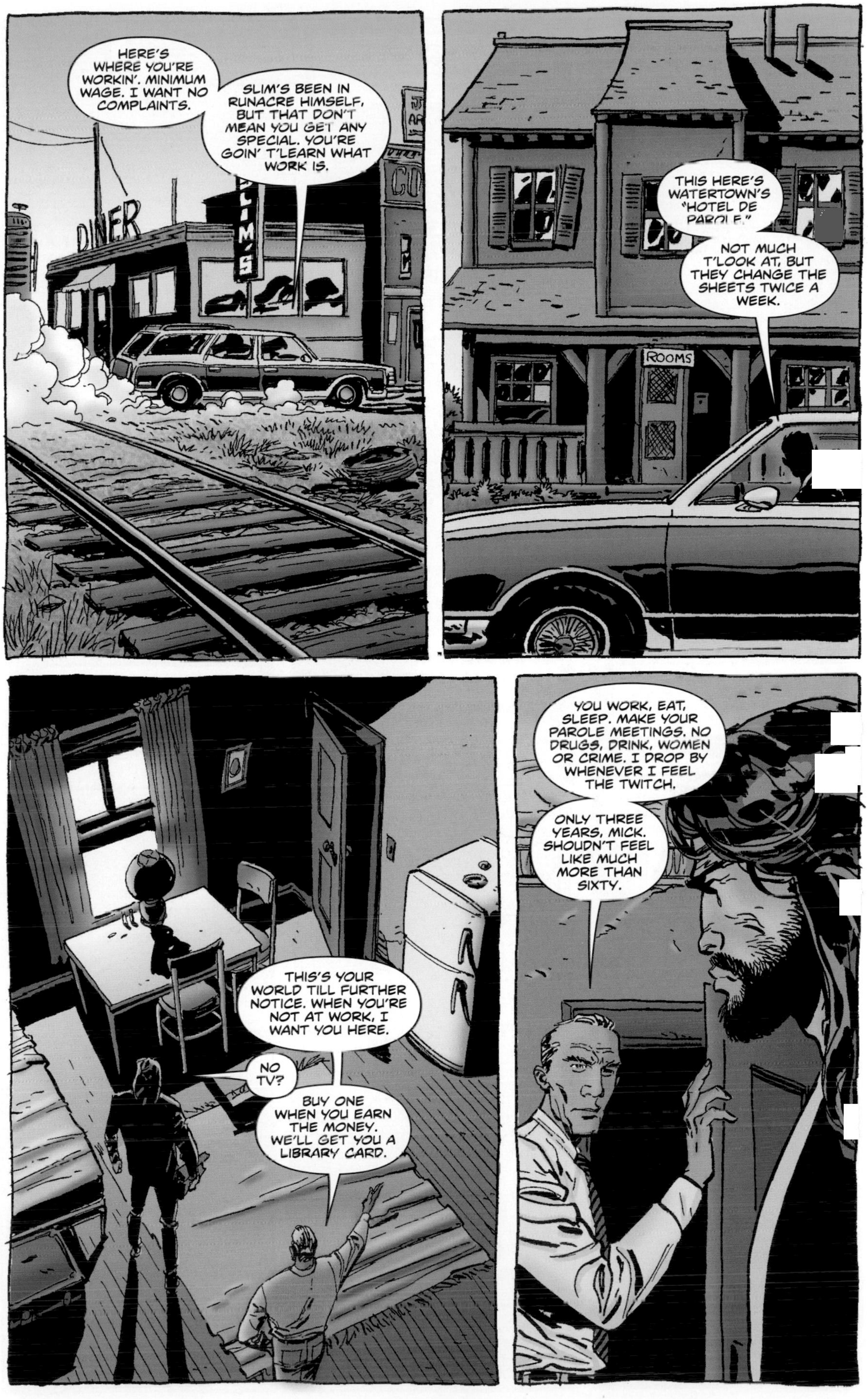
HERE'S WHERE YOU'RE WORKIN'. MINIMUM WAGE. I WANT NO COMPLAINTS.
SLIM'S BEEN IN RUNACRE HIMSELF, BUT THAT DON'T MEAN YOU GET ANY SPECIAL. YOU'RE GOIN' T'LEARN WHAT WORK IS.
DINER
SLIM'S
THIS HERE'S WATERTOWN'S "HOTEL DE PAROLE."
NOT MUCH T'LOOK AT, BUT THEY CHANGE THE SHEETS TWICE A WEEK.
ROOMS
THIS'S YOUR WORLD TILL FURTHER NOTICE. WHEN YOU'RE NOT AT WORK, I WANT YOU HERE.
NO TV?
BUY ONE WHEN YOU EARN THE MONEY. WE'LL GET YOU A LIBRARY CARD.
YOU WORK, EAT, SLEEP. MAKE YOUR PAROLE MEETINGS. NO DRUGS, DRINK, WOMEN OR CRIME. I DROP BY WHENEVER I FEEL THE TWITCH.
ONLY THREE YEARS, MICK. SHOUDN'T FEEL LIKE MUCH MORE THAN SIXTY.

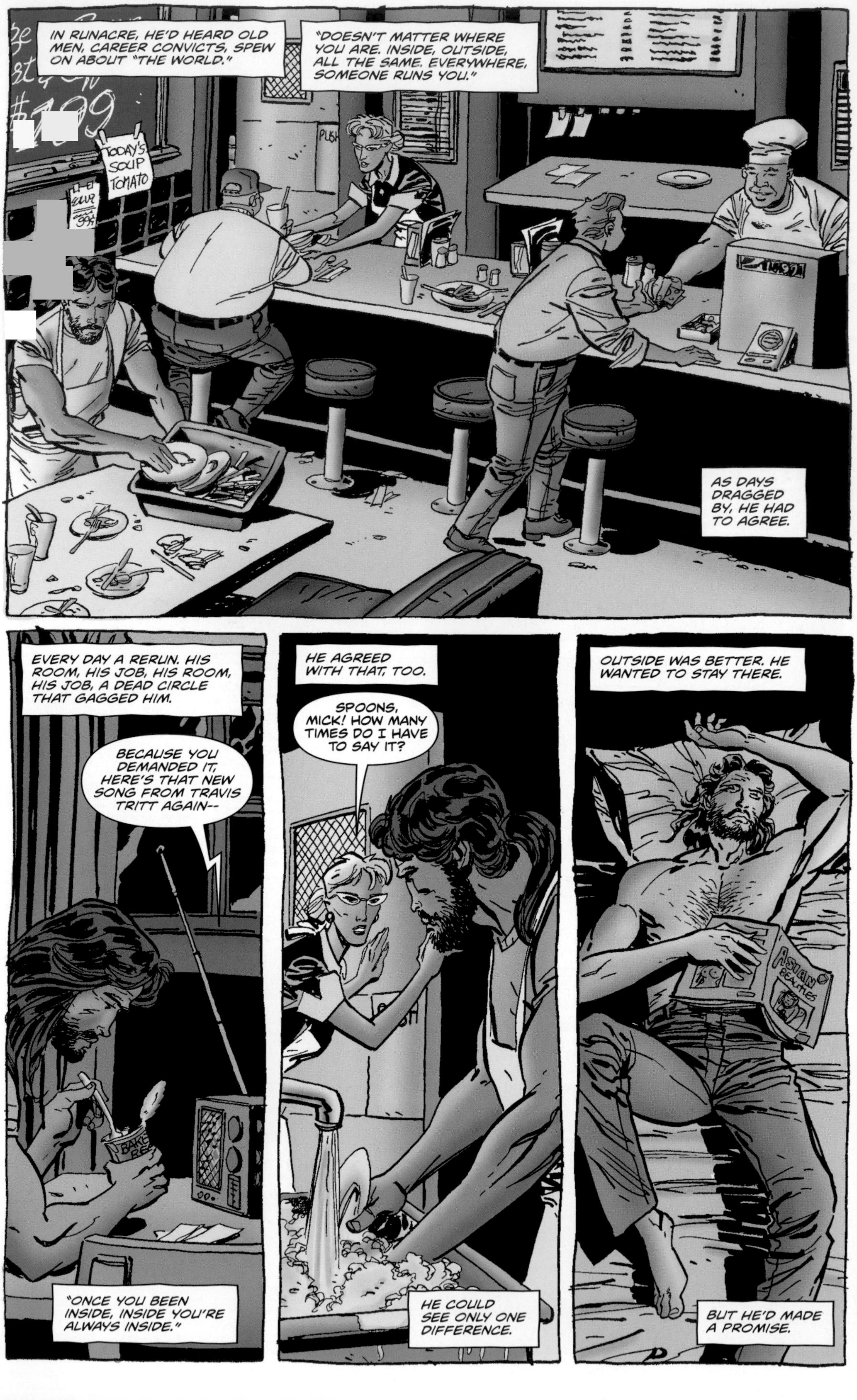
IN RUNACRE, HE'D HEARD OLD MEN, CAREER CONVICTS, SPEW ON ABOUT "THE WORLD."
"DOESN'T MATTER WHERE YOU ARE. INSIDE, OUTSIDE, ALL THE SAME. EVERYWHERE, SOMEONE RUNS YOU."
TODAY'S SOUP TOMATO
PUSH
AS DAYS DRAGGED BY, HE HAD TO AGREE.
EVERY DAY A RERUN. HIS ROOM, HIS JOB, HIS ROOM, HIS JOB, A DEAD CIRCLE THAT GAGGED HIM.
BECAUSE YOU DEMANDED IT, HERE'S THAT NEW SONG FROM TRAVIS TRITT AGAIN--
"ONCE YOU BEEN INSIDE, INSIDE YOU'RE ALWAYS INSIDE."
HE AGREED WITH THAT, TOO.
SPOONS, MICK! HOW MANY TIMES DO I HAVE TO SAY IT?
HE COULD SEE ONLY ONE DIFFERENCE.
OUTSIDE WAS BETTER. HE WANTED TO STAY THERE.
ASIAN BEAUTIES
BUT HE'D MADE A PROMISE.

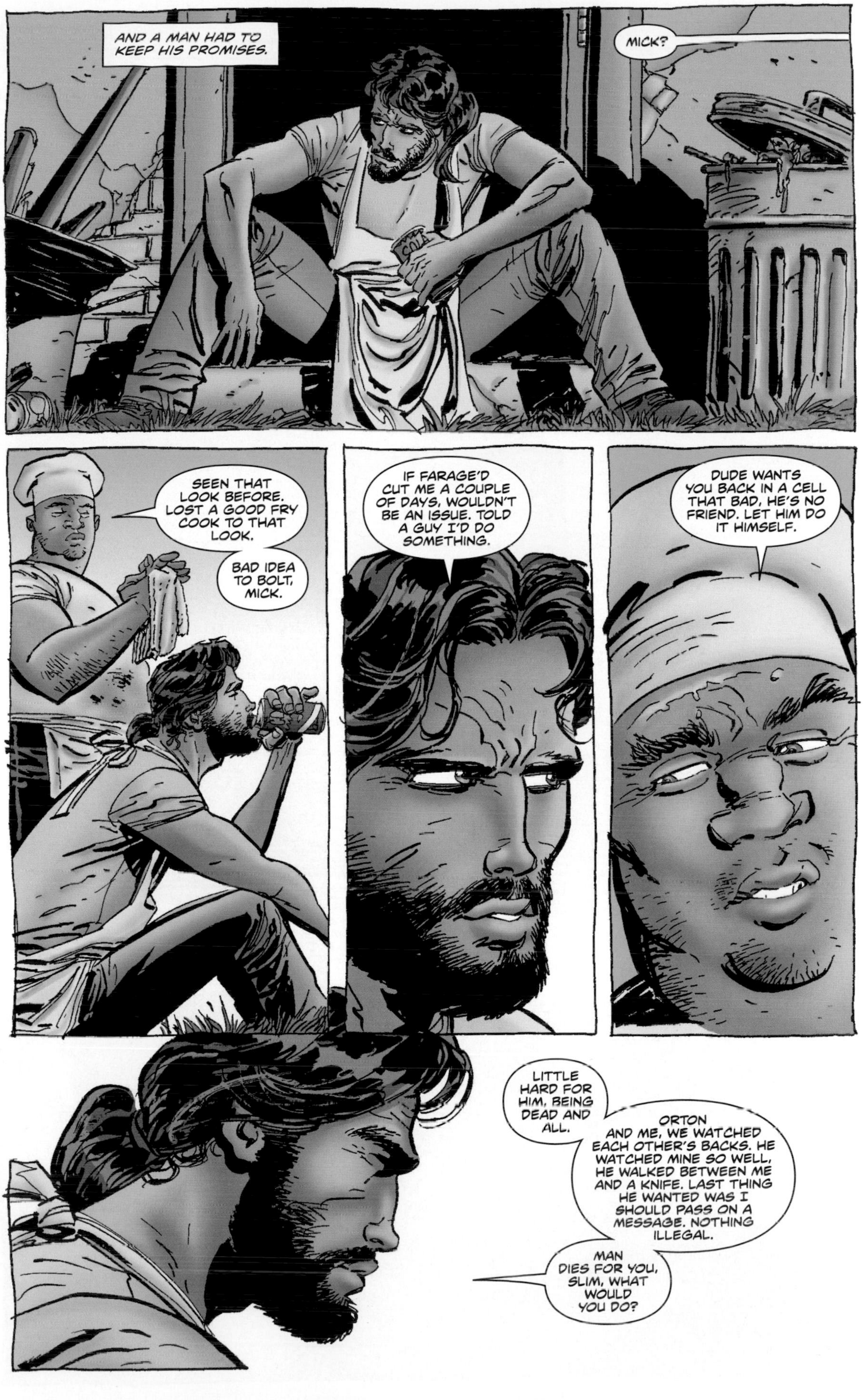
AND A MAN HAD TO KEEP HIS PROMISES.
MICK?
SEEN THAT LOOK BEFORE. LOST A GOOD FRY COOK TO THAT LOOK.
BAD IDEA TO BOLT, MICK.
IF FARAGE'D CUT ME A COUPLE OF DAYS, WOULDN'T BE AN ISSUE. TOLD A GUY I'D DO SOMETHING.
DUDE WANTS YOU BACK IN A CELL THAT BAD, HE'S NO FRIEND. LET HIM DO IT HIMSELF.
LITTLE HARD FOR HIM, BEING DEAD AND ALL.
ORTON AND ME, WE WATCHED EACH OTHER'S BACKS. HE WATCHED MINE SO WELL, HE WALKED BETWEEN ME AND A KNIFE. LAST THING HE WANTED WAS I SHOULD PASS ON A MESSAGE. NOTHING ILLEGAL.
MAN DIES FOR YOU, SLIM, WHAT WOULD YOU DO?

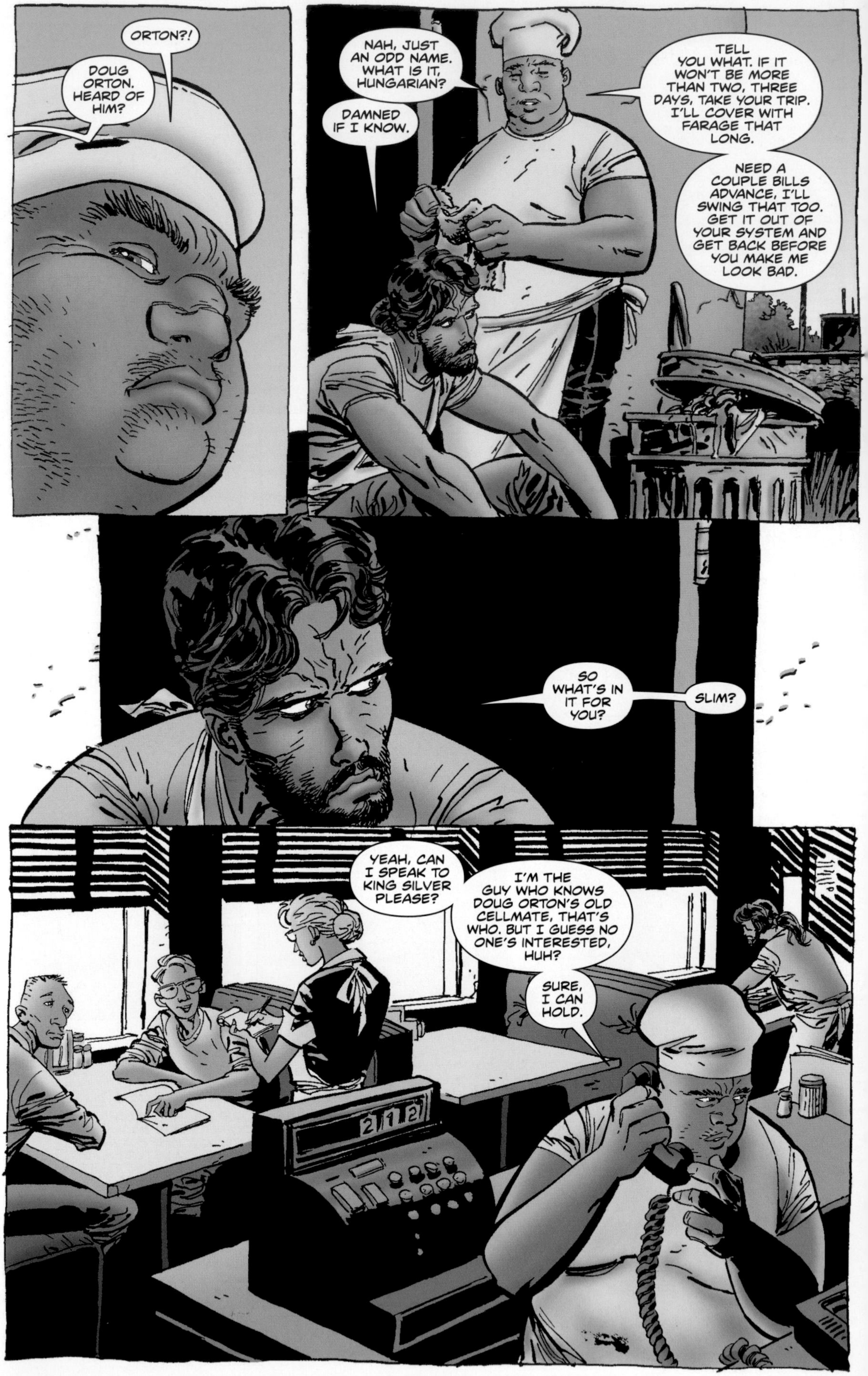
DOUG ORTON. HEARD OF HIM?
ORTON?!
NAH, JUST AN ODD NAME. WHAT IS IT, HUNGARIAN?
DAMNED IF I KNOW.
TELL YOU WHAT. IF IT WON'T BE MORE THAN TWO, THREE DAYS, TAKE YOUR TRIP. I'LL COVER WITH FARAGE THAT LONG.
NEED A COUPLE BILLS ADVANCE, I'LL SWING THAT TOO. GET IT OUT OF YOUR SYSTEM AND GET BACK BEFORE YOU MAKE ME LOOK BAD.
SO WHAT'S IN IT FOR YOU?
SLIM?
YEAH, CAN I SPEAK TO KING SILVER PLEASE?
I'M THE GUY WHO KNOWS DOUG ORTON'S OLD CELLMATE, THAT'S WHO. BUT I GUESS NO ONE'S INTERESTED, HUH?
SURE, I CAN HOLD.

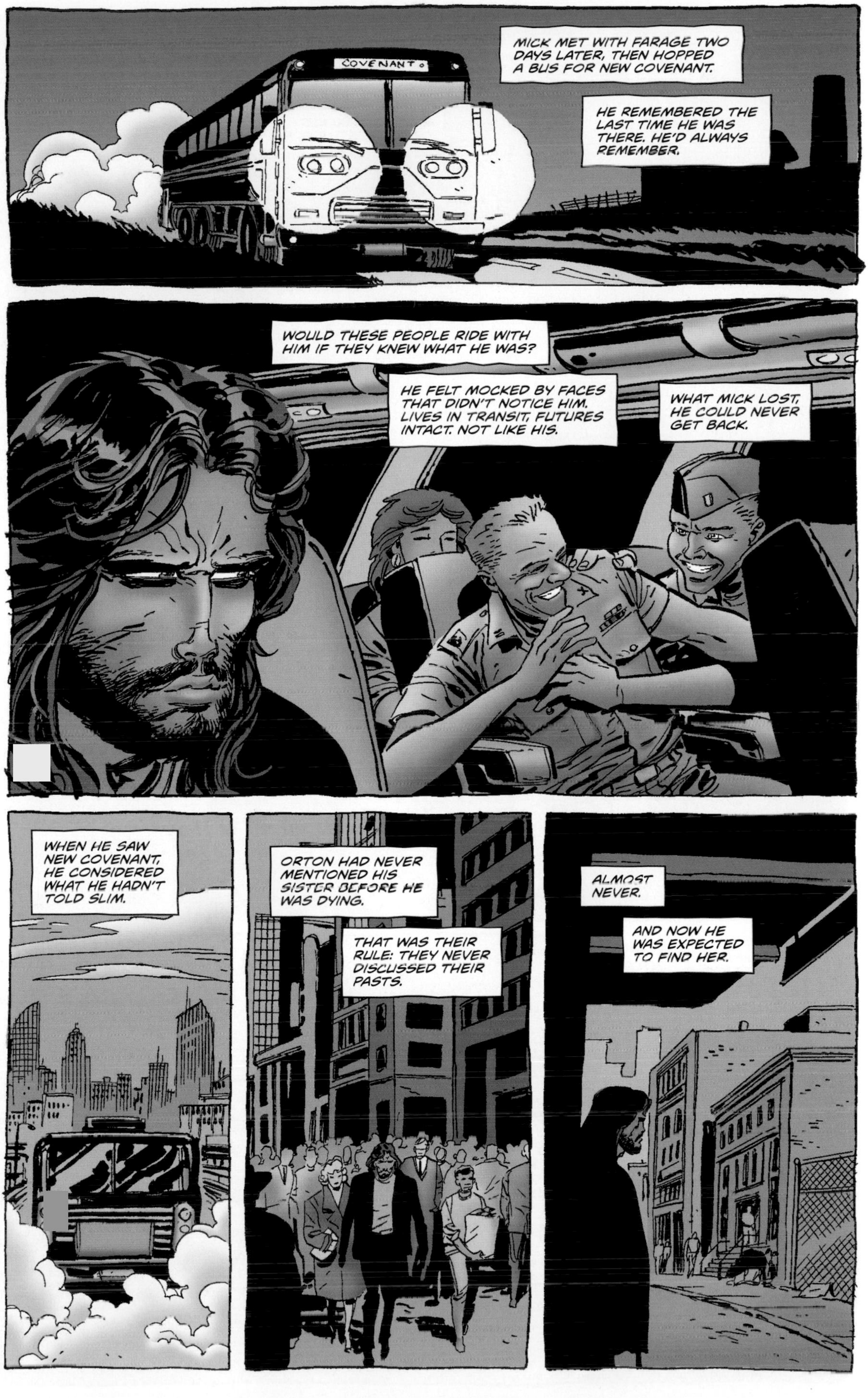
COVENANT
MICK MET WITH FARAGE TWO DAYS LATER, THEN HOPPED A BUS FOR NEW COVENANT.
HE REMEMBERED THE LAST TIME HE WAS THERE. HE'D ALWAYS REMEMBER.
WOULD THESE PEOPLE RIDE WITH HIM IF THEY KNEW WHAT HE WAS?
HE FELT MOCKED BY FACES THAT DIDN'T NOTICE HIM. LIVES IN TRANSIT, FUTURES INTACT. NOT LIKE HIS.
WHAT MICK LOST, HE COULD NEVER GET BACK.
WHEN HE SAW NEW COVENANT, HE CONSIDERED WHAT HE HADN'T TOLD SLIM.
ORTON HAD NEVER MENTIONED HIS SISTER BEFORE HE WAS DYING.
THAT WAS THEIR RULE: THEY NEVER DISCUSSED THEIR PASTS.
ALMOST NEVER.
AND NOW HE WAS EXPECTED TO FIND HER.

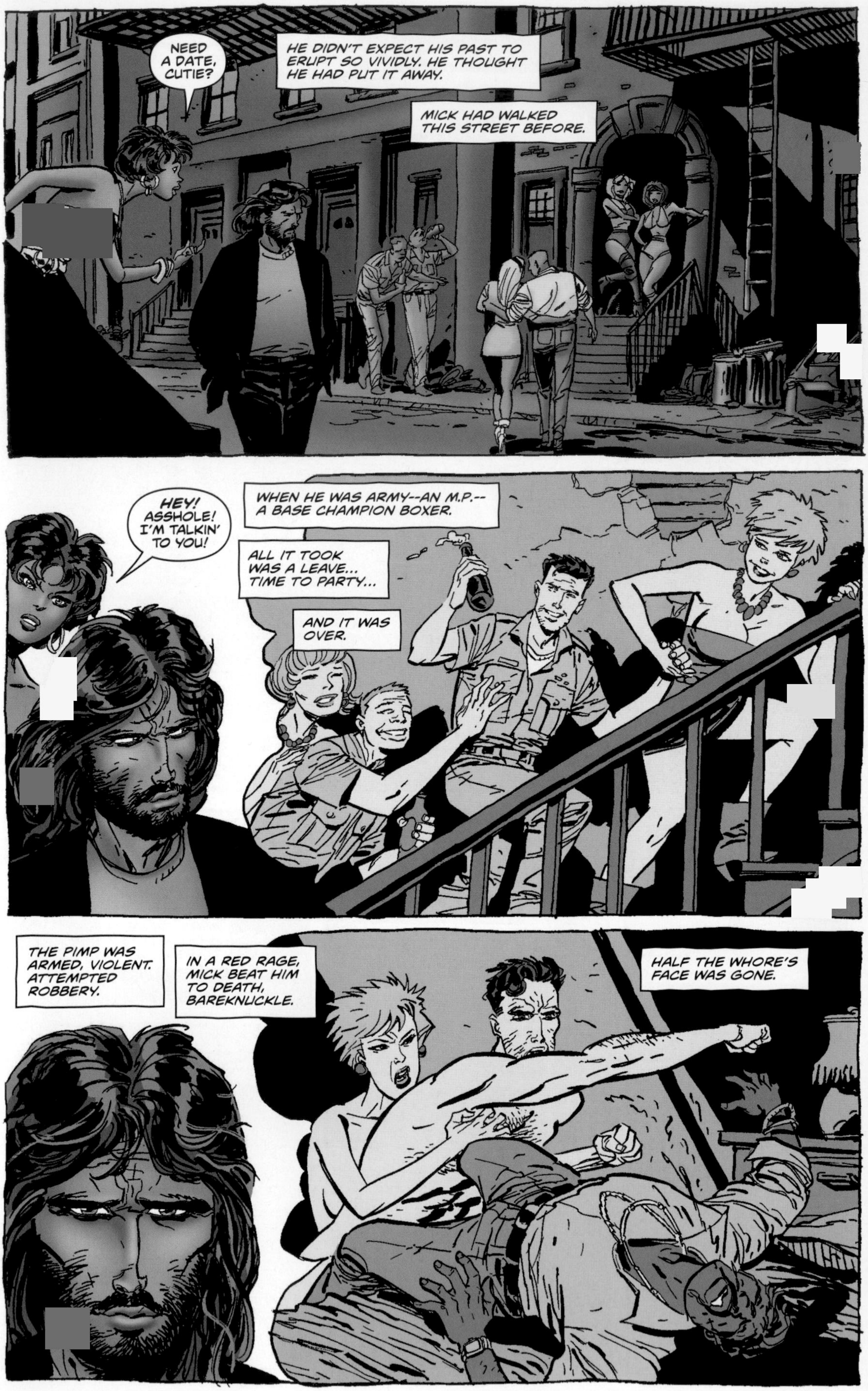
NEED A DATE, CUTIE?
HE DIDN'T EXPECT HIS PAST TO ERUPT SO VIVIDLY. HE THOUGHT HE HAD PUT IT AWAY.
MICK HAD WALKED THIS STREET BEFORE.
HEY! ASSHOLE! I'M TALKIN' TO YOU!
WHEN HE WAS ARMY--AN M.P.--A BASE CHAMPION BOXER.
ALL IT TOOK WAS A LEAVE... TIME TO PARTY...
AND IT WAS OVER.
THE PIMP WAS ARMED, VIOLENT. ATTEMPTED ROBBERY.
IN A RED RAGE, MICK BEAT HIM TO DEATH, BAREKNUCKLE.
HALF THE WHORE'S FACE WAS GONE.

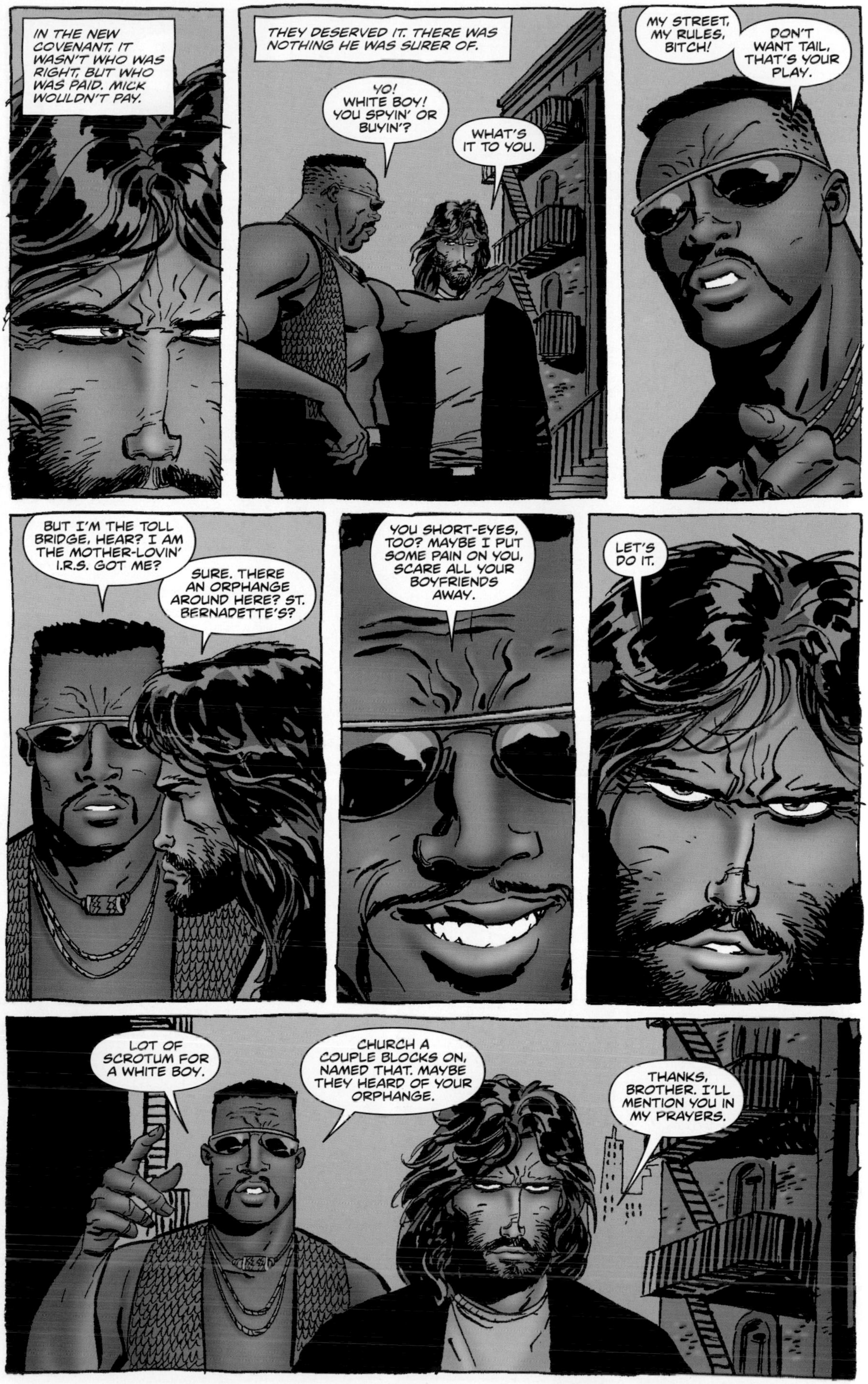
IN THE NEW COVENANT, IT WASN'T WHO WAS RIGHT, BUT WHO WAS PAID. MICK WOULDN'T PAY.
THEY DESERVED IT. THERE WAS NOTHING HE WAS SURER OF.
YO! WHITE BOY! YOU SPYIN' OR BUYIN'?
WHAT'S IT TO YOU.
MY STREET, MY RULES, BITCH!
DON'T WANT TAIL, THAT'S YOUR PLAY.
BUT I'M THE TOLL BRIDGE, HEAR? I AM THE MOTHER-LOVIN' I.R.S. GOT ME?
SURE. THERE AN ORPHANGE AROUND HERE? ST. BERNADETTE'S?
YOU SHORT-EYES, TOO? MAYBE I PUT SOME PAIN ON YOU, SCARE ALL YOUR BOYFRIENDS AWAY.
LET'S DO IT.
LOT OF SCROTUM FOR A WHITE BOY.
CHURCH A COUPLE BLOCKS ON, NAMED THAT. MAYBE THEY HEARD OF YOUR ORPHANGE.
THANKS, BROTHER. I'LL MENTION YOU IN MY PRAYERS.

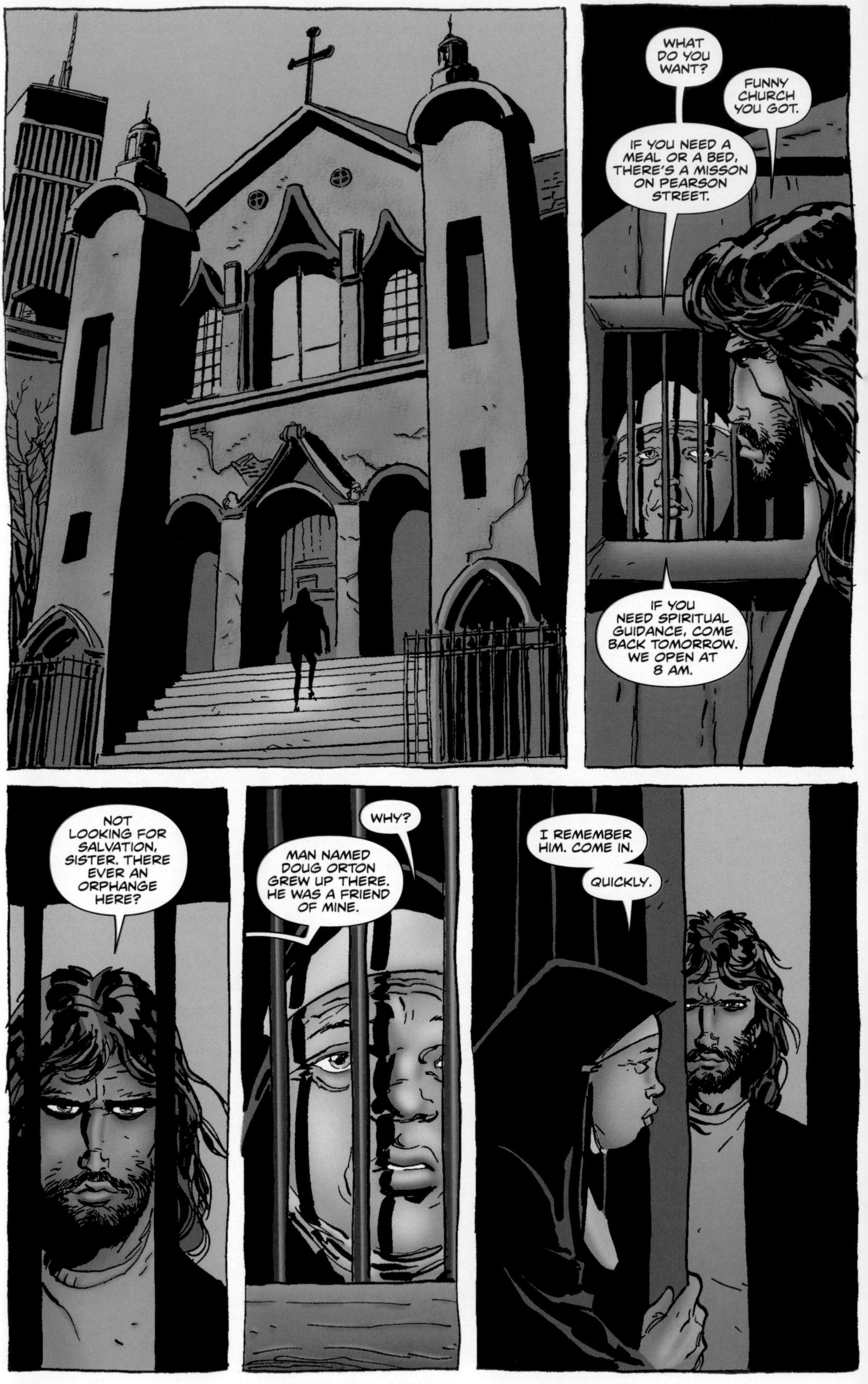
WHAT DO YOU WANT?
FUNNY CHURCH YOU GOT.
IF YOU NEED A MEAL OR A BED, THERE'S A MISSON ON PEARSON STREET.
IF YOU NEED SPIRITUAL GUIDANCE, COME BACK TOMORROW. WE OPEN AT 8 AM.
NOT LOOKING FOR SALVATION, SISTER. THERE EVER AN ORPHANGE HERE?
WHY?
MAN NAMED DOUG ORTON GREW UP THERE. HE WAS A FRIEND OF MINE.
I REMEMBER HIM. COME IN.
QUICKLY.

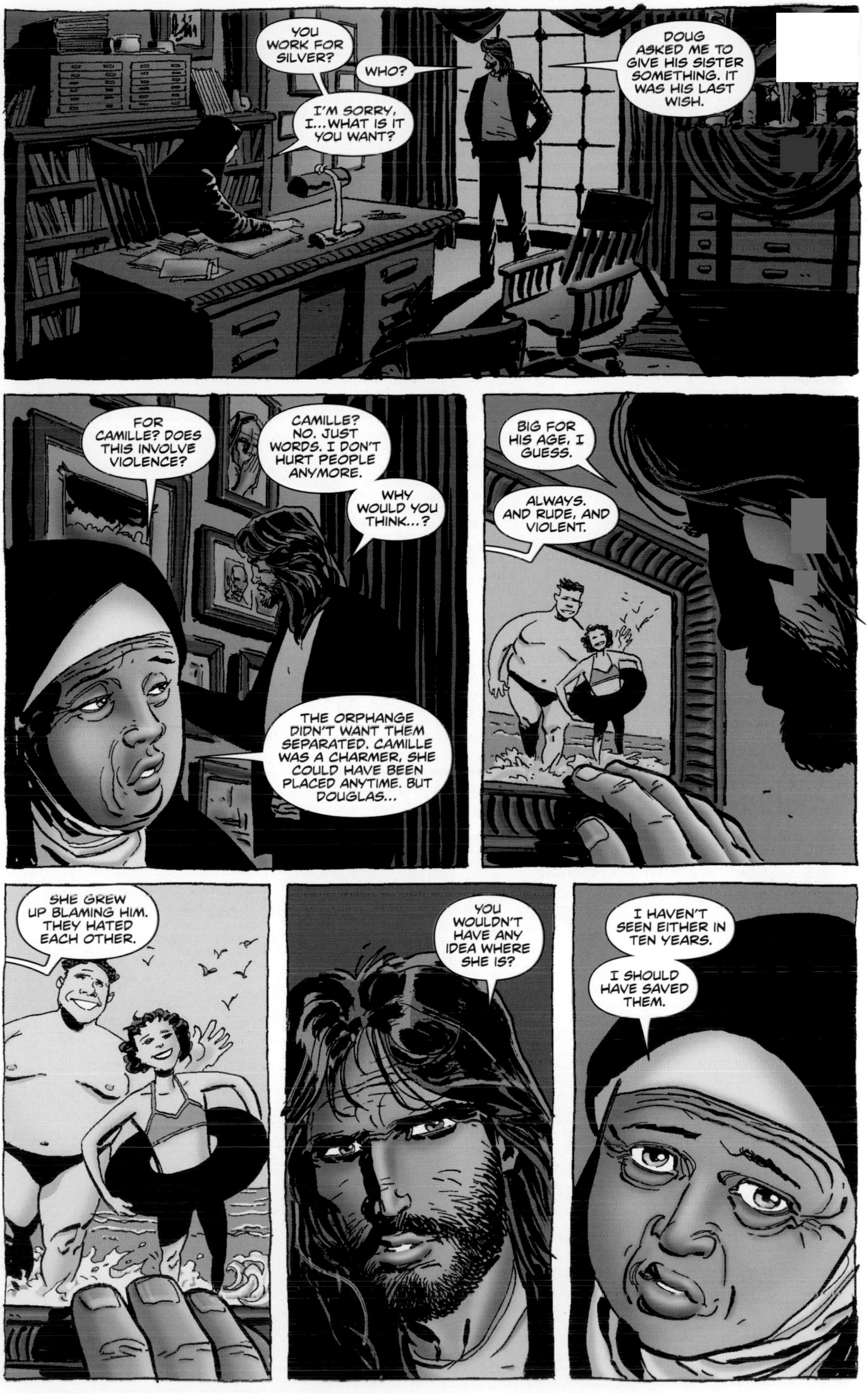
YOU WORK FOR SILVER?
WHO?
I'M SORRY, I...WHAT IS IT YOU WANT?
DOUG ASKED ME TO GIVE HIS SISTER SOMETHING. IT WAS HIS LAST WISH.
FOR CAMILLE? DOES THIS INVOLVE VIOLENCE?
CAMILLE? NO. JUST WORDS. I DON'T HURT PEOPLE ANYMORE.
WHY WOULD YOU THINK...?
THE ORPHANGE DIDN'T WANT THEM SEPARATED. CAMILLE WAS A CHARMER, SHE COULD HAVE BEEN PLACED ANYTIME. BUT DOUGLAS...
BIG FOR HIS AGE, I GUESS.
ALWAYS. AND RUDE, AND VIOLENT.
SHE GREW UP BLAMING HIM. THEY HATED EACH OTHER.
YOU WOULDN'T HAVE ANY IDEA WHERE SHE IS?
I HAVEN'T SEEN EITHER IN TEN YEARS.
I SHOULD HAVE SAVED THEM.

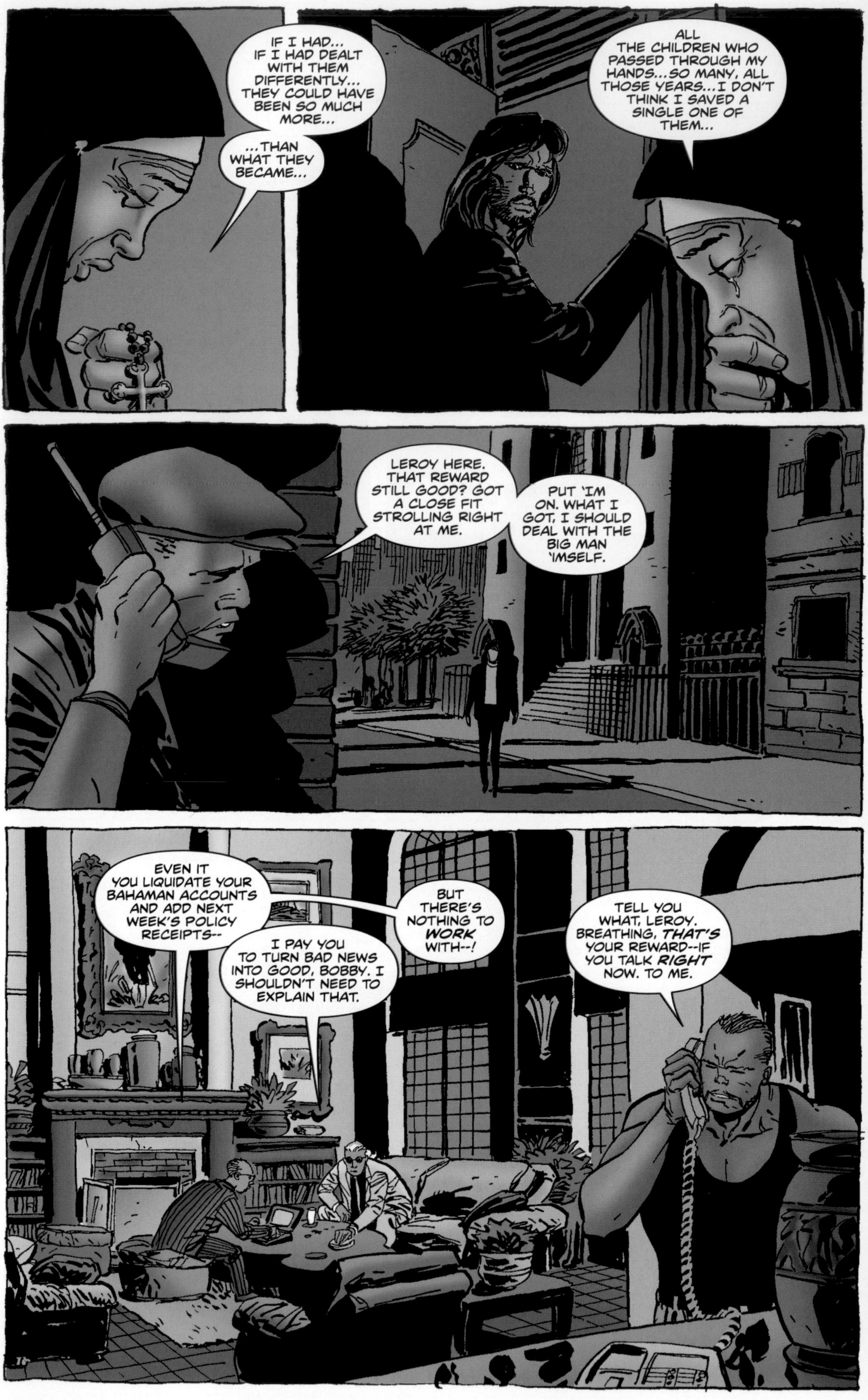
IF I HAD... IF I HAD DEALT WITH THEM DIFFERENTLY... THEY COULD HAVE BEEN SO MUCH MORE...
...THAN WHAT THEY BECAME...
ALL THE CHILDREN WHO PASSED THROUGH MY HANDS...SO MANY, ALL THOSE YEARS...I DON'T THINK I SAVED A SINGLE ONE OF THEM...
LEROY HERE. THAT REWARD STILL GOOD? GOT A CLOSE FIT STROLLING RIGHT AT ME.
PUT 'IM ON. WHAT I GOT, I SHOULD DEAL WITH THE BIG MAN 'IMSELF.
EVEN IT YOU LIQUIDATE YOUR BAHAMAN ACCOUNTS AND ADD NEXT WEEK'S POLICY RECEIPTS--
BUT THERE'S NOTHING TO *WORK* WITH--!
I PAY YOU TO TURN BAD NEWS INTO GOOD, BOBBY. I SHOULDN'T NEED TO EXPLAIN THAT.
TELL YOU WHAT, LEROY. BREATHING, *THAT'S* YOUR REWARD--IF YOU TALK *RIGHT* NOW. TO ME.

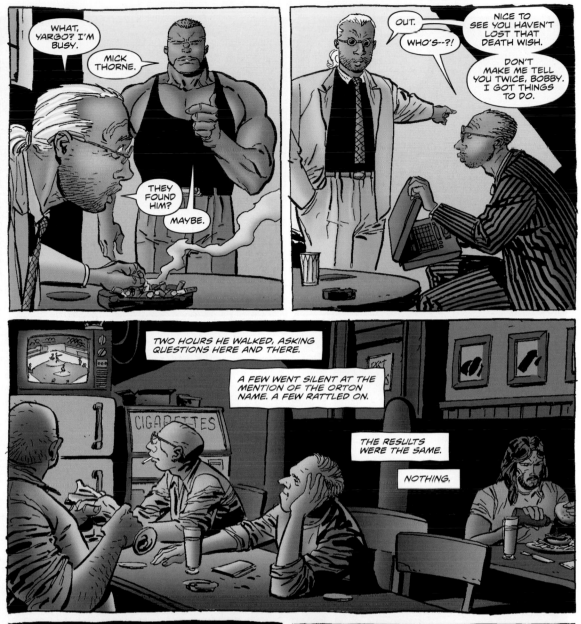

WHAT, YARGO? I'M BUSY.

MICK THORNE.

THEY FOUND HIM?

MAYBE.

OUT.

WHO'S--?!

NICE TO SEE YOU HAVEN'T LOST THAT DEATH WISH.

DON'T MAKE ME TELL YOU TWICE, BOBBY. I GOT THINGS TO DO.

TWO HOURS HE WALKED, ASKING QUESTIONS HERE AND THERE.

A FEW WENT SILENT AT THE MENTION OF THE ORTON NAME. A FEW RATTLED ON.

THE RESULTS WERE THE SAME.

NOTHING.

CIGARETTES

HEY, SLUGGER. LONELY?

YEAH, AND POOR.

THAT'S FUNNY. I HEAR YOU'VE BEEN ASKING FOR CAM ORTON?

SO?

SO I'M HER.

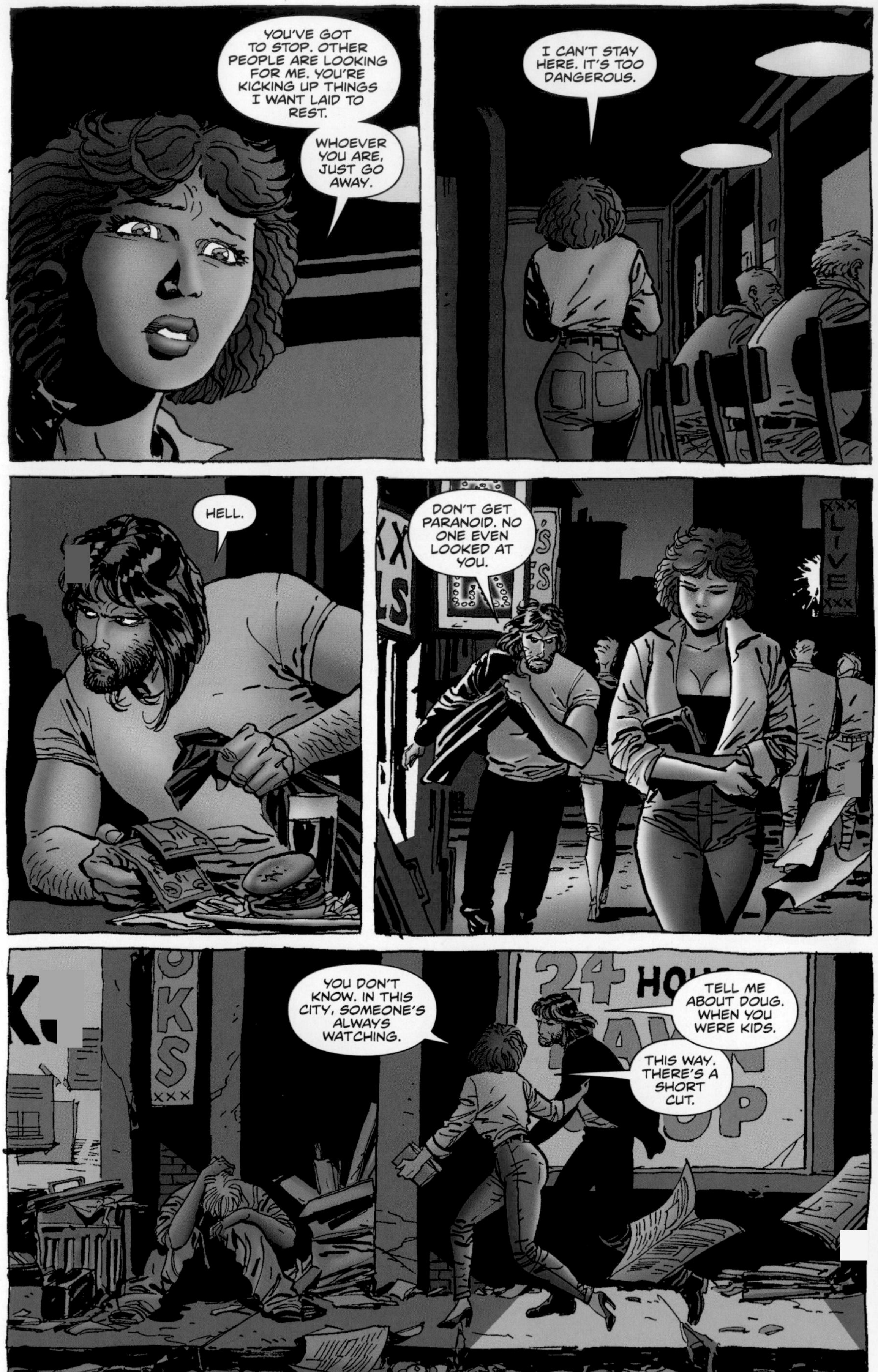
YOU'VE GOT TO STOP. OTHER PEOPLE ARE LOOKING FOR ME. YOU'RE KICKING UP THINGS I WANT LAID TO REST.
WHOEVER YOU ARE, JUST GO AWAY.
I CAN'T STAY HERE. IT'S TOO DANGEROUS.
HELL.
DON'T GET PARANOID. NO ONE EVEN LOOKED AT YOU.
XXX LIVE XXX
YOU DON'T KNOW. IN THIS CITY, SOMEONE'S ALWAYS WATCHING.
TELL ME ABOUT DOUG. WHEN YOU WERE KIDS.
THIS WAY. THERE'S A SHORT CUT.

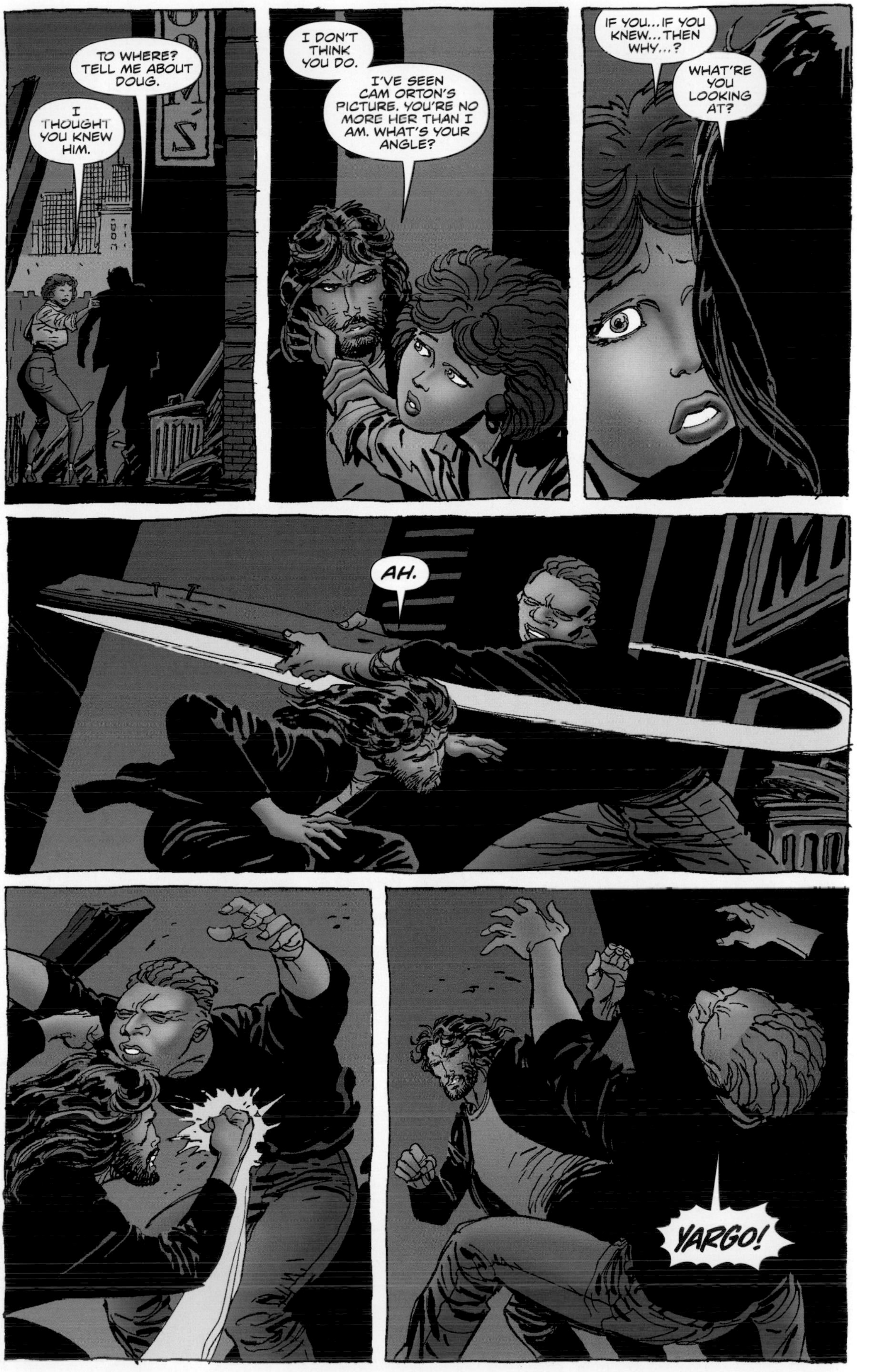
I THOUGHT YOU KNEW HIM.
TO WHERE? TELL ME ABOUT DOUG.
I DON'T THINK YOU DO.
I'VE SEEN CAM ORTON'S PICTURE. YOU'RE NO MORE HER THAN I AM. WHAT'S YOUR ANGLE?
IF YOU... IF YOU KNEW... THEN WHY...?
WHAT'RE YOU LOOKING AT?
AH.
YARGO!

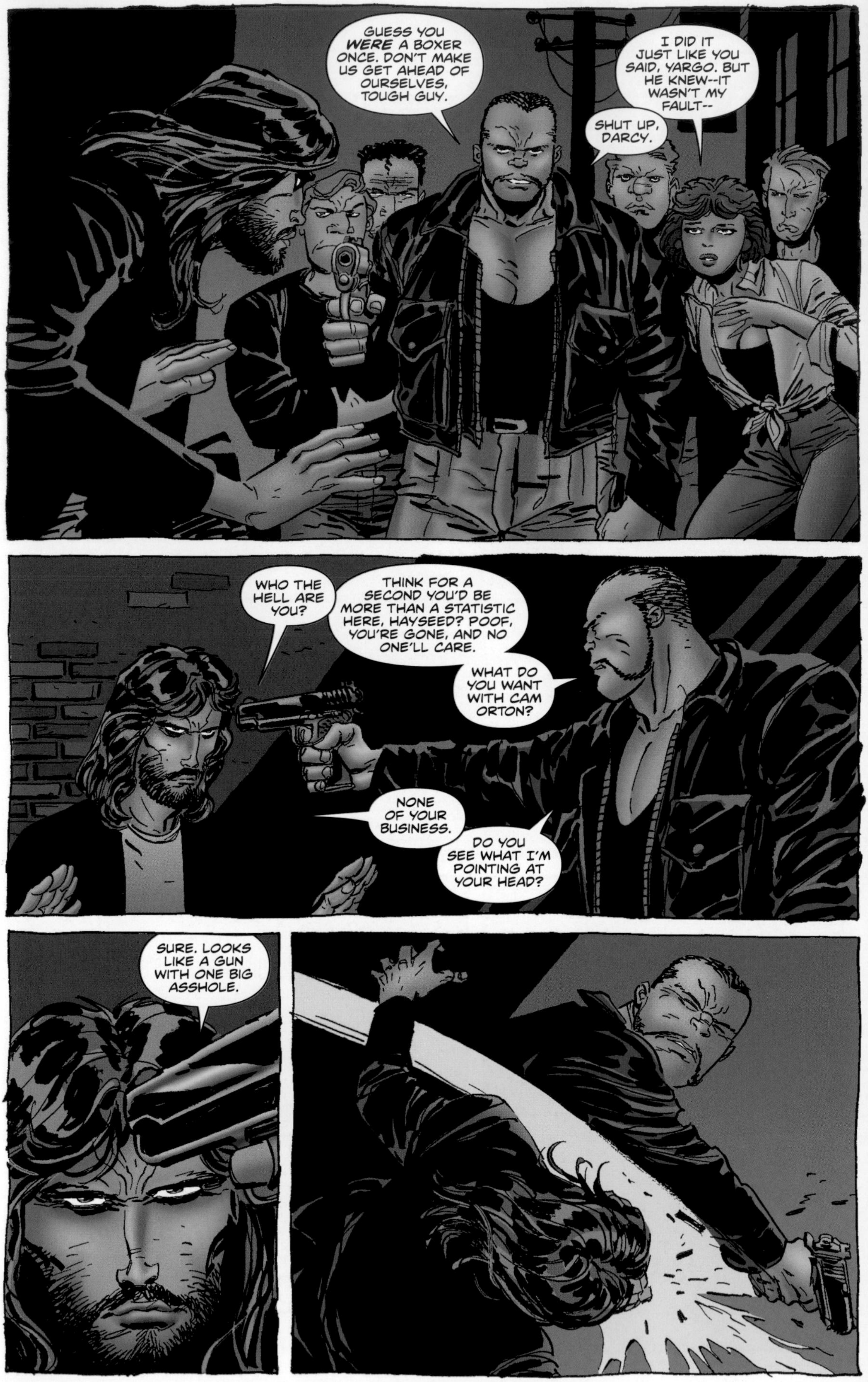
GUESS YOU *WERE* A BOXER ONCE. DON'T MAKE US GET AHEAD OF OURSELVES, TOUGH GUY.
I DID IT JUST LIKE YOU SAID, YARGO. BUT HE KNEW--IT WASN'T MY FAULT--
SHUT UP, DARCY.
WHO THE HELL ARE YOU?
THINK FOR A SECOND YOU'D BE MORE THAN A STATISTIC HERE, HAYSEED? POOF, YOU'RE GONE, AND NO ONE'LL CARE.
WHAT DO YOU WANT WITH CAM ORTON?
NONE OF YOUR BUSINESS.
DO YOU SEE WHAT I'M POINTING AT YOUR HEAD?
SURE. LOOKS LIKE A GUN WITH ONE BIG ASSHOLE.

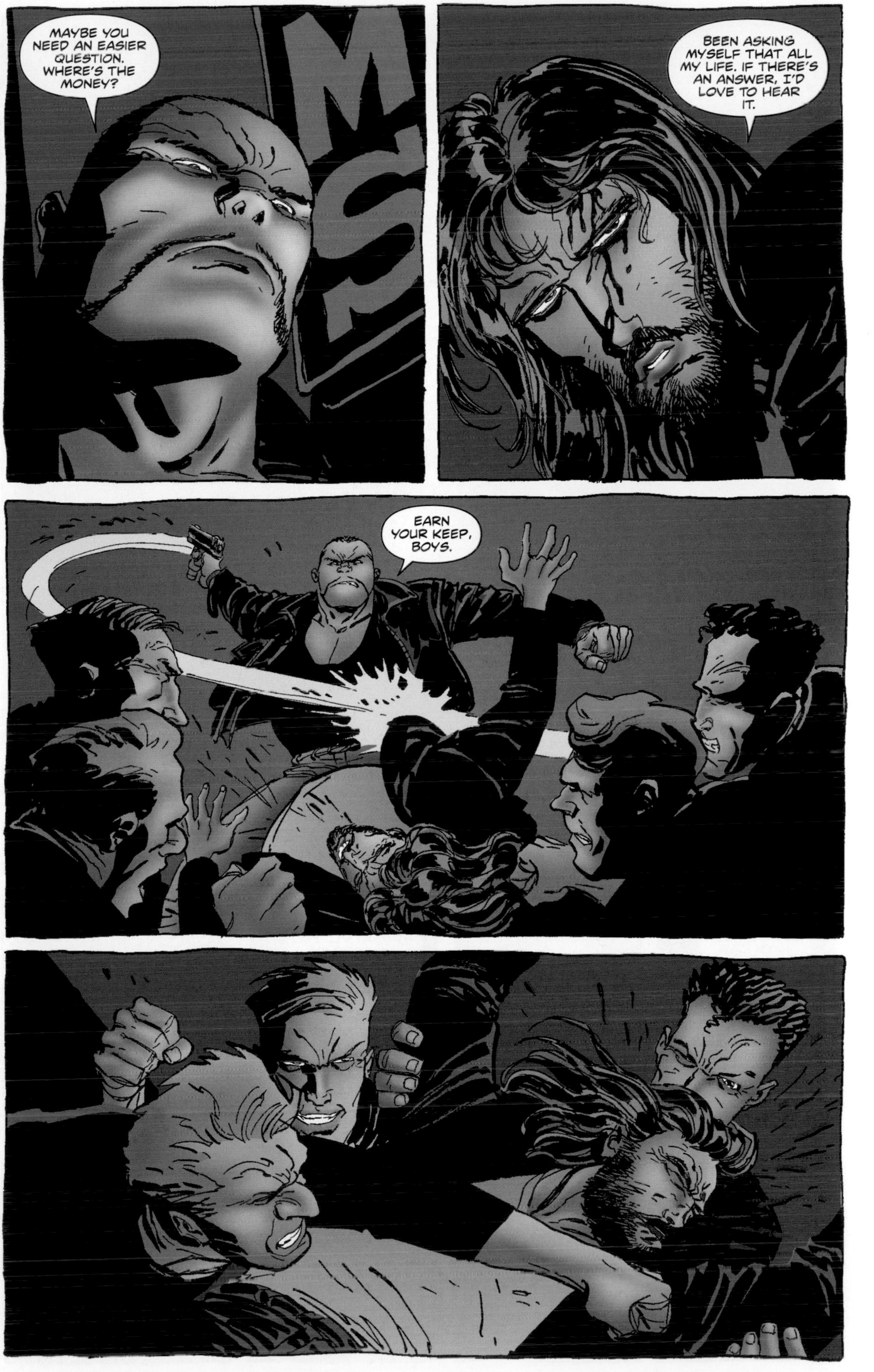
MAYBE YOU NEED AN EASIER QUESTION. WHERE'S THE MONEY?
BEEN ASKING MYSELF THAT ALL MY LIFE. IF THERE'S AN ANSWER, I'D LOVE TO HEAR IT.
EARN YOUR KEEP, BOYS.

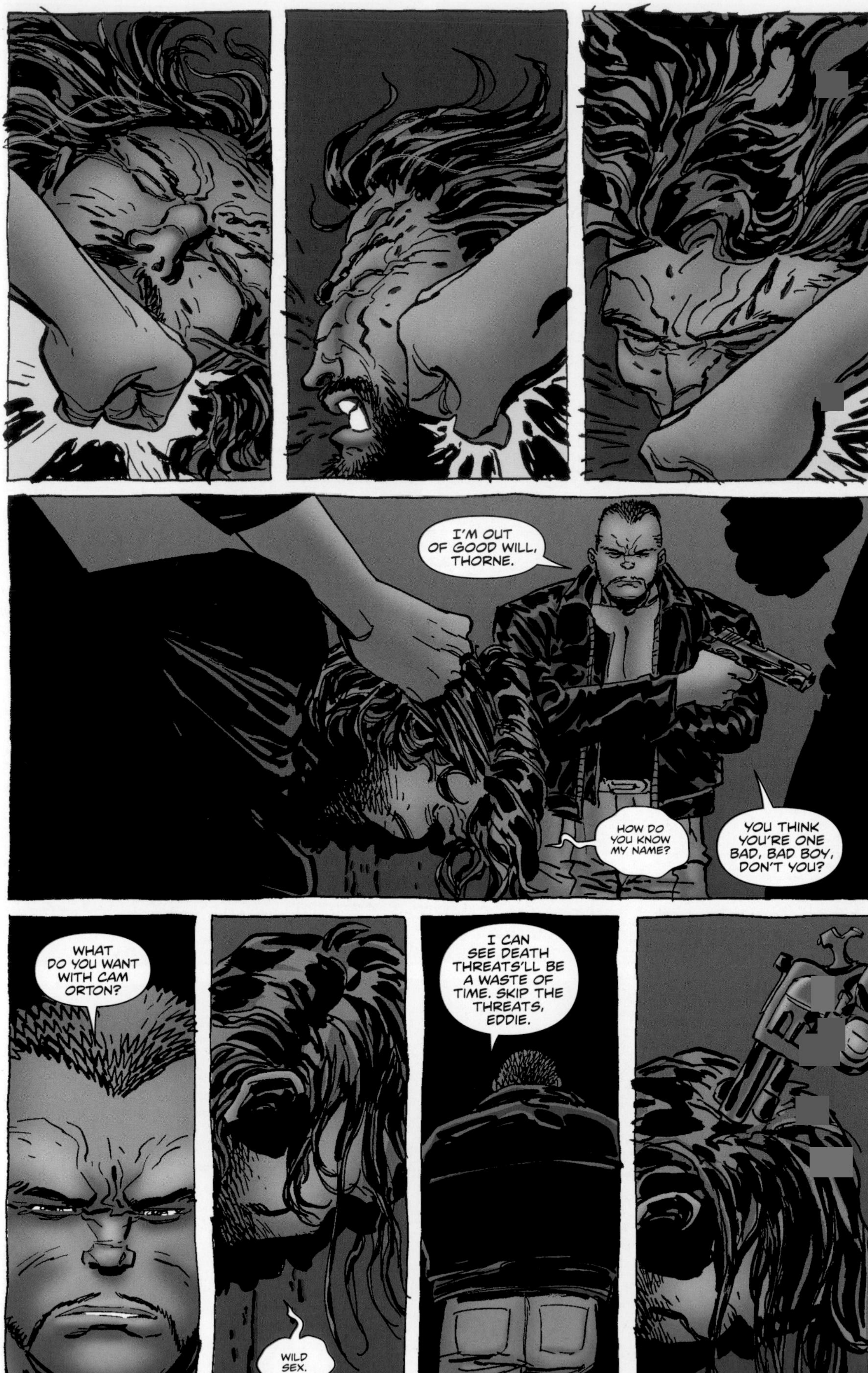
I'M OUT OF GOOD WILL, THORNE.
HOW DO YOU KNOW MY NAME?
YOU THINK YOU'RE ONE BAD, BAD BOY, DON'T YOU?
WHAT DO YOU WANT WITH CAM ORTON?
WILD SEX.
I CAN SEE DEATH THREATS'LL BE A WASTE OF TIME. SKIP THE THREATS, EDDIE.

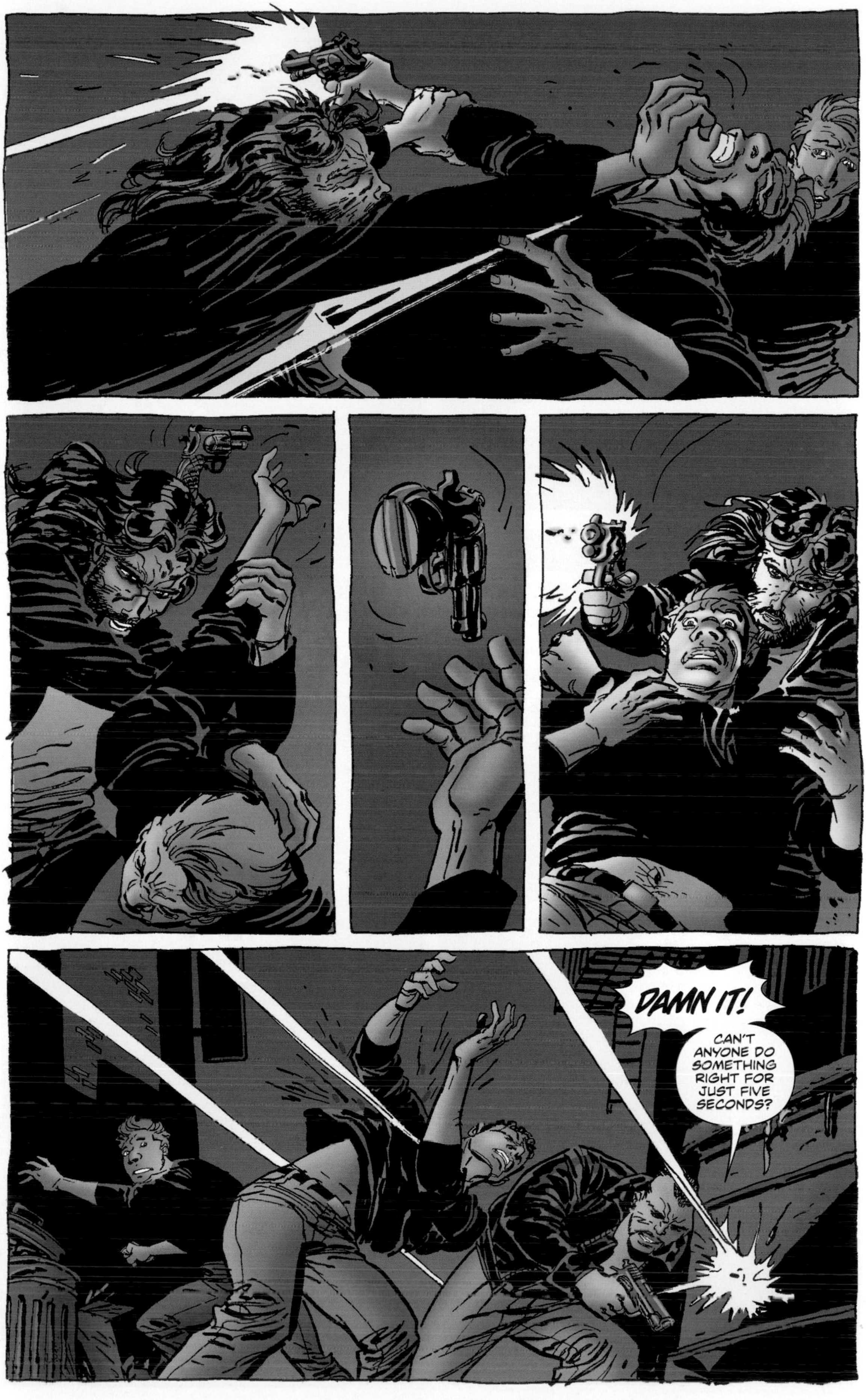
DAMN IT!
CAN'T ANYONE DO SOMETHING RIGHT FOR JUST FIVE SECONDS?

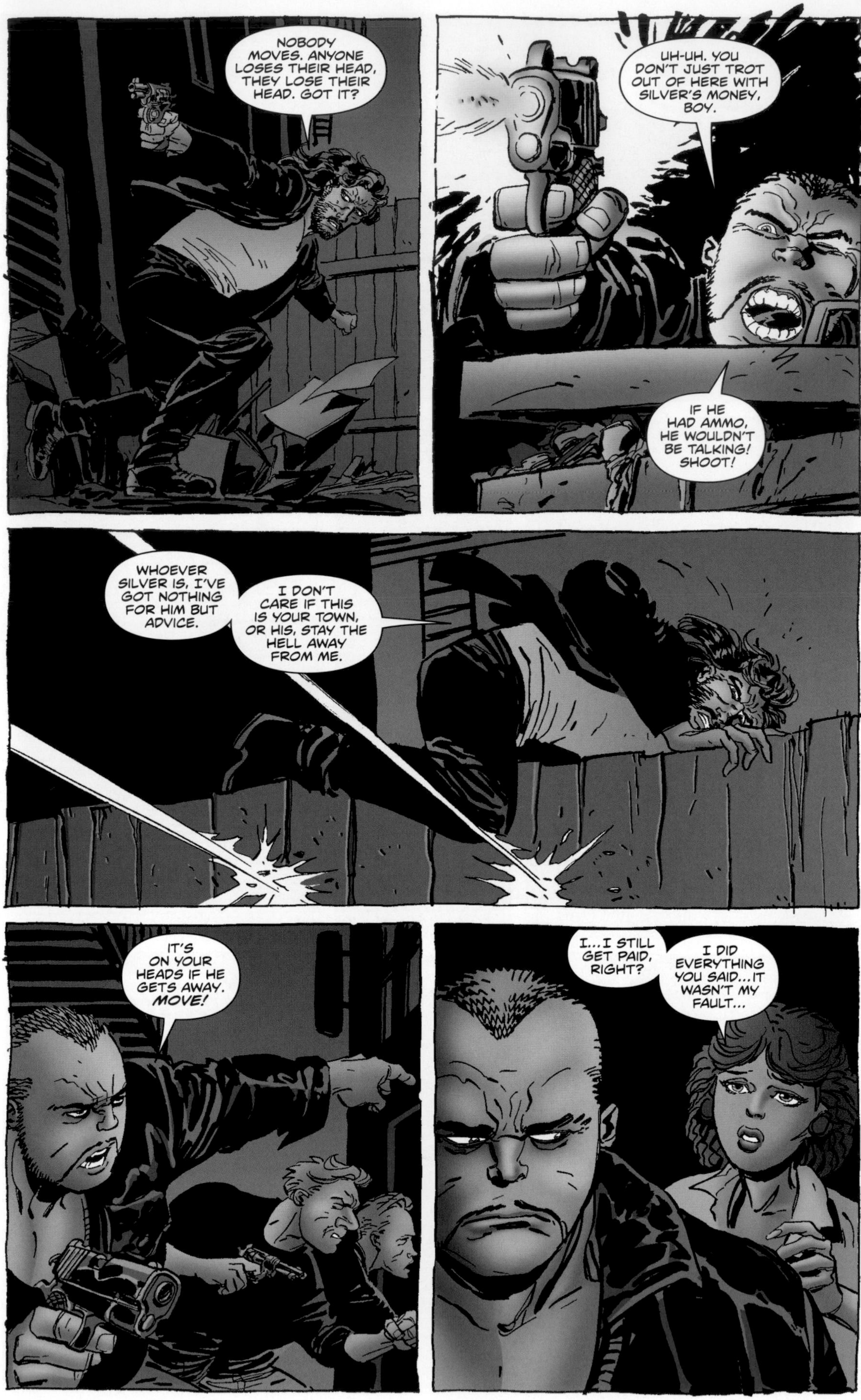
NOBODY MOVES. ANYONE LOSES THEIR HEAD, THEY LOSE THEIR HEAD. GOT IT?
UH-UH. YOU DON'T JUST TROT OUT OF HERE WITH SILVER'S MONEY, BOY.
IF HE HAD AMMO, HE WOULDN'T BE TALKING! SHOOT!
WHOEVER SILVER IS, I'VE GOT NOTHING FOR HIM BUT ADVICE.
I DON'T CARE IF THIS IS YOUR TOWN, OR HIS, STAY THE HELL AWAY FROM ME.
IT'S ON YOUR HEADS IF HE GETS AWAY. *MOVE!*
I...I STILL GET PAID, RIGHT?
I DID EVERYTHING YOU SAID...IT WASN'T MY FAULT...

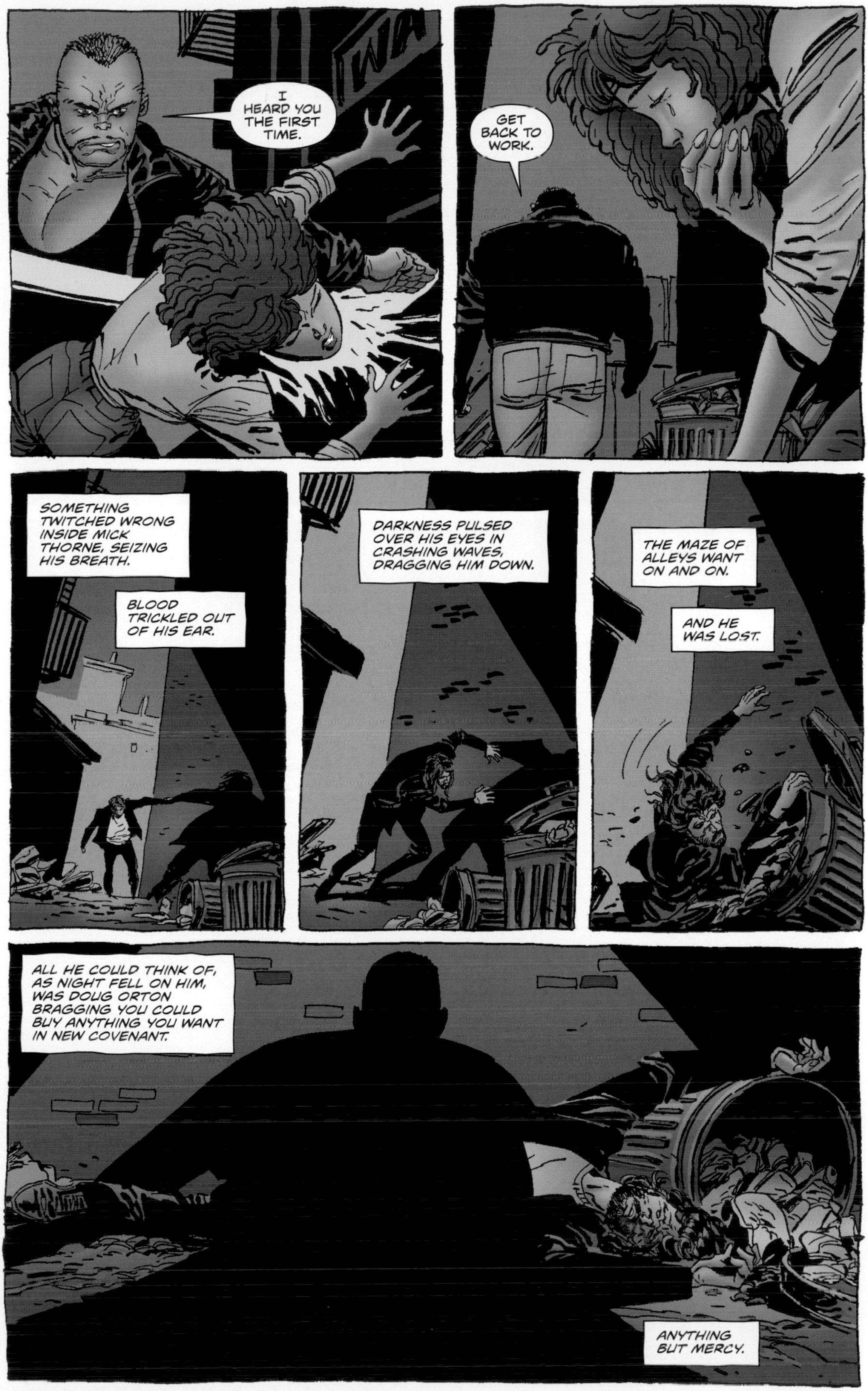
I HEARD YOU THE FIRST TIME.
GET BACK TO WORK.
SOMETHING TWITCHED WRONG INSIDE MICK THORNE, SEIZING HIS BREATH.
BLOOD TRICKLED OUT OF HIS EAR.
DARKNESS PULSED OVER HIS EYES IN CRASHING WAVES, DRAGGING HIM DOWN.
THE MAZE OF ALLEYS WANT ON AND ON.
AND HE WAS LOST.
ALL HE COULD THINK OF, AS NIGHT FELL ON HIM, WAS DOUG ORTON BRAGGING YOU COULD BUY ANYTHING YOU WANT IN NEW COVENANT.
ANYTHING BUT MERCY.

"ALL HIS LIFE, MICK THORNE
NEVER RAN FROM ANYTHING."

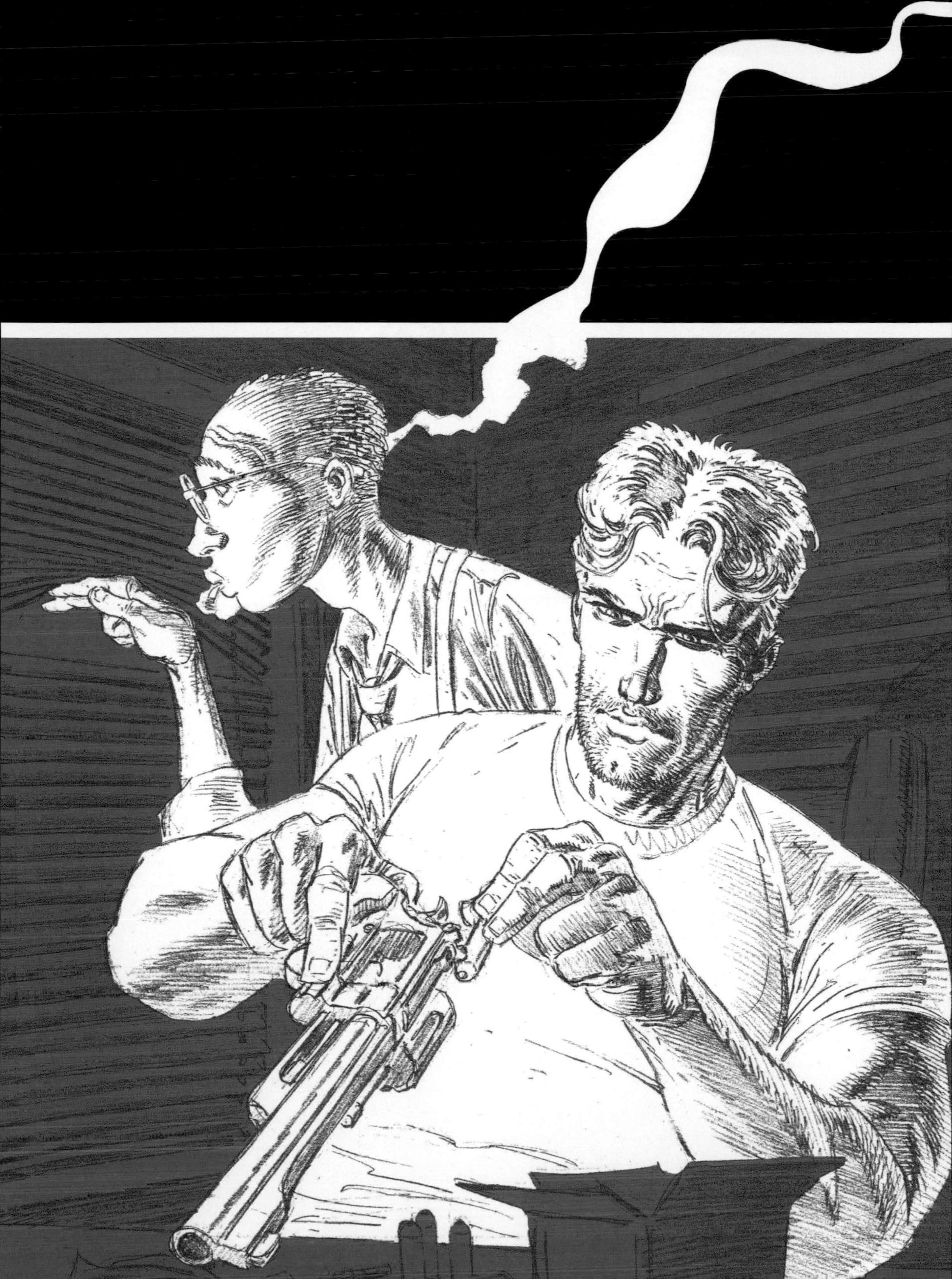

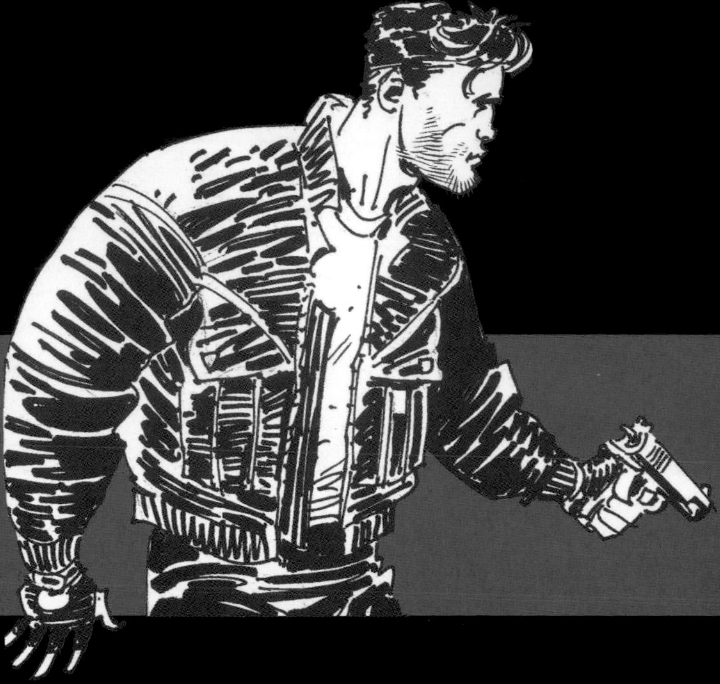

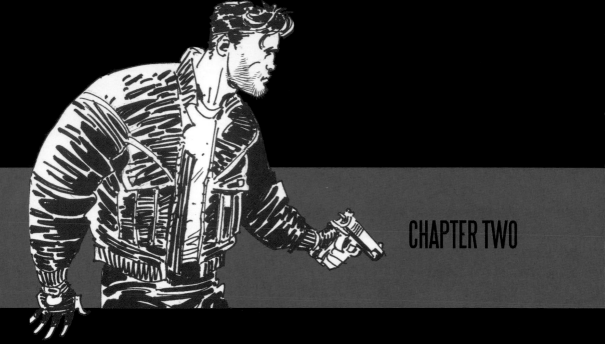

CHAPTER TWO

DRESSING UP FOR A DANCE WITH SILVER —

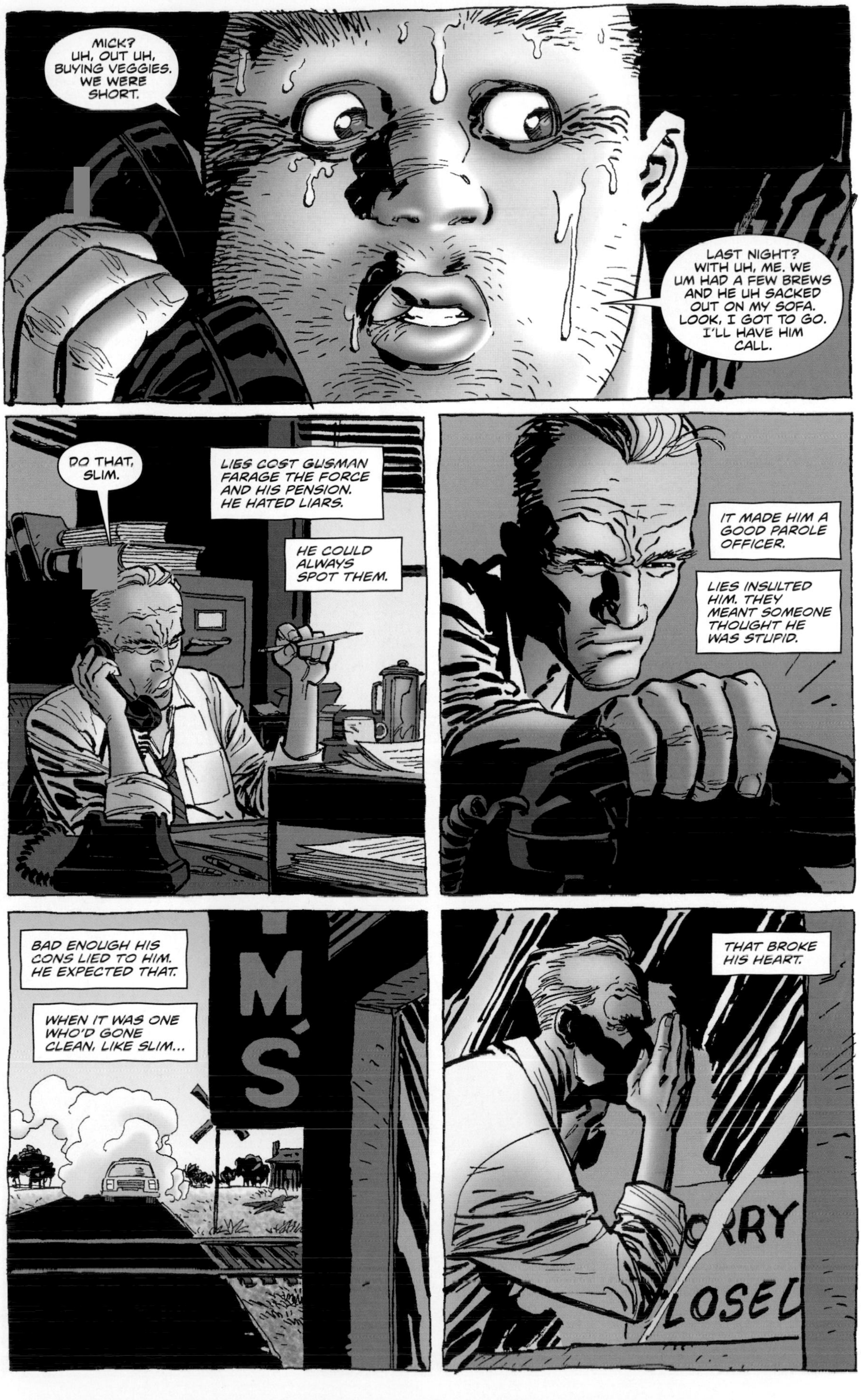
MICK? UH, OUT UH, BUYING VEGGIES. WE WERE SHORT.
LAST NIGHT? WITH UH, ME. WE UM HAD A FEW BREWS AND HE UH SACKED OUT ON MY SOFA. LOOK, I GOT TO GO. I'LL HAVE HIM CALL.
DO THAT, SLIM.
LIES COST GUSMAN FARAGE THE FORCE AND HIS PENSION. HE HATED LIARS.
HE COULD ALWAYS SPOT THEM.
IT MADE HIM A GOOD PAROLE OFFICER.
LIES INSULTED HIM. THEY MEANT SOMEONE THOUGHT HE WAS STUPID.
BAD ENOUGH HIS CONS LIED TO HIM. HE EXPECTED THAT.
WHEN IT WAS ONE WHO'D GONE CLEAN, LIKE SLIM...
M'S
THAT BROKE HIS HEART.
ORRY
LOSED

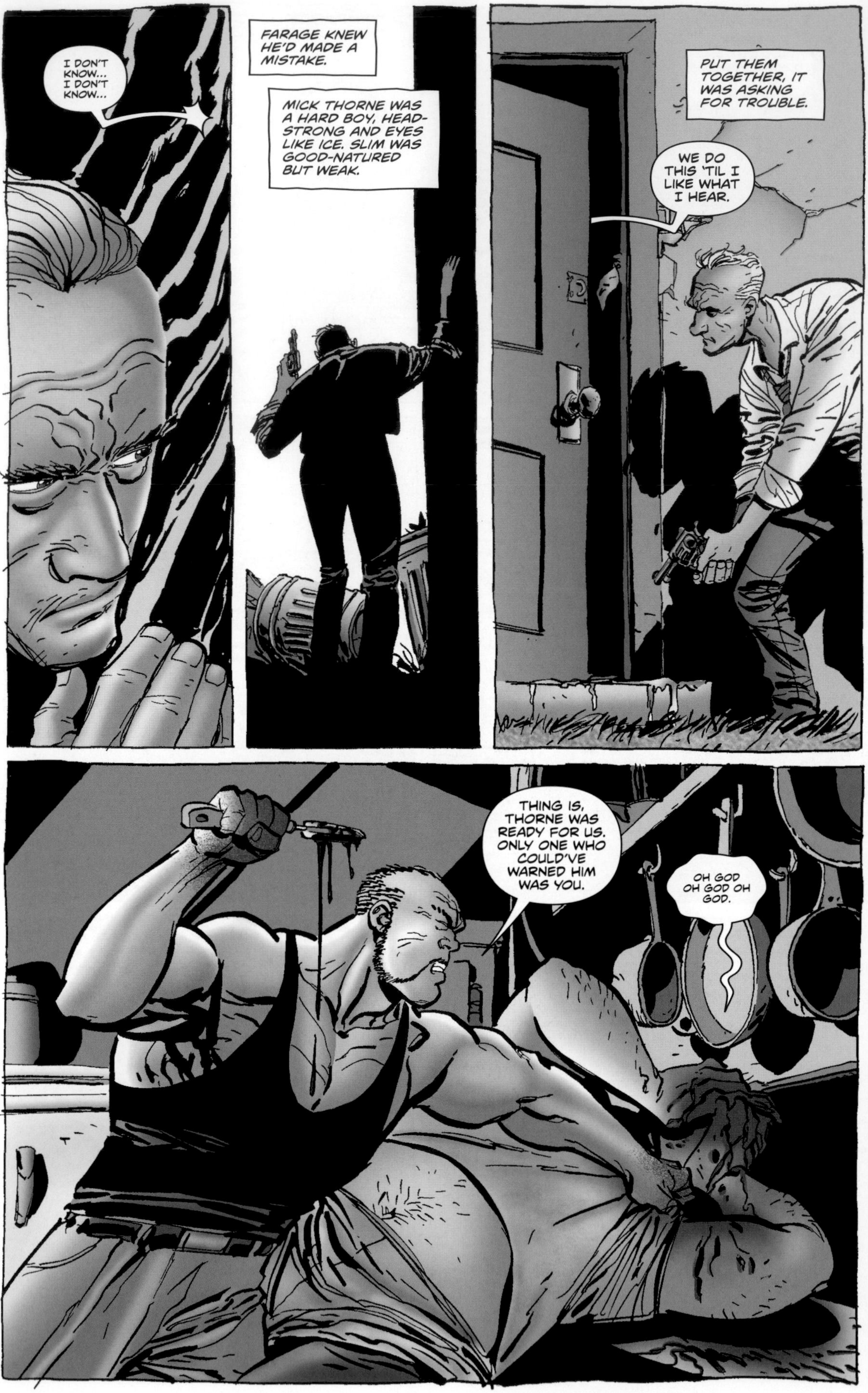
I DON'T KNOW... I DON'T KNOW...
FARAGE KNEW HE'D MADE A MISTAKE.
MICK THORNE WAS A HARD BOY, HEAD-STRONG AND EYES LIKE ICE. SLIM WAS GOOD-NATURED BUT WEAK.
PUT THEM TOGETHER, IT WAS ASKING FOR TROUBLE.
WE DO THIS 'TIL I LIKE WHAT I HEAR.
THING IS, THORNE WAS READY FOR US. ONLY ONE WHO COULD'VE WARNED HIM WAS YOU.
OH GOD OH GOD OH GOD.

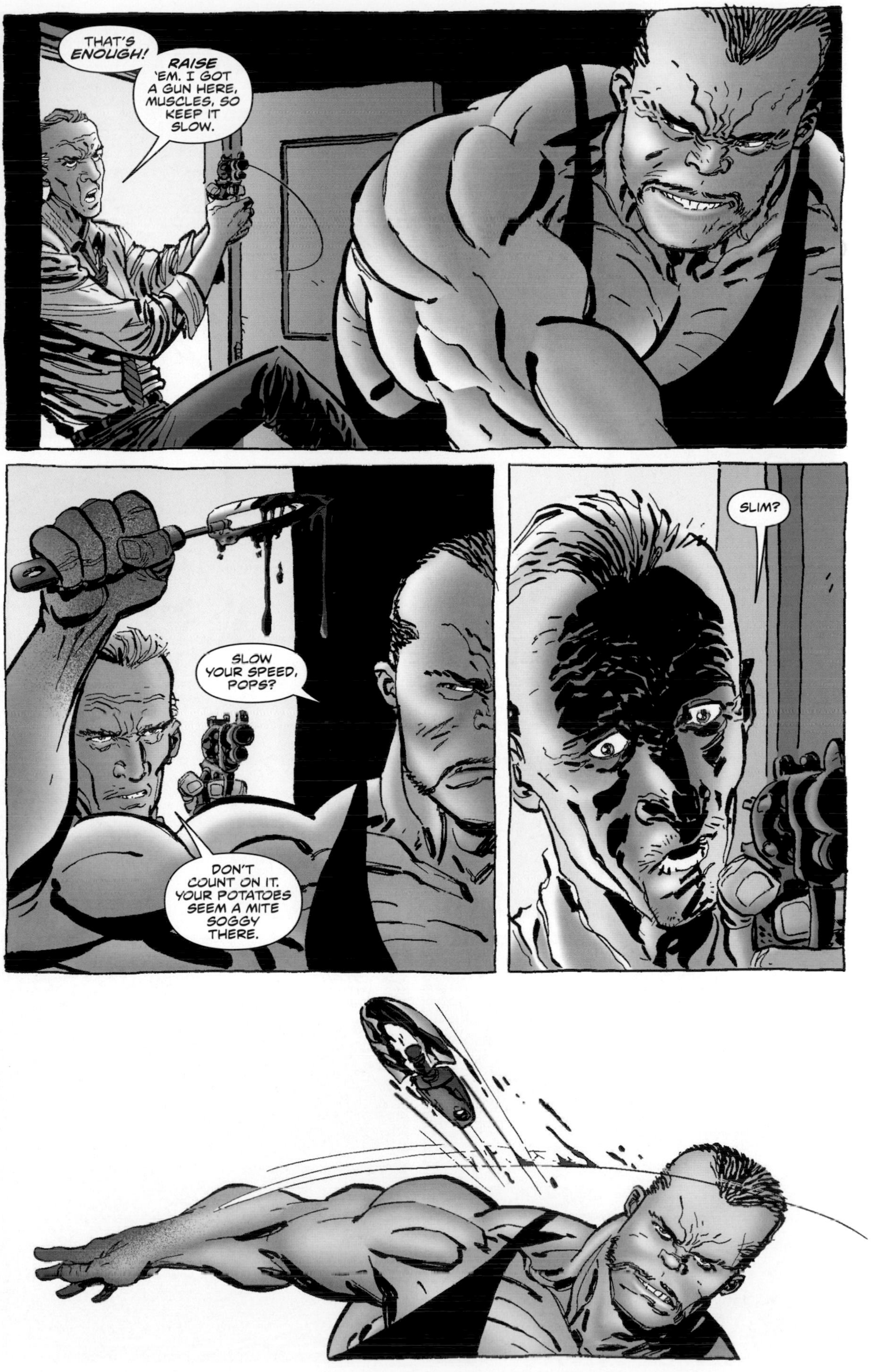
THAT'S ENOUGH!
RAISE 'EM. I GOT A GUN HERE, MUSCLES, SO KEEP IT SLOW.
SLOW YOUR SPEED, POPS?
DON'T COUNT ON IT. YOUR POTATOES SEEM A MITE SOGGY THERE.
SLIM?

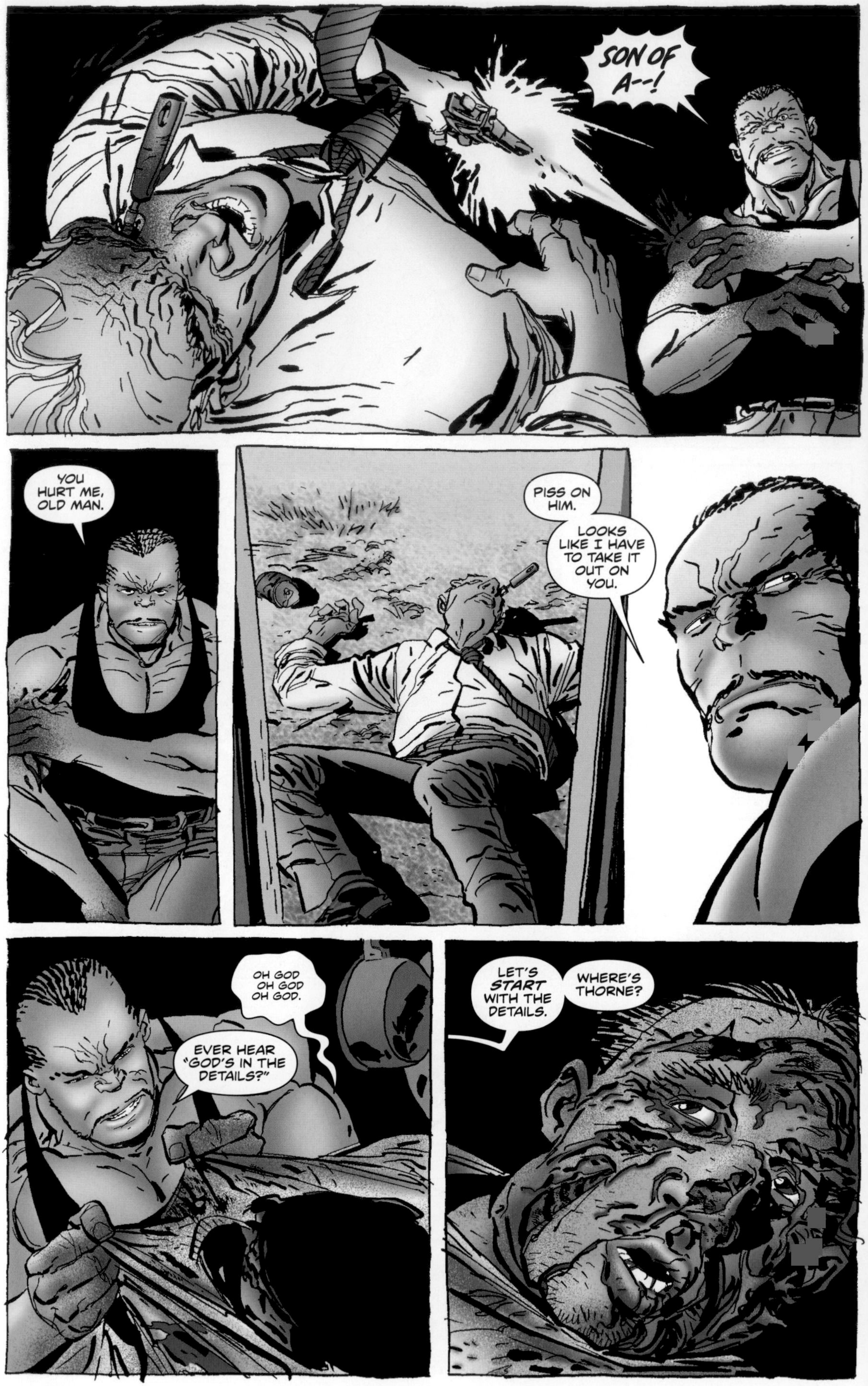
SON OF A--!
YOU HURT ME, OLD MAN.
PISS ON HIM.
LOOKS LIKE I HAVE TO TAKE IT OUT ON YOU.
EVER HEAR "GOD'S IN THE DETAILS?"
OH GOD OH GOD OH GOD.
LET'S START WITH THE DETAILS.
WHERE'S THORNE?

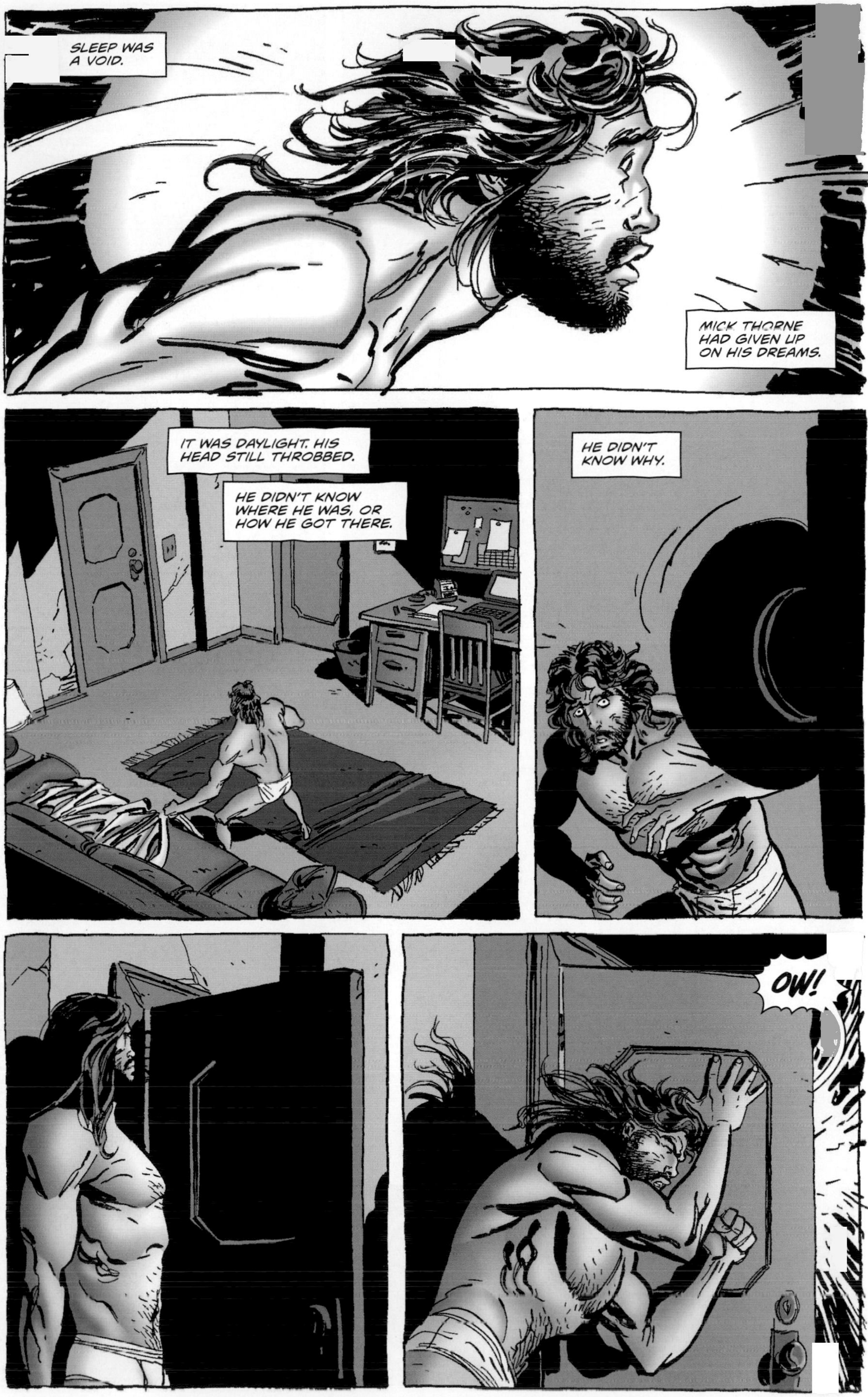
SLEEP WAS A VOID.
MICK THORNE HAD GIVEN UP ON HIS DREAMS.
IT WAS DAYLIGHT. HIS HEAD STILL THROBBED.
HE DIDN'T KNOW WHERE HE WAS, OR HOW HE GOT THERE.
HE DIDN'T KNOW WHY.
OW!

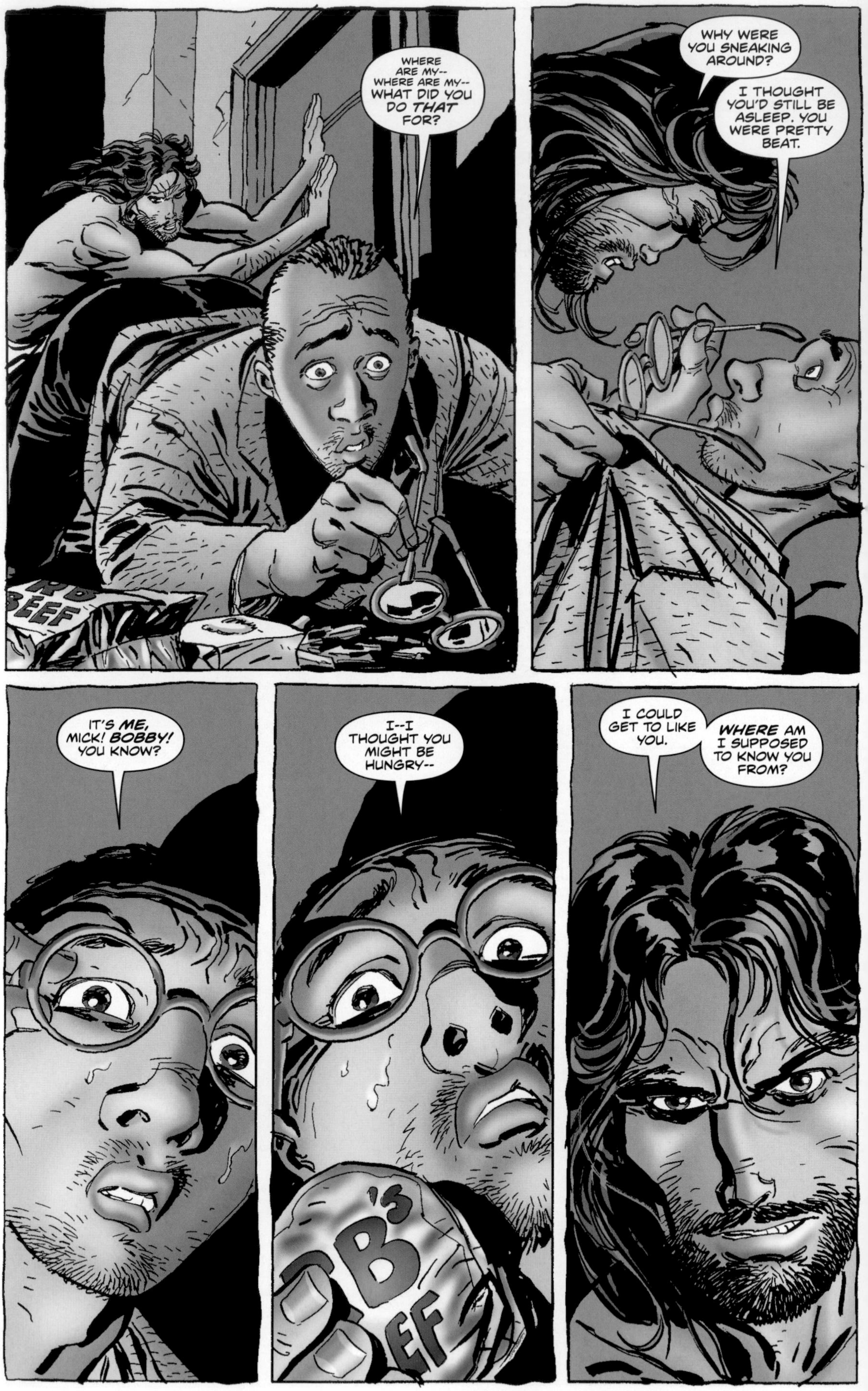
WHERE ARE MY-- WHERE ARE MY-- WHAT DID YOU DO THAT FOR?
WHY WERE YOU SNEAKING AROUND?
I THOUGHT YOU'D STILL BE ASLEEP. YOU WERE PRETTY BEAT.
IT'S ME, MICK! BOBBY! YOU KNOW?
I--I THOUGHT YOU MIGHT BE HUNGRY--
I COULD GET TO LIKE YOU.
WHERE AM I SUPPOSED TO KNOW YOU FROM?

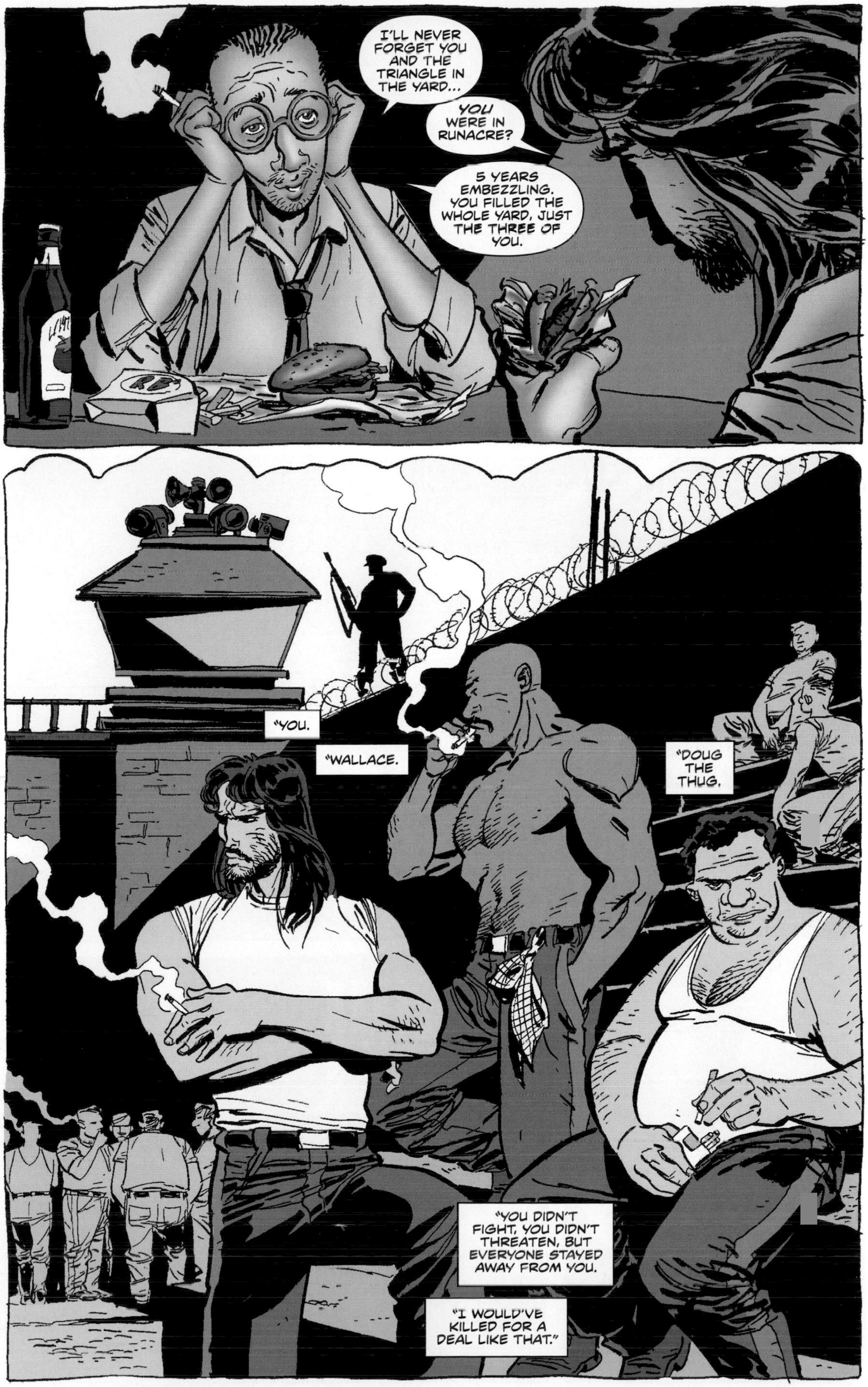
I'LL NEVER FORGET YOU AND THE TRIANGLE IN THE YARD...
YOU WERE IN RUNACRE?
5 YEARS EMBEZZLING. YOU FILLED THE WHOLE YARD, JUST THE THREE OF YOU.
"YOU.
"WALLACE.
"DOUG THE THUG.
"YOU DIDN'T FIGHT, YOU DIDN'T THREATEN, BUT EVERYONE STAYED AWAY FROM YOU.
"I WOULD'VE KILLED FOR A DEAL LIKE THAT."

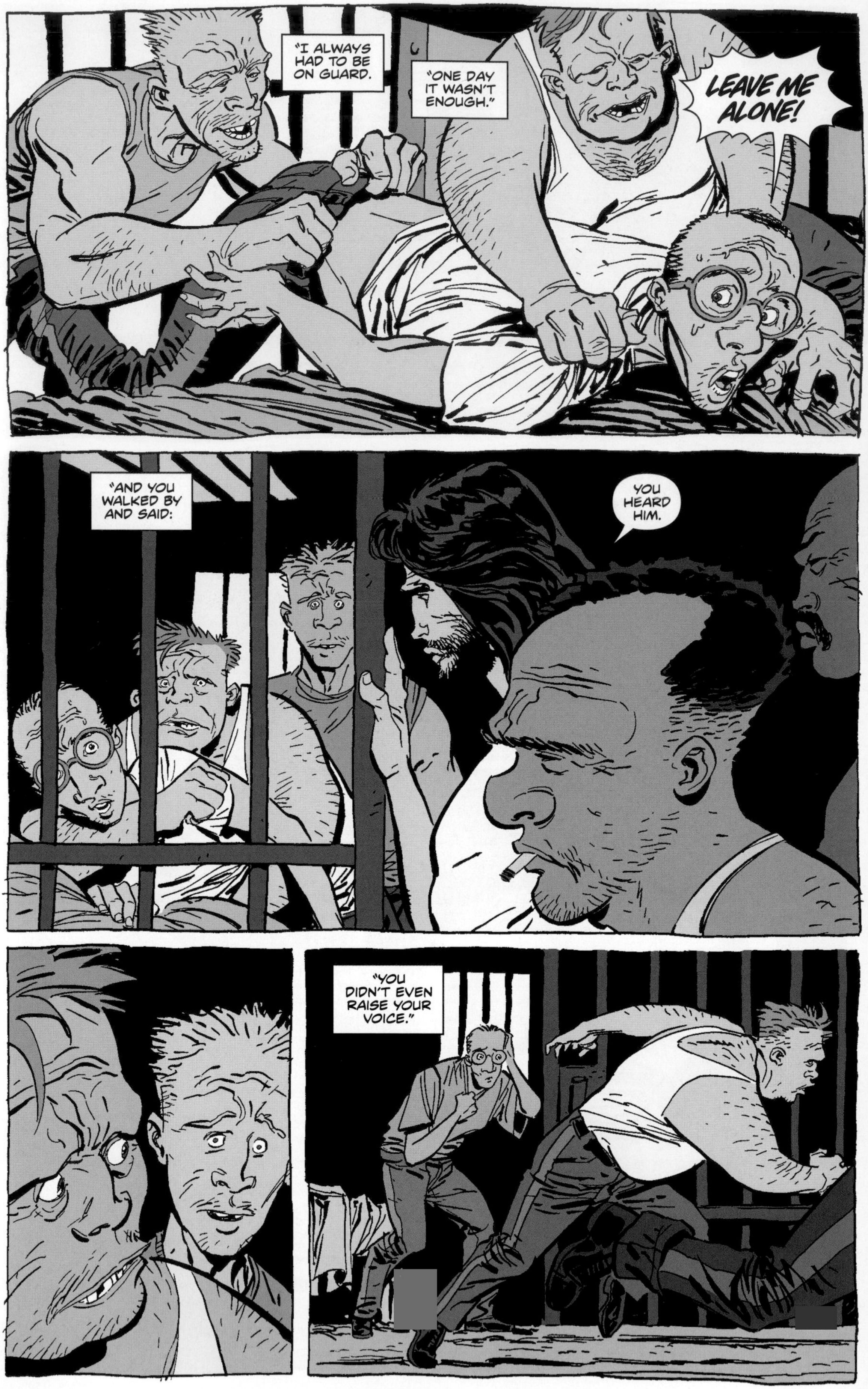
"I ALWAYS HAD TO BE ON GUARD.
"ONE DAY IT WASN'T ENOUGH."
LEAVE ME ALONE!
"AND YOU WALKED BY AND SAID:
YOU HEARD HIM.
"YOU DIDN'T EVEN RAISE YOUR VOICE."

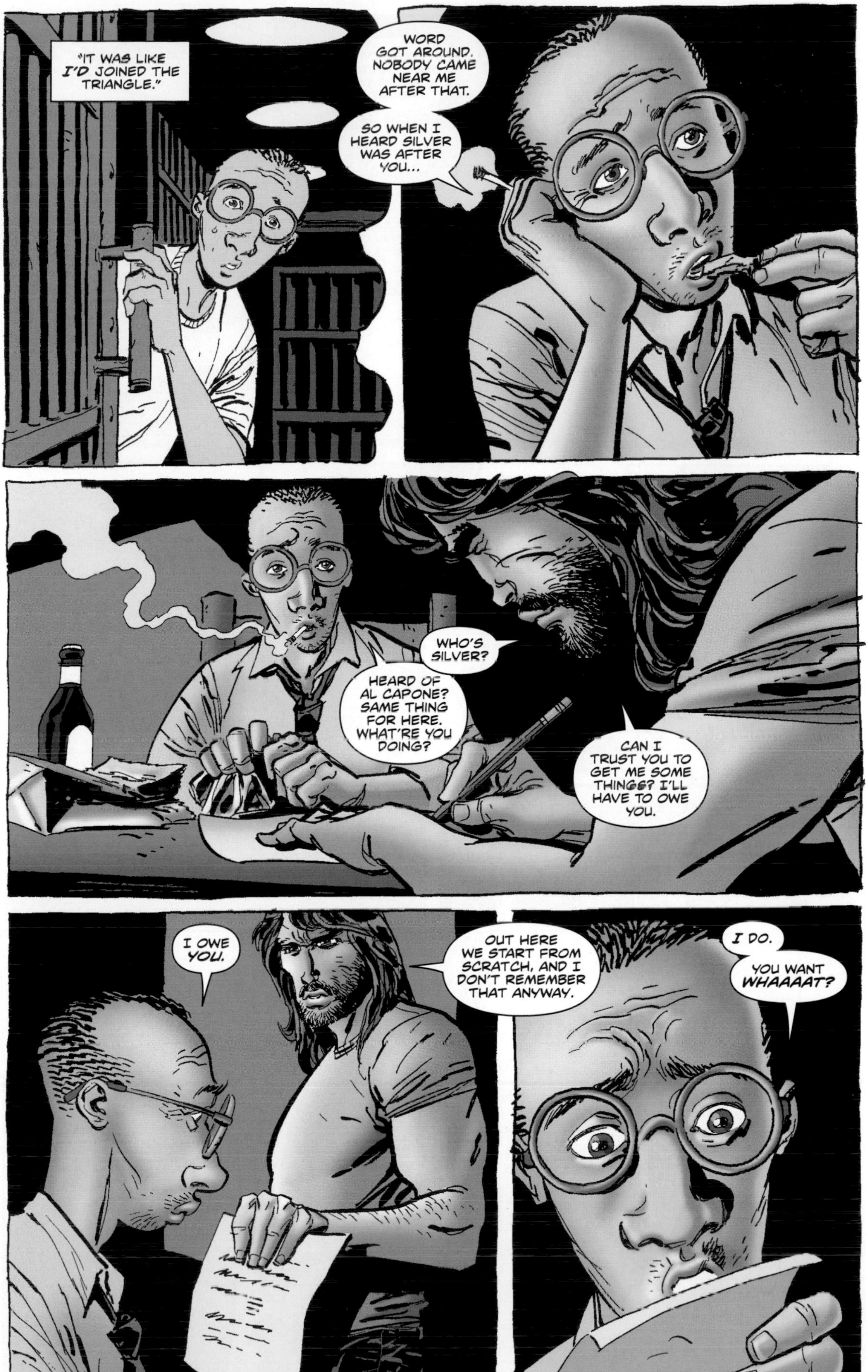
"IT WAS LIKE I'D JOINED THE TRIANGLE."
WORD GOT AROUND. NOBODY CAME NEAR ME AFTER THAT.
SO WHEN I HEARD SILVER WAS AFTER YOU...
WHO'S SILVER?
HEARD OF AL CAPONE? SAME THING FOR HERE. WHAT'RE YOU DOING?
CAN I TRUST YOU TO GET ME SOME THINGS? I'LL HAVE TO OWE YOU.
I OWE YOU.
OUT HERE WE START FROM SCRATCH, AND I DON'T REMEMBER THAT ANYWAY.
I DO.
YOU WANT WHAAAAT?

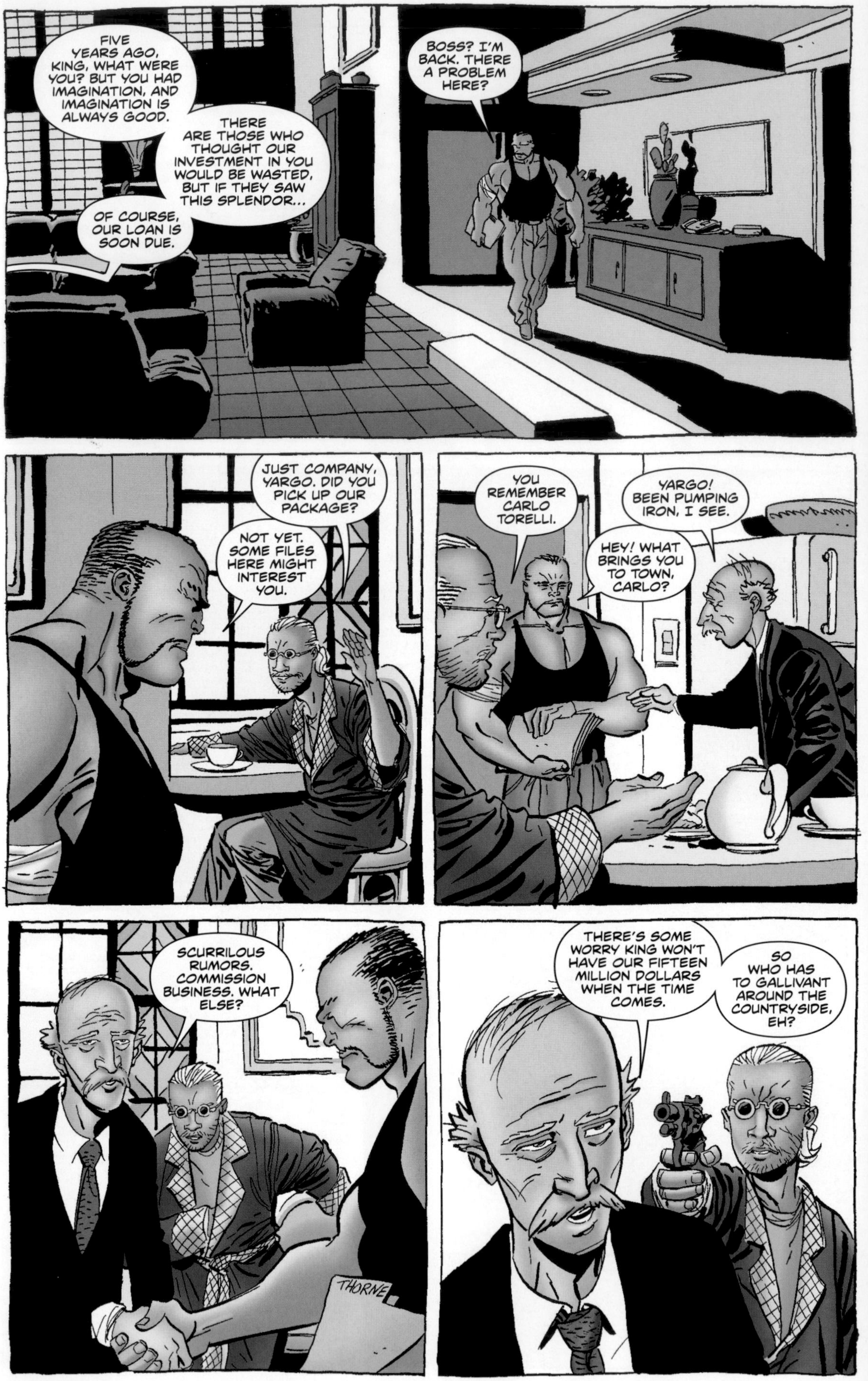
FIVE YEARS AGO, KING, WHAT WERE YOU? BUT YOU HAD IMAGINATION, AND IMAGINATION IS ALWAYS GOOD.
THERE ARE THOSE WHO THOUGHT OUR INVESTMENT IN YOU WOULD BE WASTED, BUT IF THEY SAW THIS SPLENDOR...
OF COURSE, OUR LOAN IS SOON DUE.
BOSS? I'M BACK. THERE A PROBLEM HERE?
JUST COMPANY, YARGO. DID YOU PICK UP OUR PACKAGE?
NOT YET. SOME FILES HERE MIGHT INTEREST YOU.
YOU REMEMBER CARLO TORELLI.
YARGO! BEEN PUMPING IRON, I SEE.
HEY! WHAT BRINGS YOU TO TOWN, CARLO?
SCURRILOUS RUMORS. COMMISSION BUSINESS. WHAT ELSE?
THORNE
THERE'S SOME WORRY KING WON'T HAVE OUR FIFTEEN MILLION DOLLARS WHEN THE TIME COMES.
SO WHO HAS TO GALLIVANT AROUND THE COUNTRYSIDE, EH?

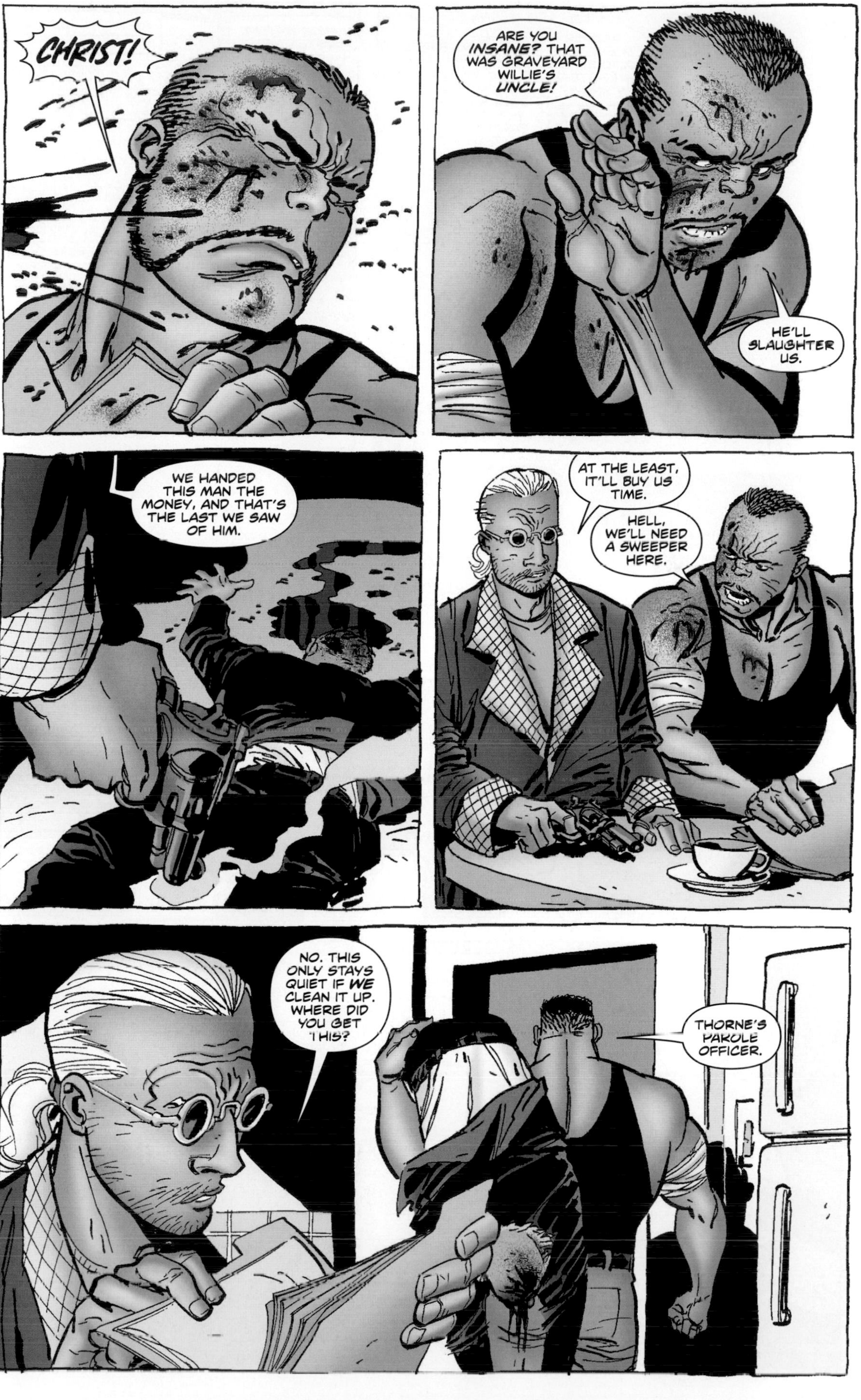
CHRIST!
ARE YOU INSANE? THAT WAS GRAVEYARD WILLIE'S UNCLE!
HE'LL SLAUGHTER US.
WE HANDED THIS MAN THE MONEY, AND THAT'S THE LAST WE SAW OF HIM.
AT THE LEAST, IT'LL BUY US TIME.
HELL, WE'LL NEED A SWEEPER HERE.
NO. THIS ONLY STAYS QUIET IF WE CLEAN IT UP. WHERE DID YOU GET THIS?
THORNE'S PAROLE OFFICER.

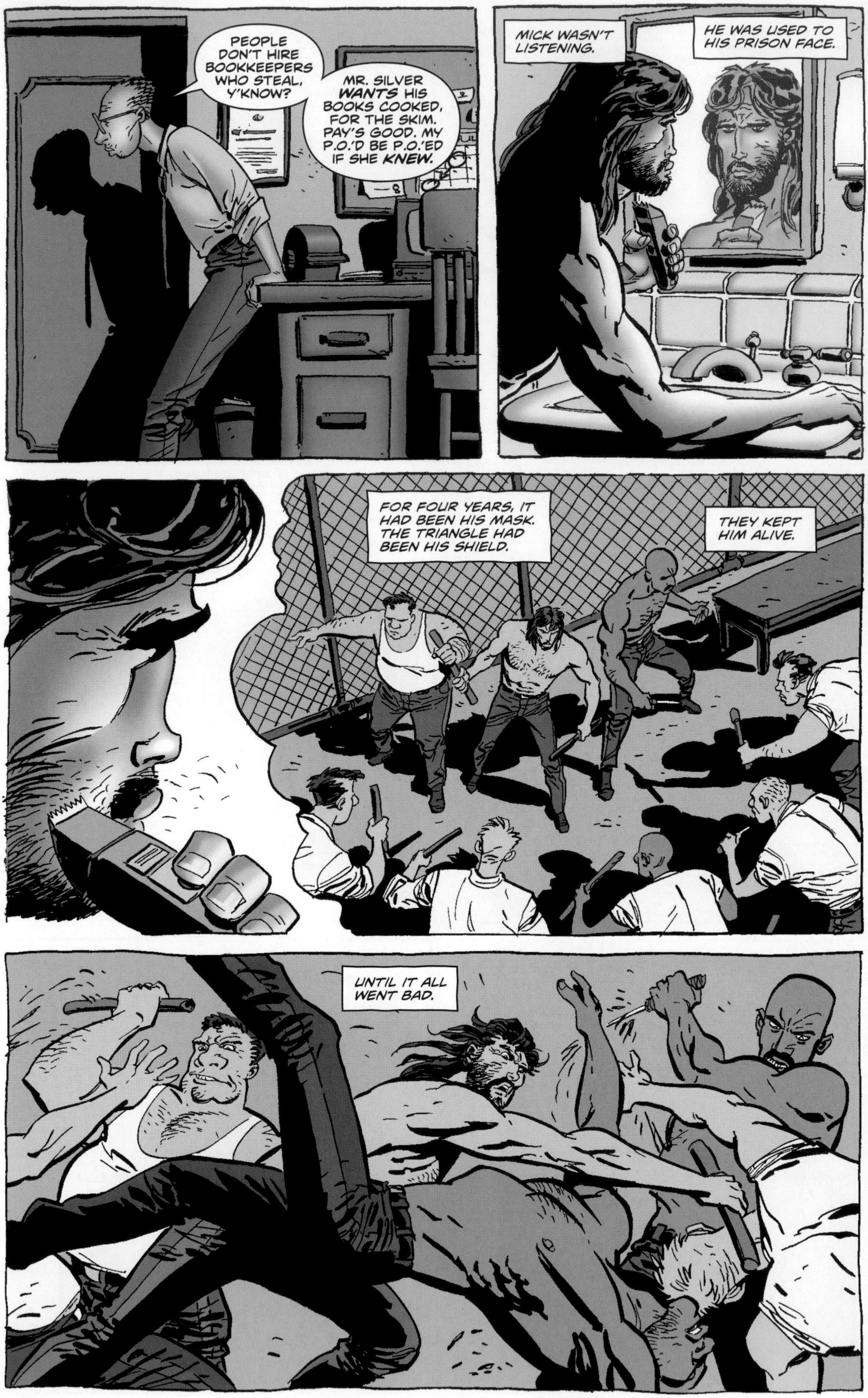
PEOPLE DON'T HIRE BOOKKEEPERS WHO STEAL, Y'KNOW?
MR. SILVER WANTS HIS BOOKS COOKED, FOR THE SKIM. PAY'S GOOD. MY P.O.'D BE P.O.'ED IF SHE KNEW.
MICK WASN'T LISTENING.
HE WAS USED TO HIS PRISON FACE.
FOR FOUR YEARS, IT HAD BEEN HIS MASK. THE TRIANGLE HAD BEEN HIS SHIELD.
THEY KEPT HIM ALIVE.
UNTIL IT ALL WENT BAD.

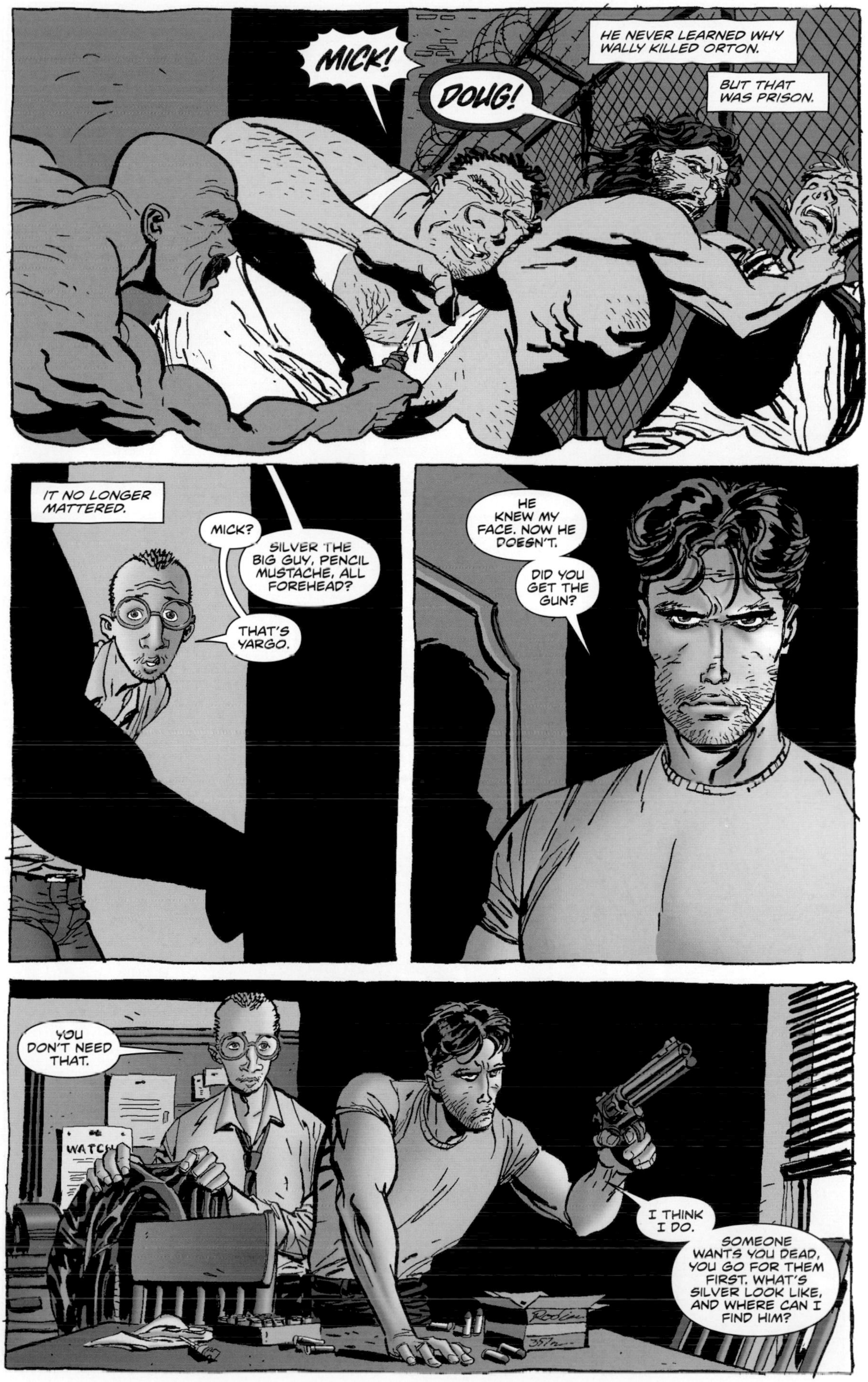
HE NEVER LEARNED WHY WALLY KILLED ORTON.
BUT THAT WAS PRISON.
MICK!
DOUG!
IT NO LONGER MATTERED.
SILVER THE BIG GUY, PENCIL MUSTACHE, ALL FOREHEAD?
MICK?
THAT'S YARGO.
HE KNEW MY FACE. NOW HE DOESN'T.
DID YOU GET THE GUN?
YOU DON'T NEED THAT.
I THINK I DO.
SOMEONE WANTS YOU DEAD, YOU GO FOR THEM FIRST. WHAT'S SILVER LOOK LIKE, AND WHERE CAN I FIND HIM?

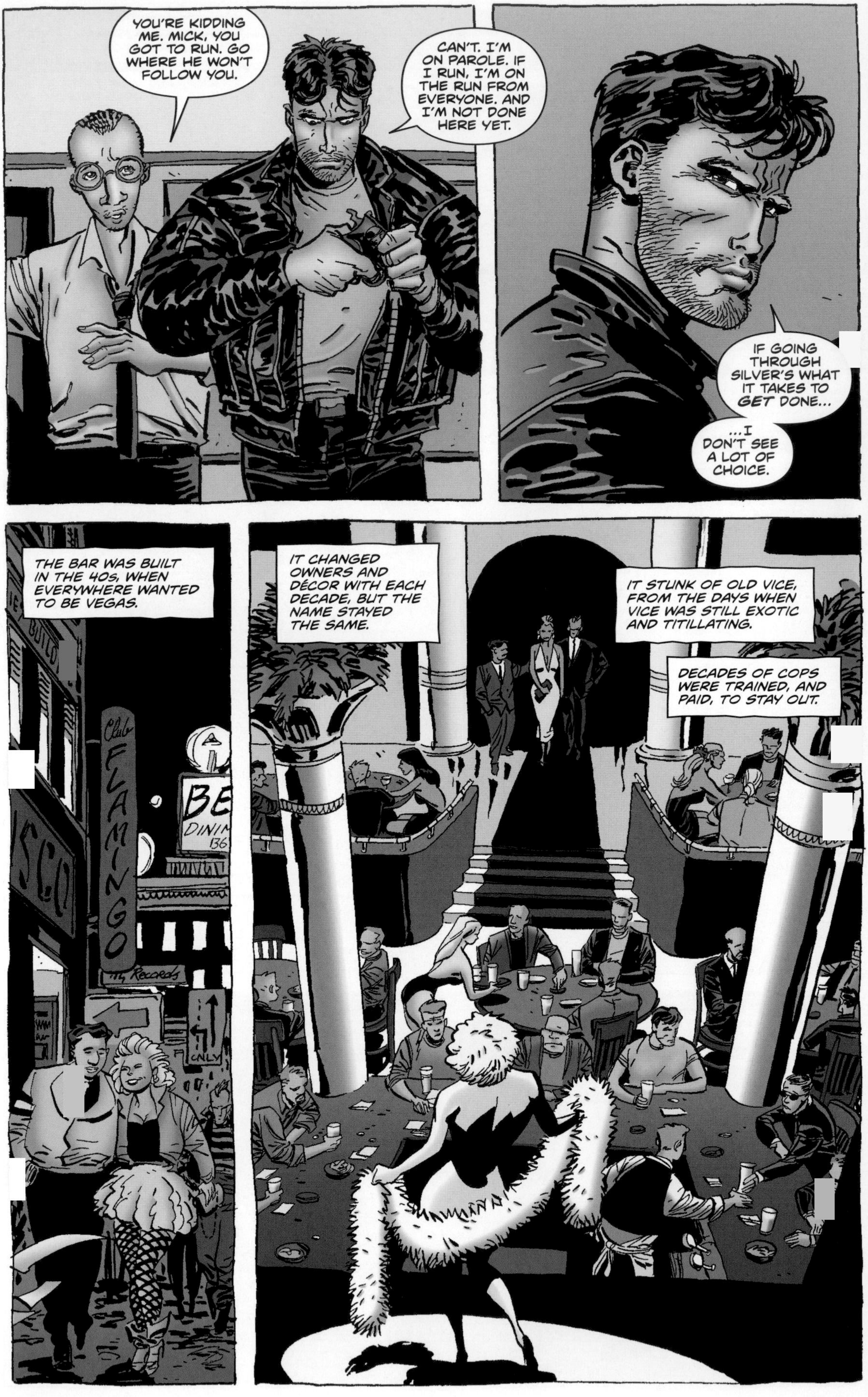
YOU'RE KIDDING ME. MICK, YOU GOT TO RUN. GO WHERE HE WON'T FOLLOW YOU.
CAN'T. I'M ON PAROLE. IF I RUN, I'M ON THE RUN FROM EVERYONE. AND I'M NOT DONE HERE YET.
IF GOING THROUGH SILVER'S WHAT IT TAKES TO GET DONE...
...I DON'T SEE A LOT OF CHOICE.
THE BAR WAS BUILT IN THE 40s, WHEN EVERYWHERE WANTED TO BE VEGAS.
Club FLAMINGO
IT CHANGED OWNERS AND DÉCOR WITH EACH DECADE, BUT THE NAME STAYED THE SAME.
IT STUNK OF OLD VICE, FROM THE DAYS WHEN VICE WAS STILL EXOTIC AND TITILLATING.
DECADES OF COPS WERE TRAINED, AND PAID, TO STAY OUT.

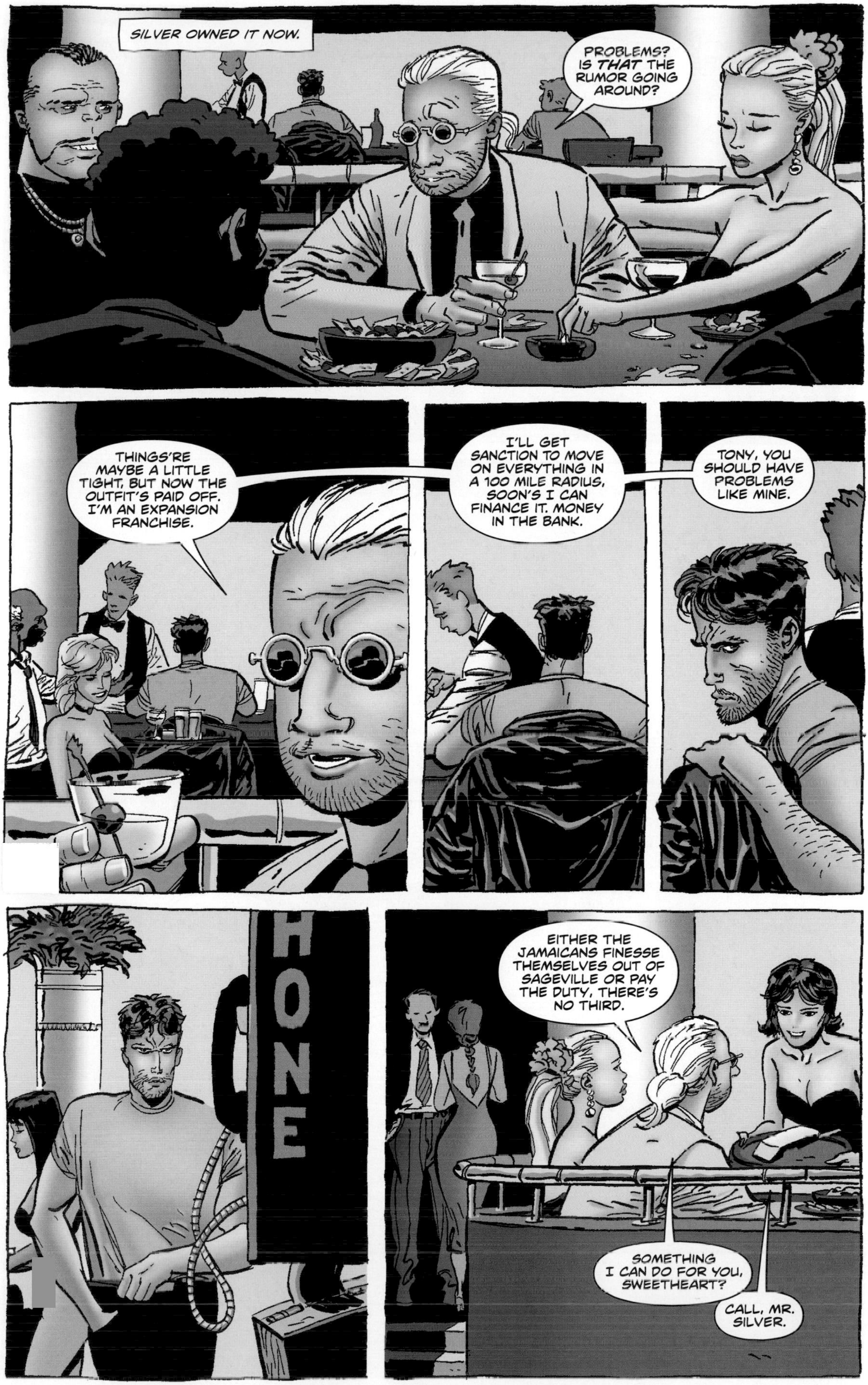
SILVER OWNED IT NOW.
PROBLEMS? IS THAT THE RUMOR GOING AROUND?
THINGS'RE MAYBE A LITTLE TIGHT, BUT NOW THE OUTFIT'S PAID OFF. I'M AN EXPANSION FRANCHISE.
I'LL GET SANCTION TO MOVE ON EVERYTHING IN A 100 MILE RADIUS, SOON'S I CAN FINANCE IT. MONEY IN THE BANK.
TONY, YOU SHOULD HAVE PROBLEMS LIKE MINE.
HONE
EITHER THE JAMAICANS FINESSE THEMSELVES OUT OF SAGEVILLE OR PAY THE DUTY, THERE'S NO THIRD.
SOMETHING I CAN DO FOR YOU, SWEETHEART?
CALL, MR. SILVER.

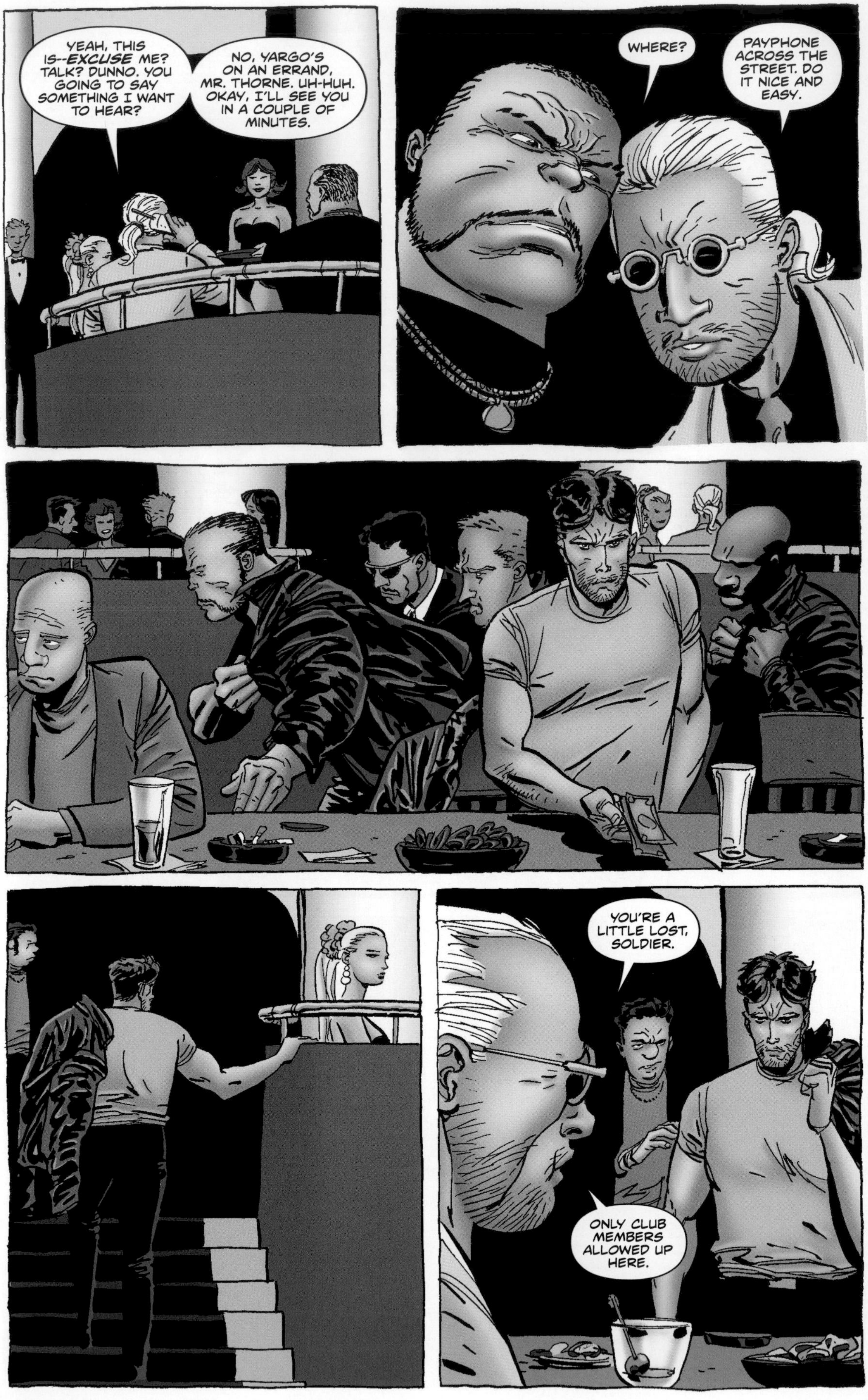
YEAH, THIS IS--*EXCUSE* ME? TALK? DUNNO. YOU GOING TO SAY SOMETHING I WANT TO HEAR?
NO, YARGO'S ON AN ERRAND, MR. THORNE. UH-HUH. OKAY, I'LL SEE YOU IN A COUPLE OF MINUTES.
WHERE?
PAYPHONE ACROSS THE STREET. DO IT NICE AND EASY.
YOU'RE A LITTLE LOST, SOLDIER.
ONLY CLUB MEMBERS ALLOWED UP HERE.

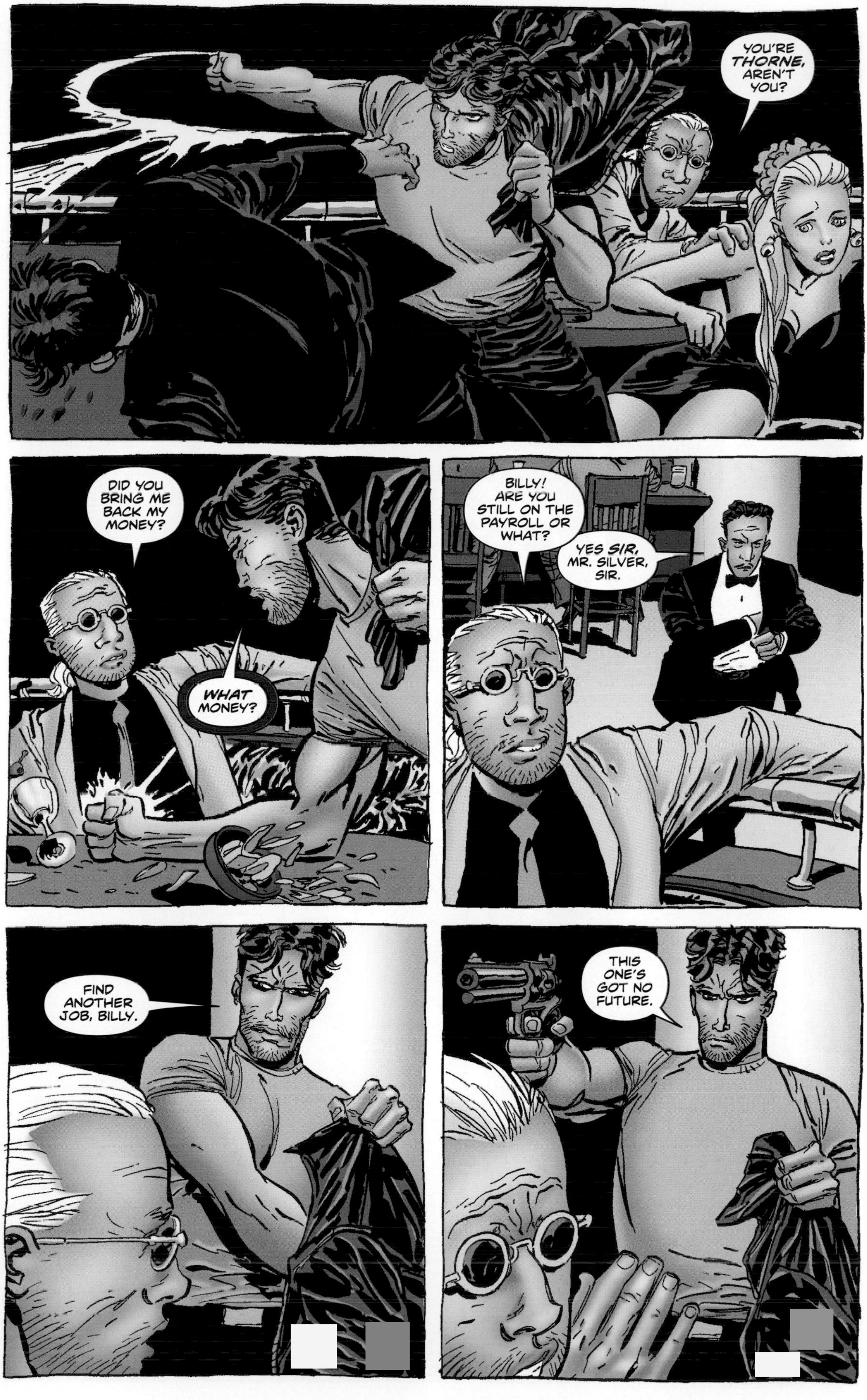
YOU'RE THORNE, AREN'T YOU?
DID YOU BRING ME BACK MY MONEY?
WHAT MONEY?
BILLY! ARE YOU STILL ON THE PAYROLL OR WHAT?
YES SIR, MR. SILVER, SIR.
FIND ANOTHER JOB, BILLY.
THIS ONE'S GOT NO FUTURE.

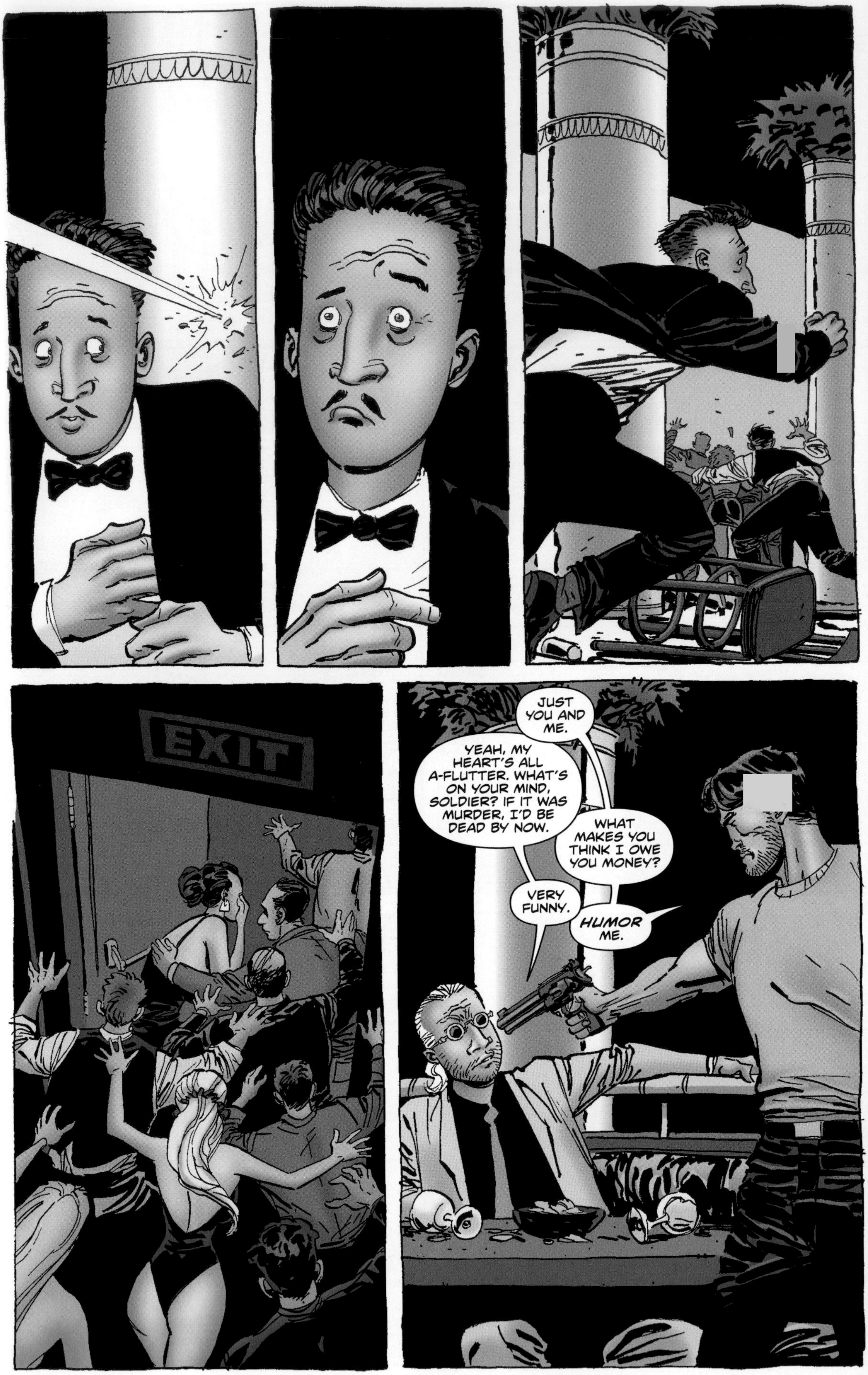
EXIT
JUST YOU AND ME.
YEAH, MY HEART'S ALL A-FLUTTER. WHAT'S ON YOUR MIND, SOLDIER? IF IT WAS MURDER, I'D BE DEAD BY NOW.
WHAT MAKES YOU THINK I OWE YOU MONEY?
VERY FUNNY.
HUMOR ME.

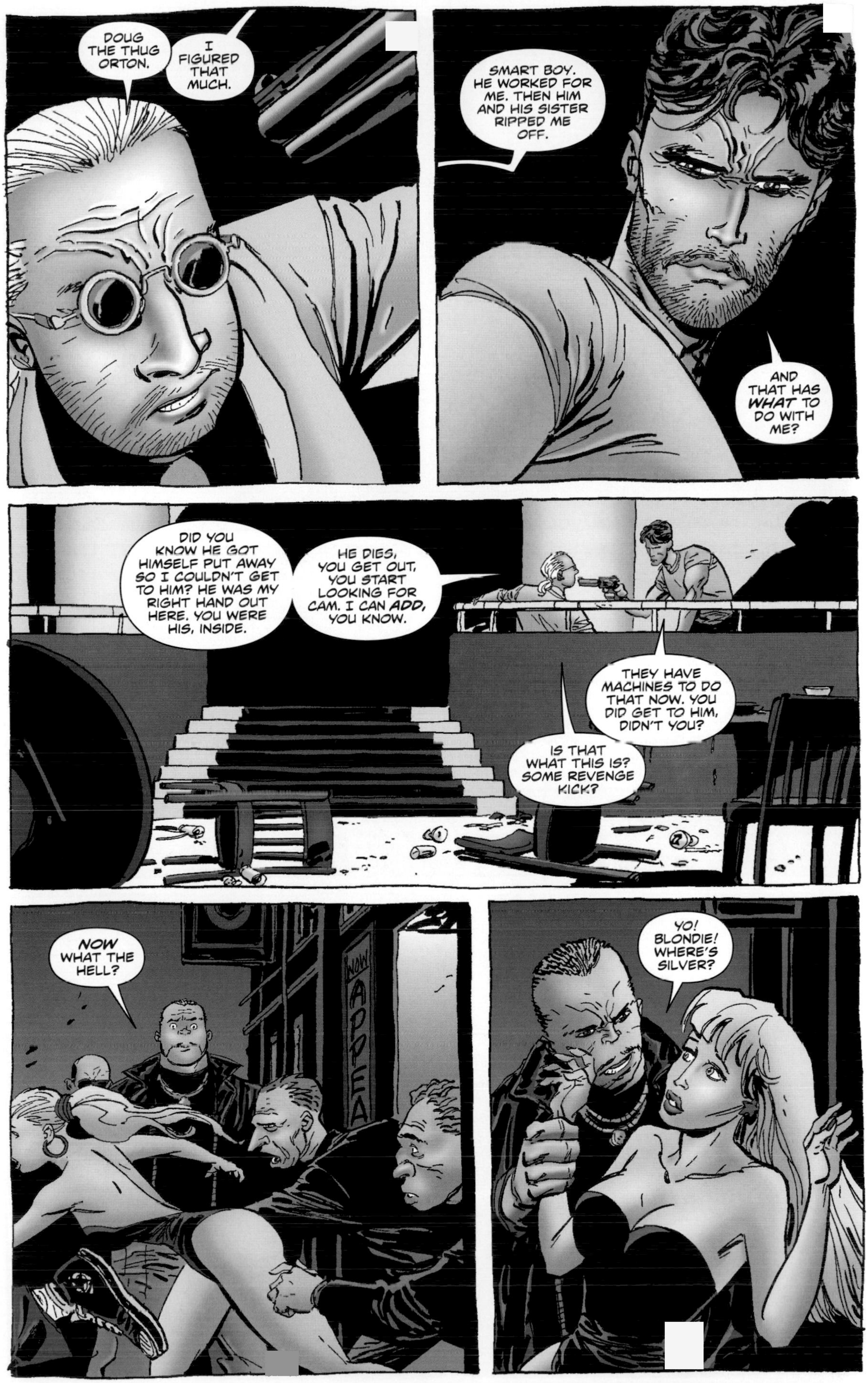
DOUG THE THUG ORTON.
I FIGURED THAT MUCH.
SMART BOY. HE WORKED FOR ME. THEN HIM AND HIS SISTER RIPPED ME OFF.
AND THAT HAS *WHAT* TO DO WITH ME?
DID YOU KNOW HE GOT HIMSELF PUT AWAY SO I COULDN'T GET TO HIM? HE WAS MY RIGHT HAND OUT HERE. YOU WERE HIS, INSIDE.
HE DIES, YOU GET OUT, YOU START LOOKING FOR CAM. I CAN *ADD*, YOU KNOW.
IS THAT WHAT THIS IS? SOME REVENGE KICK?
THEY HAVE MACHINES TO DO THAT NOW. YOU DID GET TO HIM, DIDN'T YOU?
NOW WHAT THE HELL?
YO! BLONDIE! WHERE'S SILVER?

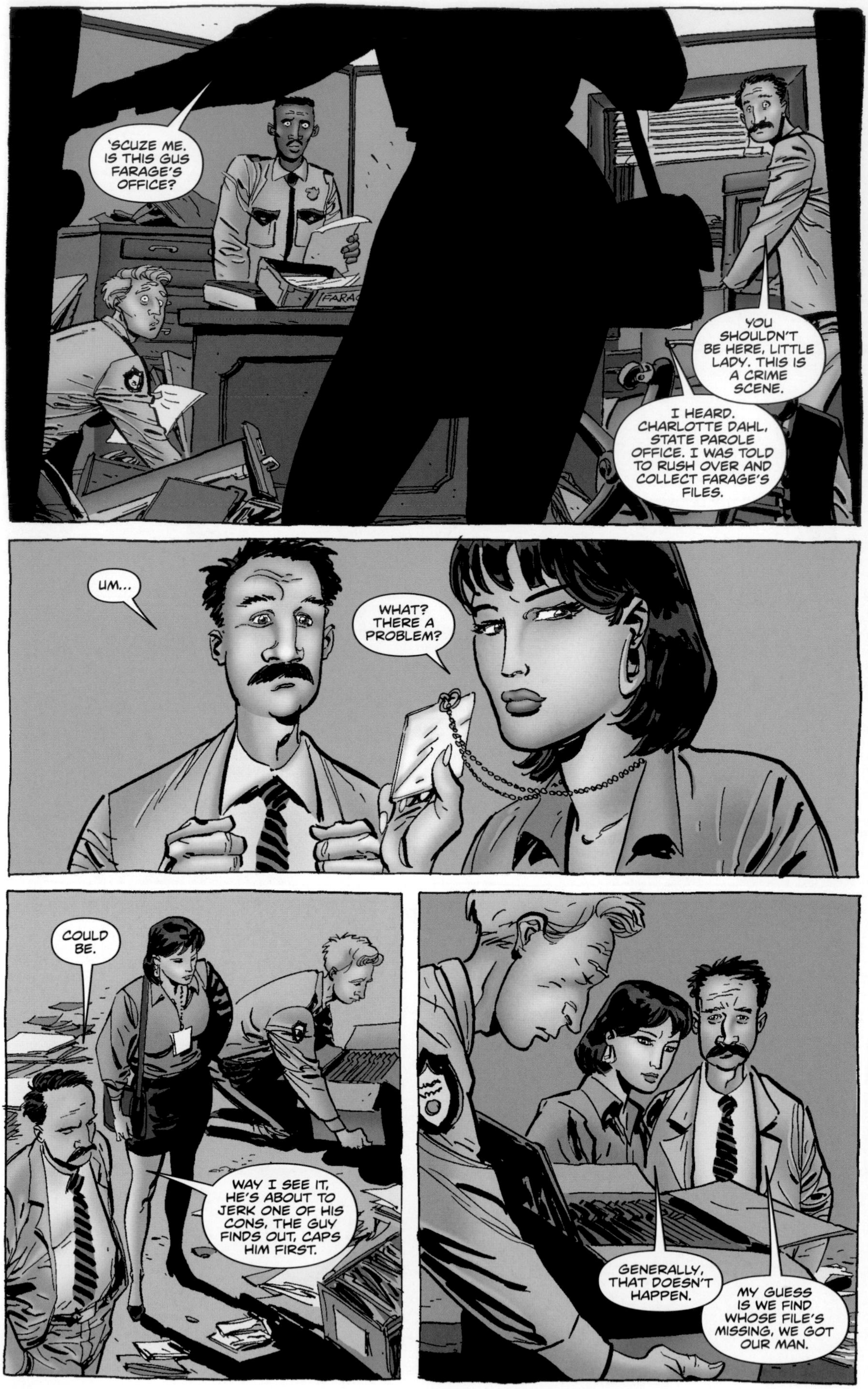

'SCUZE ME. IS THIS GUS FARAGE'S OFFICE?
FARAG
YOU SHOULDN'T BE HERE, LITTLE LADY. THIS IS A CRIME SCENE.
I HEARD. CHARLOTTE DAHL, STATE PAROLE OFFICE. I WAS TOLD TO RUSH OVER AND COLLECT FARAGE'S FILES.
UM...
WHAT? THERE A PROBLEM?
COULD BE.
WAY I SEE IT, HE'S ABOUT TO JERK ONE OF HIS CONS, THE GUY FINDS OUT, CAPS HIM FIRST.
GENERALLY, THAT DOESN'T HAPPEN.
MY GUESS IS WE FIND WHOSE FILE'S MISSING, WE GOT OUR MAN.

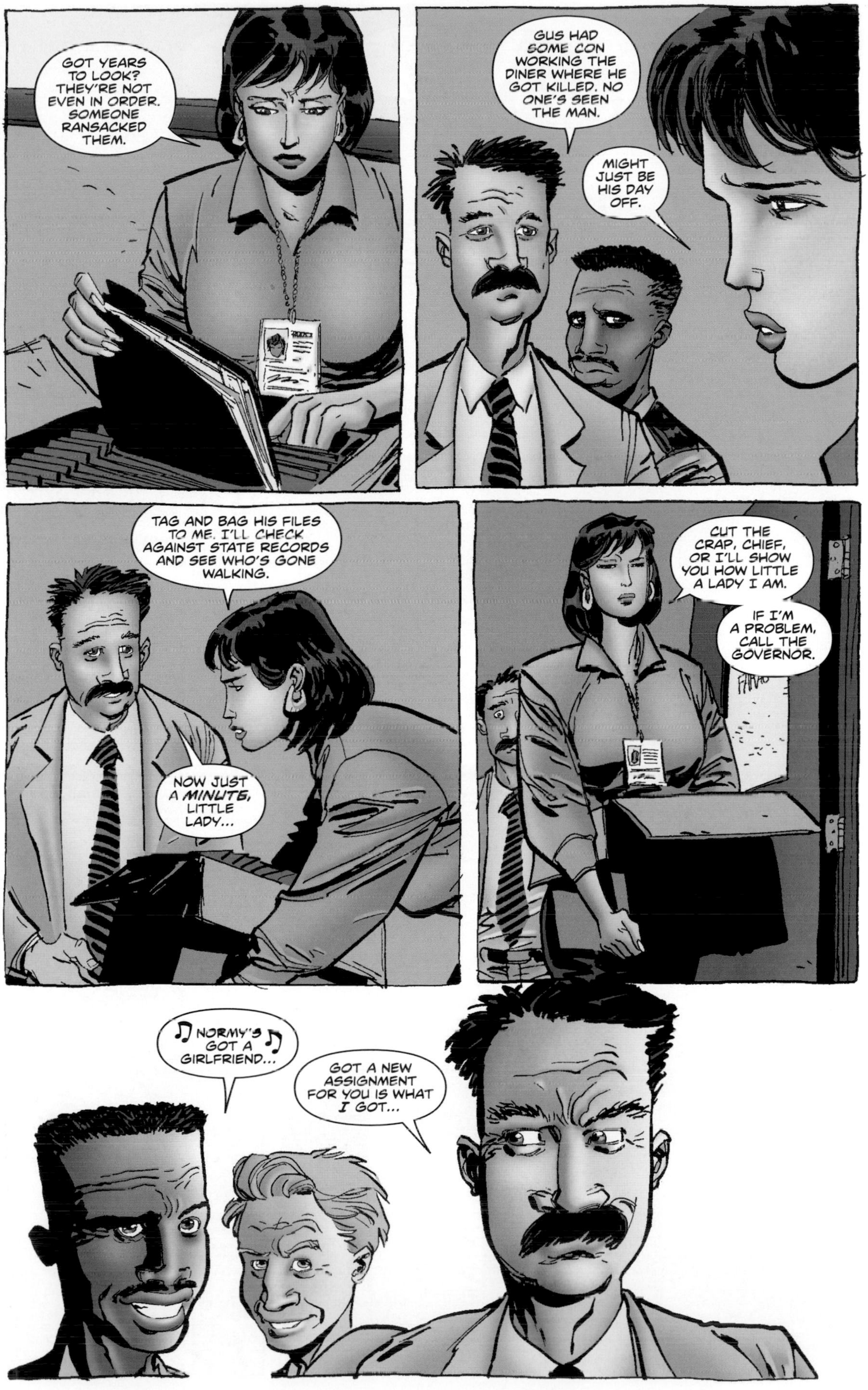
GOT YEARS TO LOOK? THEY'RE NOT EVEN IN ORDER. SOMEONE RANSACKED THEM.
GUS HAD SOME CON WORKING THE DINER WHERE HE GOT KILLED. NO ONE'S SEEN THE MAN.
MIGHT JUST BE HIS DAY OFF.
TAG AND BAG HIS FILES TO ME. I'LL CHECK AGAINST STATE RECORDS AND SEE WHO'S GONE WALKING.
NOW JUST A *MINUTE,* LITTLE LADY...
CUT THE CRAP, CHIEF, OR I'LL SHOW YOU HOW LITTLE A LADY I AM.
IF I'M A PROBLEM, CALL THE GOVERNOR.
♫ NORMY'S GOT A GIRLFRIEND... ♫
GOT A NEW ASSIGNMENT FOR YOU IS WHAT *I* GOT...

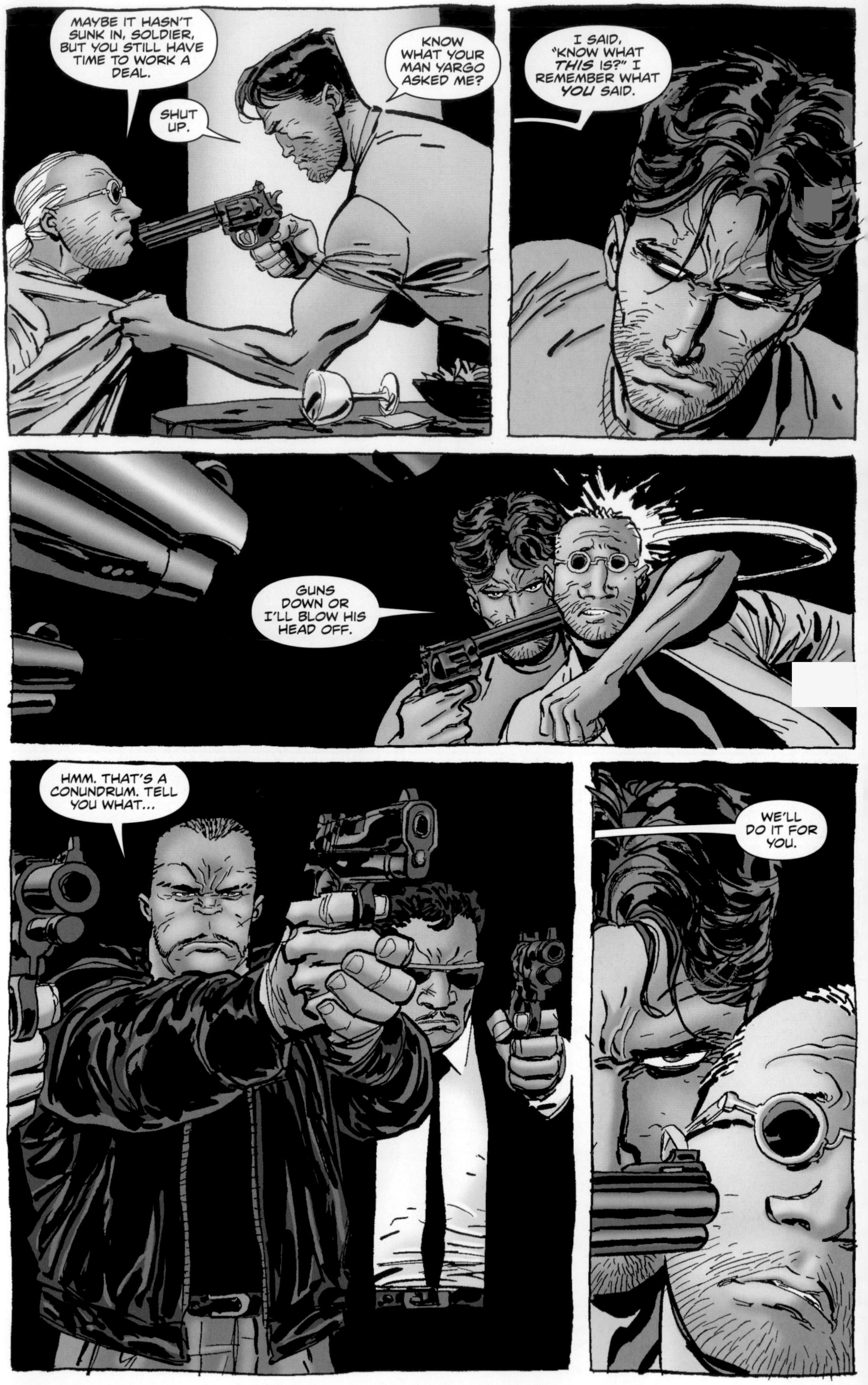
MAYBE IT HASN'T SUNK IN, SOLDIER, BUT YOU STILL HAVE TIME TO WORK A DEAL.
SHUT UP.
KNOW WHAT YOUR MAN YARGO ASKED ME?
I SAID, "KNOW WHAT THIS IS?" I REMEMBER WHAT YOU SAID.
GUNS DOWN OR I'LL BLOW HIS HEAD OFF.
HMM. THAT'S A CONUNDRUM. TELL YOU WHAT...
WE'LL DO IT FOR YOU.

DAMNED

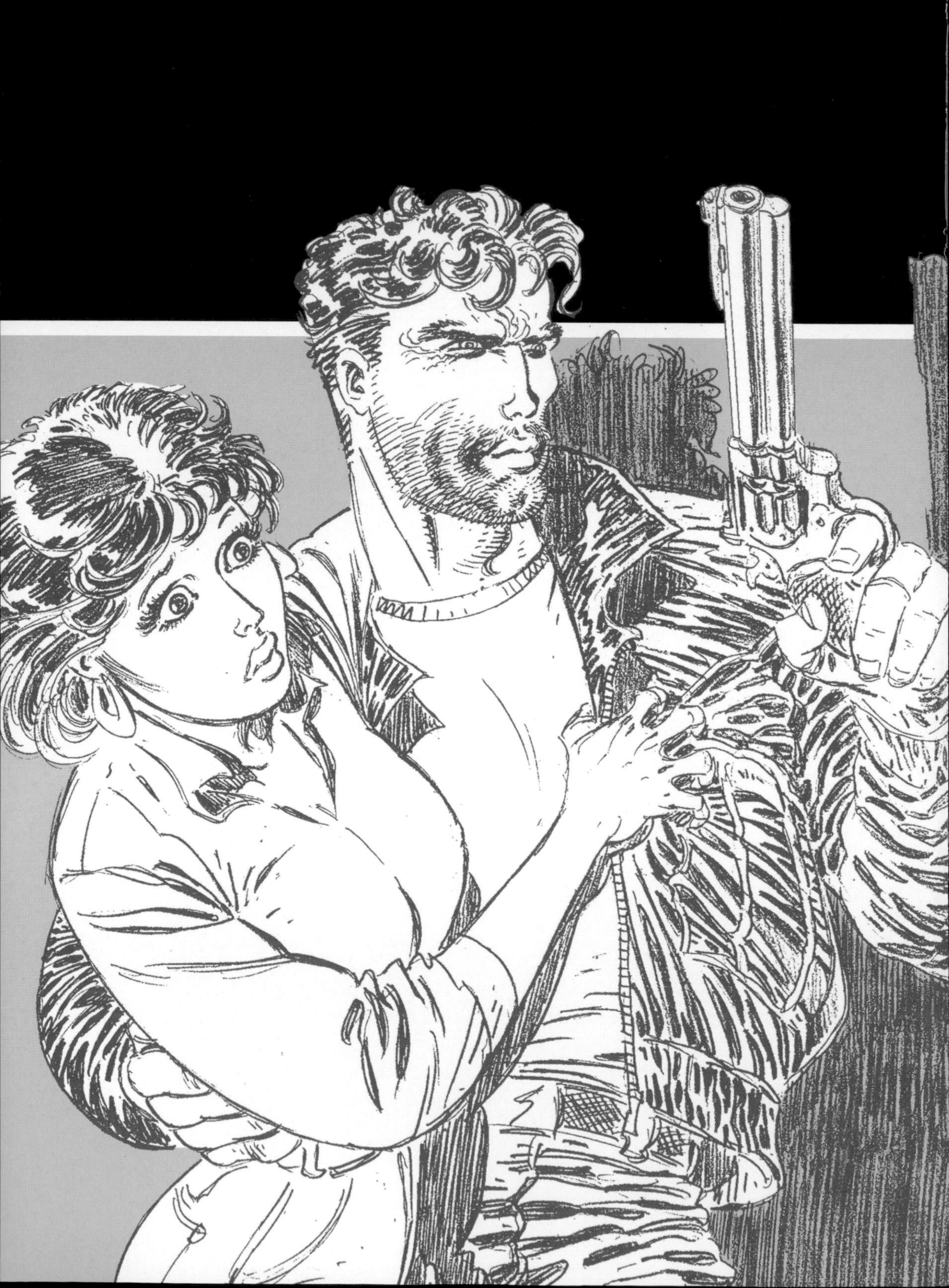

"SLEEP WAS A VOID.
MICK THORNE HAD GIVEN UP ON DREAMS."

CHAPTER THREE

IN THE BIG CITY AND
WANTED BY EVERYONE—

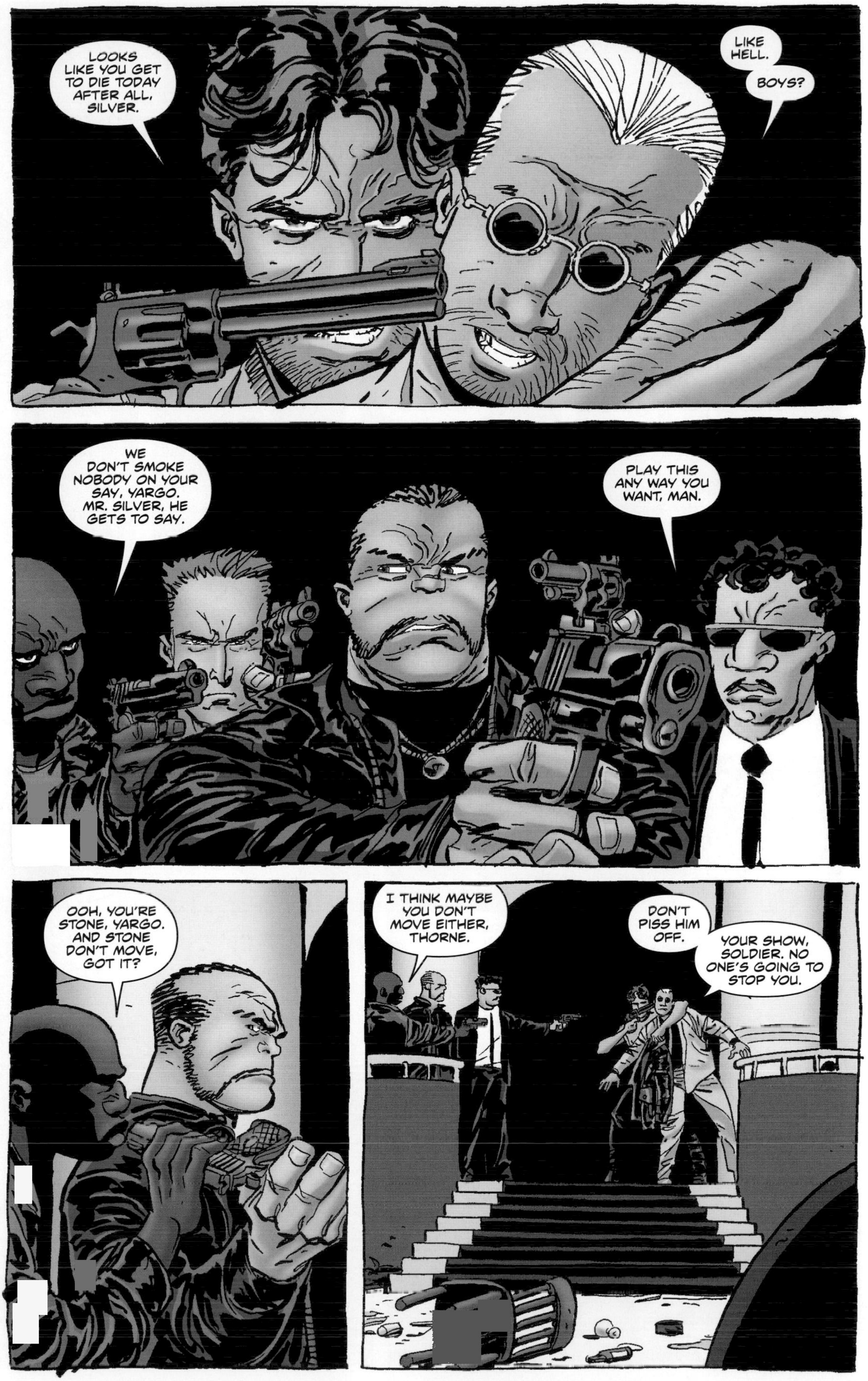
LOOKS LIKE YOU GET TO DIE TODAY AFTER ALL, SILVER.
LIKE HELL.
BOYS?
WE DON'T SMOKE NOBODY ON YOUR SAY, YARGO. MR. SILVER, HE GETS TO SAY.
PLAY THIS ANY WAY YOU WANT, MAN.
OOH, YOU'RE STONE, YARGO. AND STONE DON'T MOVE, GOT IT?
I THINK MAYBE YOU DON'T MOVE EITHER, THORNE.
DON'T PISS HIM OFF.
YOUR SHOW, SOLDIER. NO ONE'S GOING TO STOP YOU.

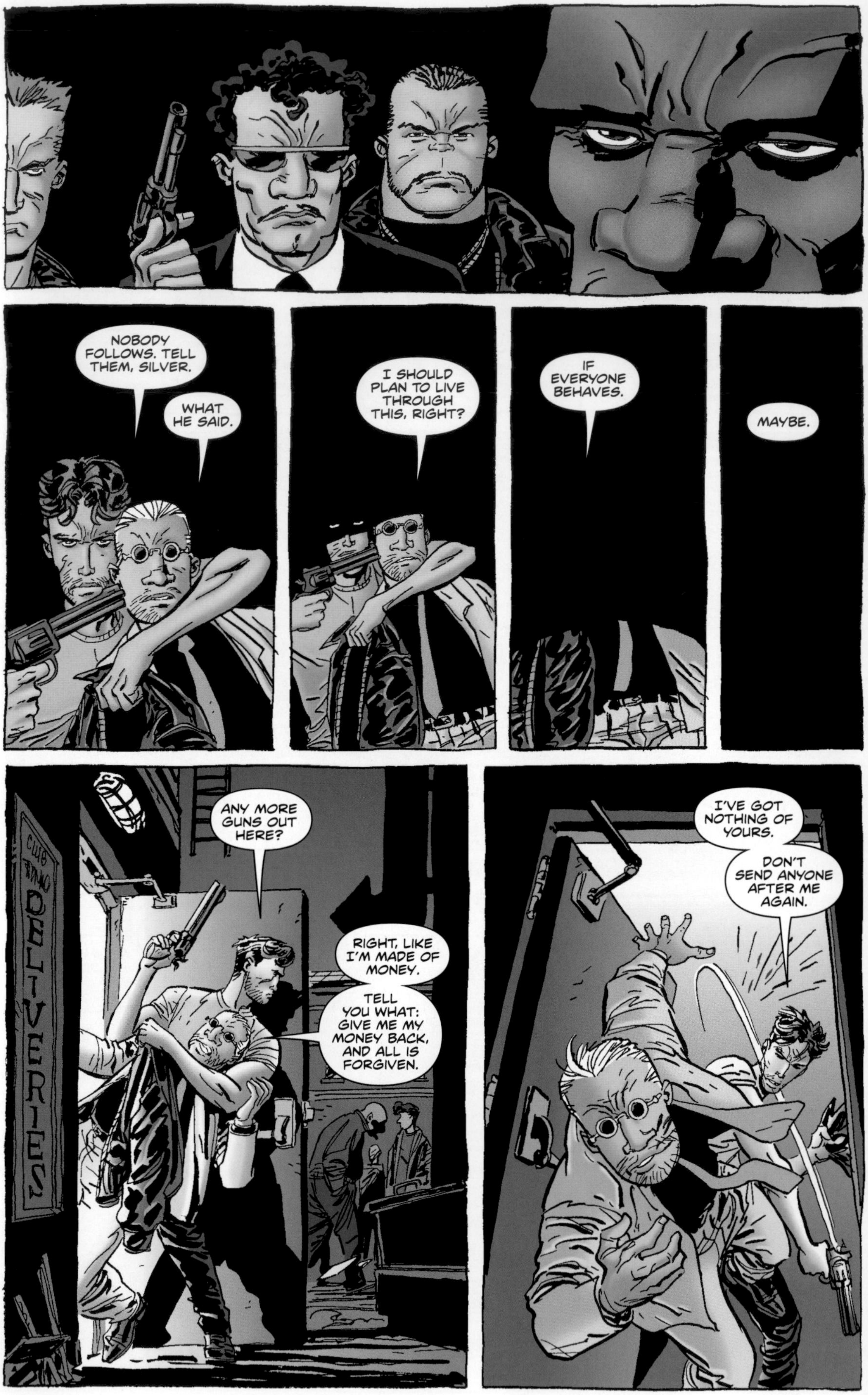
NOBODY FOLLOWS. TELL THEM, SILVER.
WHAT HE SAID.
I SHOULD PLAN TO LIVE THROUGH THIS, RIGHT?
IF EVERYONE BEHAVES.
MAYBE.
CLUB
DELIVERIES
ANY MORE GUNS OUT HERE?
RIGHT, LIKE I'M MADE OF MONEY.
TELL YOU WHAT: GIVE ME MY MONEY BACK, AND ALL IS FORGIVEN.
I'VE GOT NOTHING OF YOURS.
DON'T SEND ANYONE AFTER ME AGAIN.

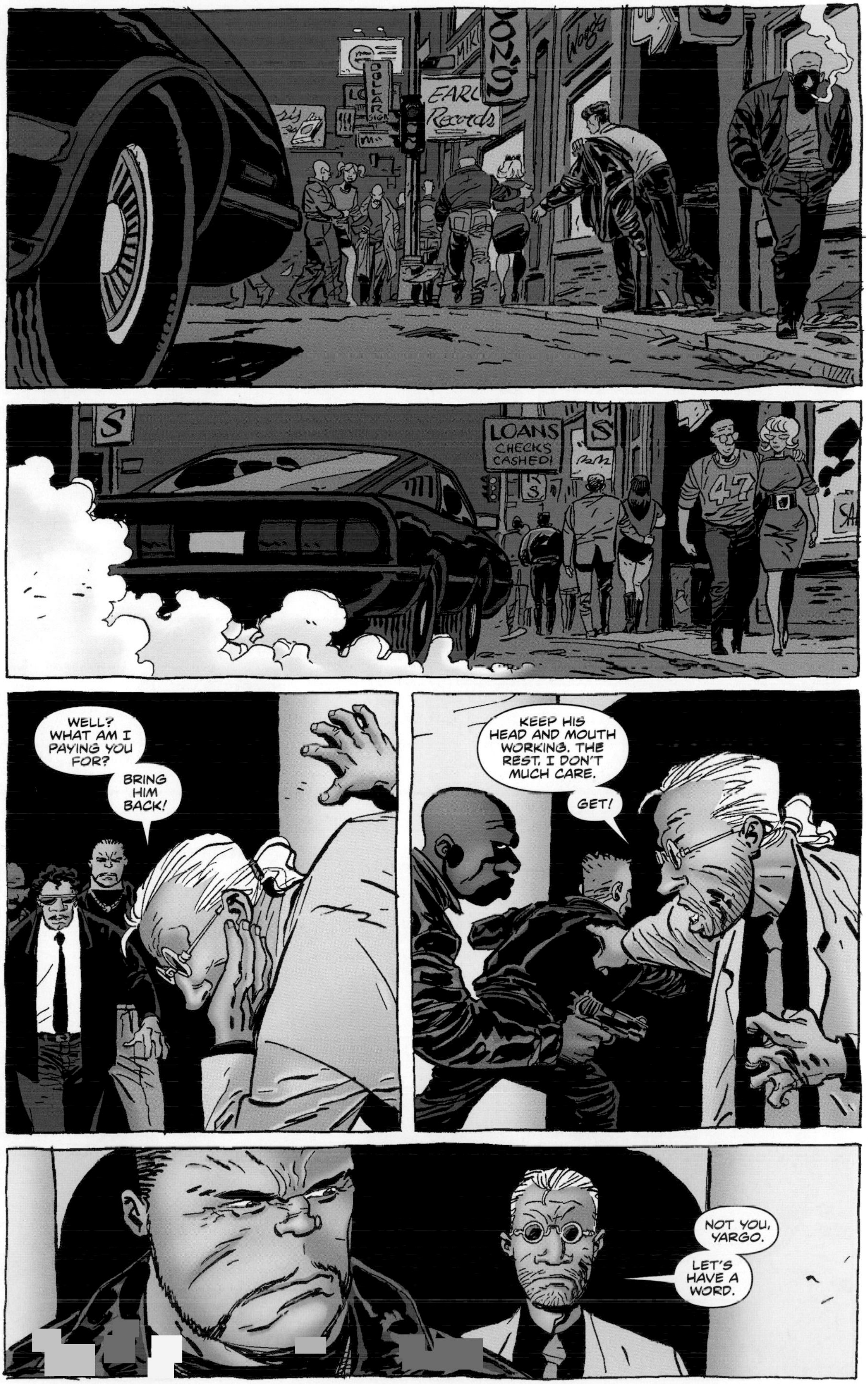

LOANS
CHECKS
CASHED!
WELL? WHAT AM I PAYING YOU FOR?
BRING HIM BACK!
KEEP HIS HEAD AND MOUTH WORKING. THE REST, I DON'T MUCH CARE.
GET!
NOT YOU, YARGO.
LET'S HAVE A WORD.

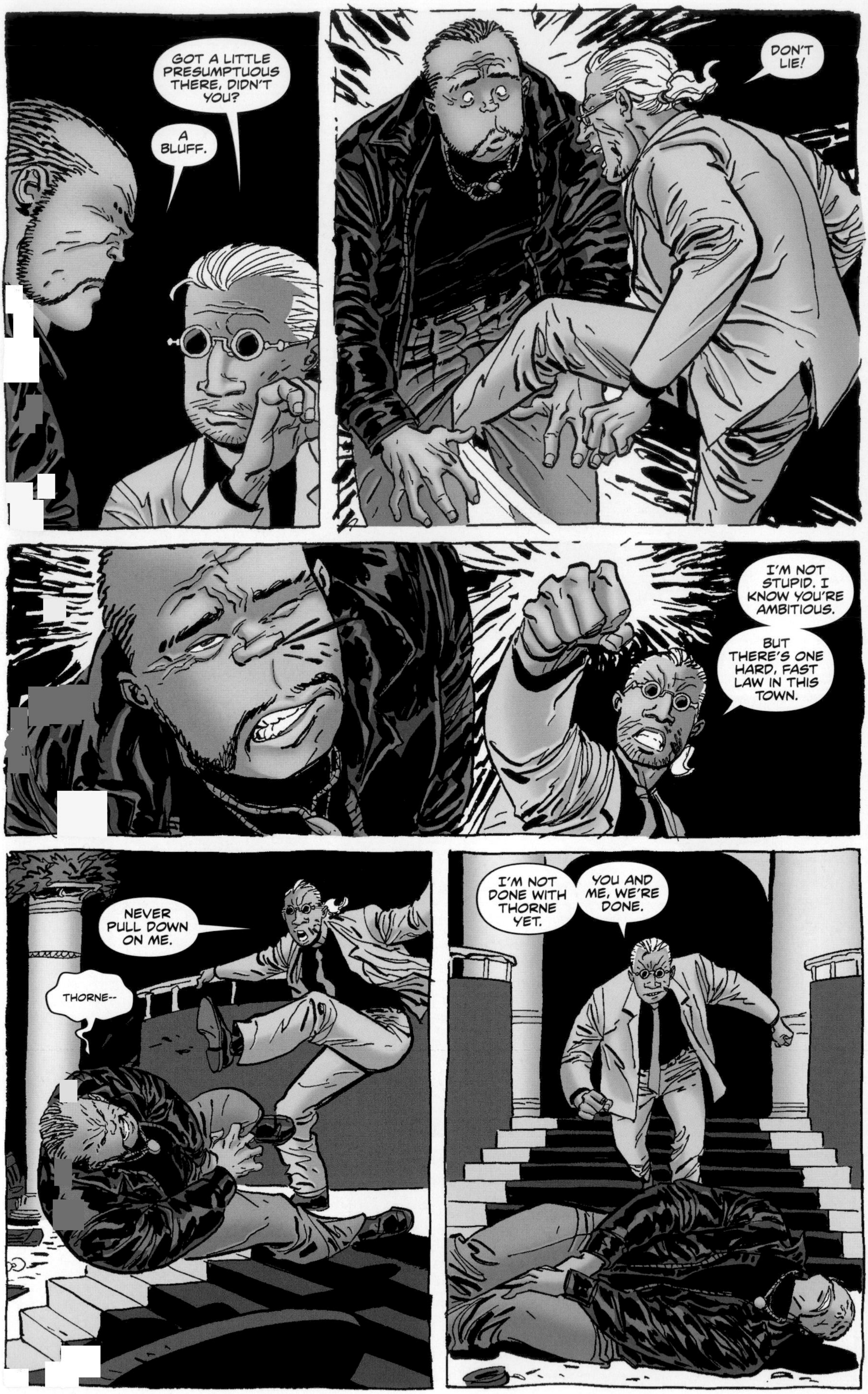
GOT A LITTLE PRESUMPTUOUS THERE, DIDN'T YOU?
A BLUFF.
DON'T LIE!
I'M NOT STUPID. I KNOW YOU'RE AMBITIOUS.
BUT THERE'S ONE HARD, FAST LAW IN THIS TOWN.
NEVER PULL DOWN ON ME.
THORNE--
I'M NOT DONE WITH THORNE YET.
YOU AND ME, WE'RE DONE.

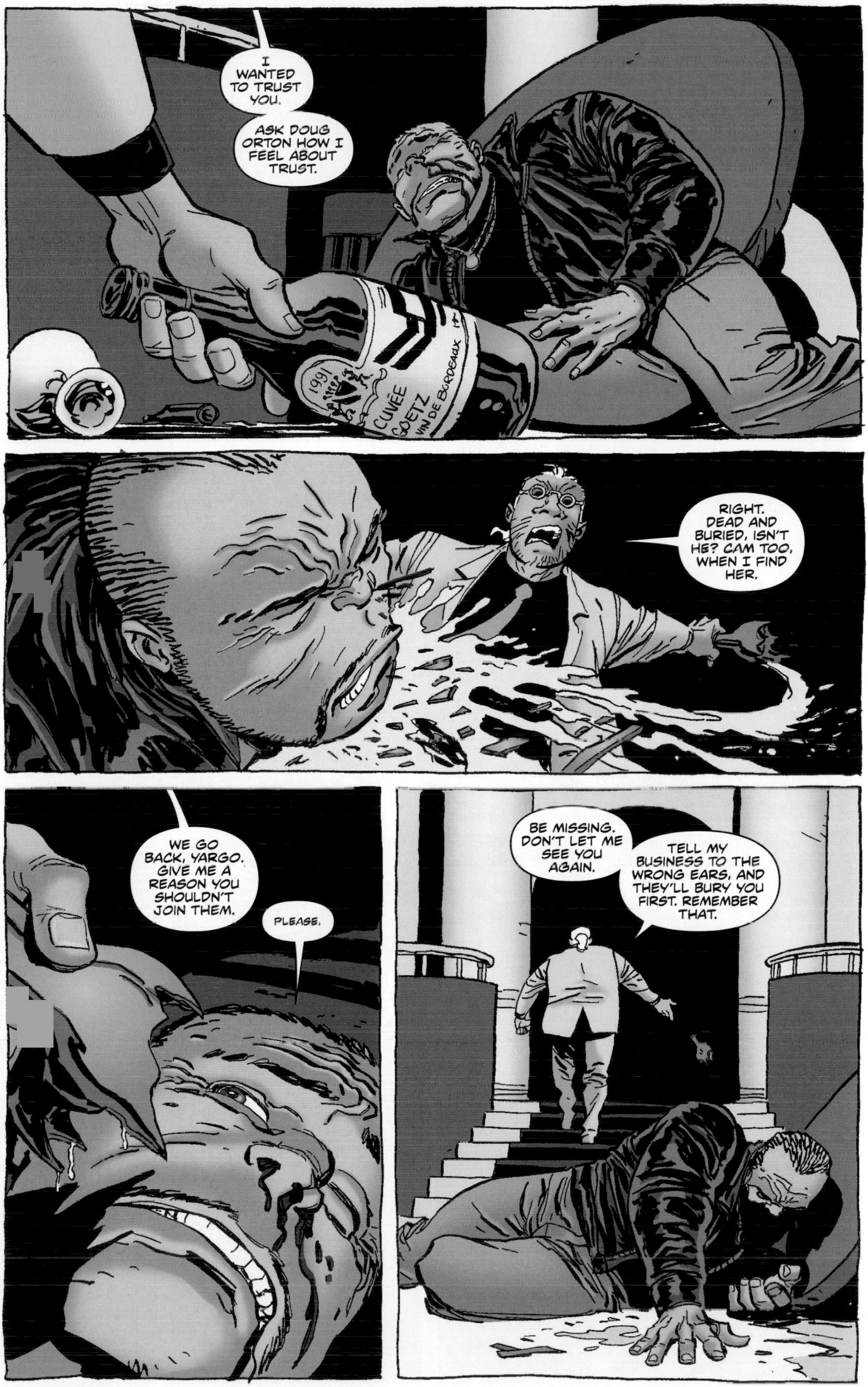
I WANTED TO TRUST YOU.
ASK DOUG ORTON HOW I FEEL ABOUT TRUST.
1991
CUVÉE GOETZ
VIN DE BORDEAUX
RIGHT. DEAD AND BURIED, ISN'T HE? CAM TOO, WHEN I FIND HER.
WE GO BACK, YARGO. GIVE ME A REASON YOU SHOULDN'T JOIN THEM.
PLEASE.
BE MISSING. DON'T LET ME SEE YOU AGAIN.
TELL MY BUSINESS TO THE WRONG EARS, AND THEY'LL BURY YOU FIRST. REMEMBER THAT.

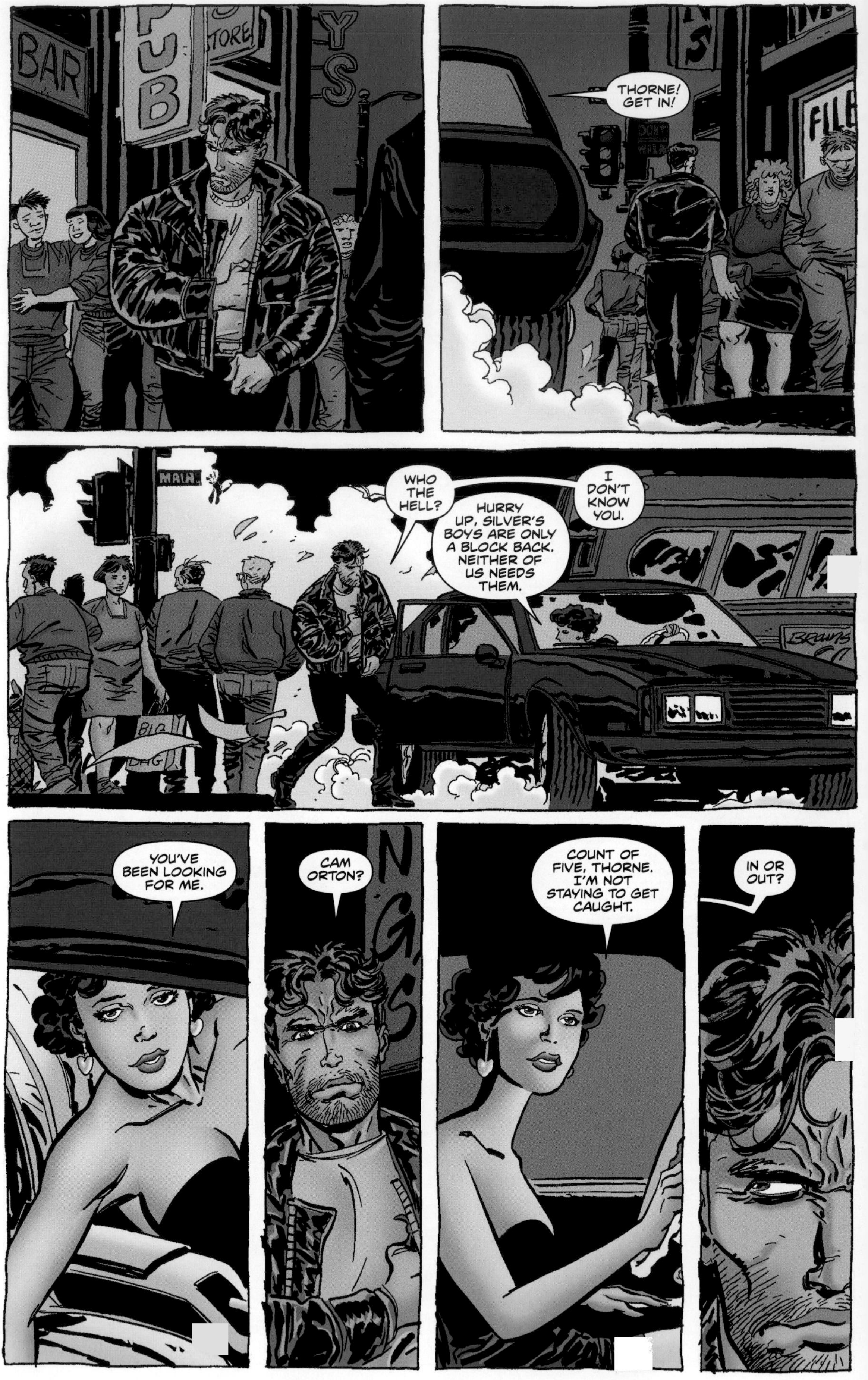
BAR
PUB
STORE
THORNE! GET IN!
DON'T WALK
FILE
MAIN
WHO THE HELL?
I DON'T KNOW YOU.
HURRY UP, SILVER'S BOYS ARE ONLY A BLOCK BACK. NEITHER OF US NEEDS THEM.
BIG BAG
YOU'VE BEEN LOOKING FOR ME.
CAM ORTON?
COUNT OF FIVE, THORNE. I'M NOT STAYING TO GET CAUGHT.
IN OR OUT?

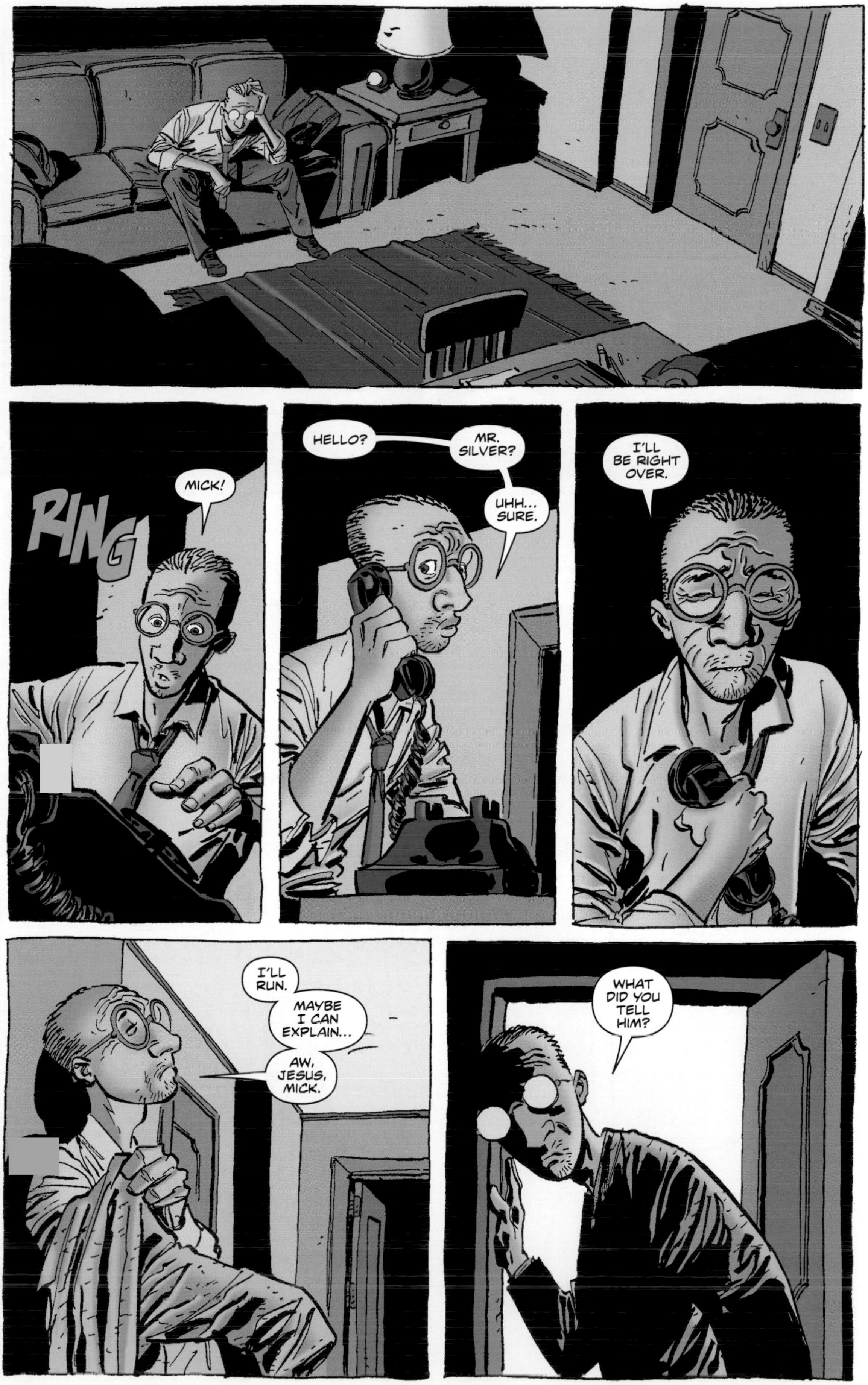
RING
MICK!
HELLO?
MR. SILVER?
UHH... SURE.
I'LL BE RIGHT OVER.
I'LL RUN.
MAYBE I CAN EXPLAIN...
AW, JESUS, MICK.
WHAT DID YOU TELL HIM?

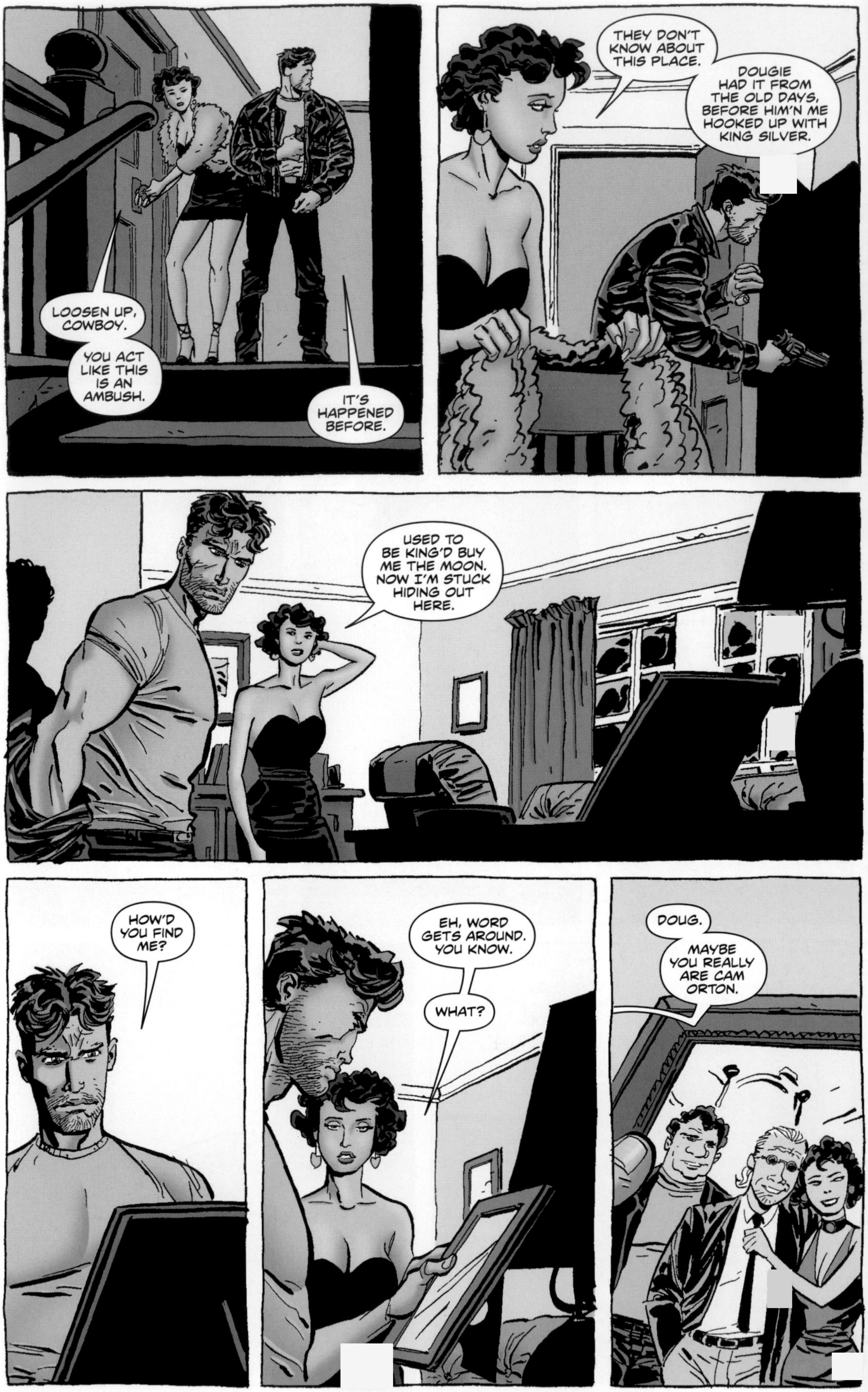
LOOSEN UP, COWBOY.
YOU ACT LIKE THIS IS AN AMBUSH.
IT'S HAPPENED BEFORE.
THEY DON'T KNOW ABOUT THIS PLACE.
DOUGIE HAD IT FROM THE OLD DAYS, BEFORE HIM'N ME HOOKED UP WITH KING SILVER.
USED TO BE KING'D BUY ME THE MOON. NOW I'M STUCK HIDING OUT HERE.
HOW'D YOU FIND ME?
EH, WORD GETS AROUND. YOU KNOW.
WHAT?
DOUG.
MAYBE YOU REALLY ARE CAM ORTON.

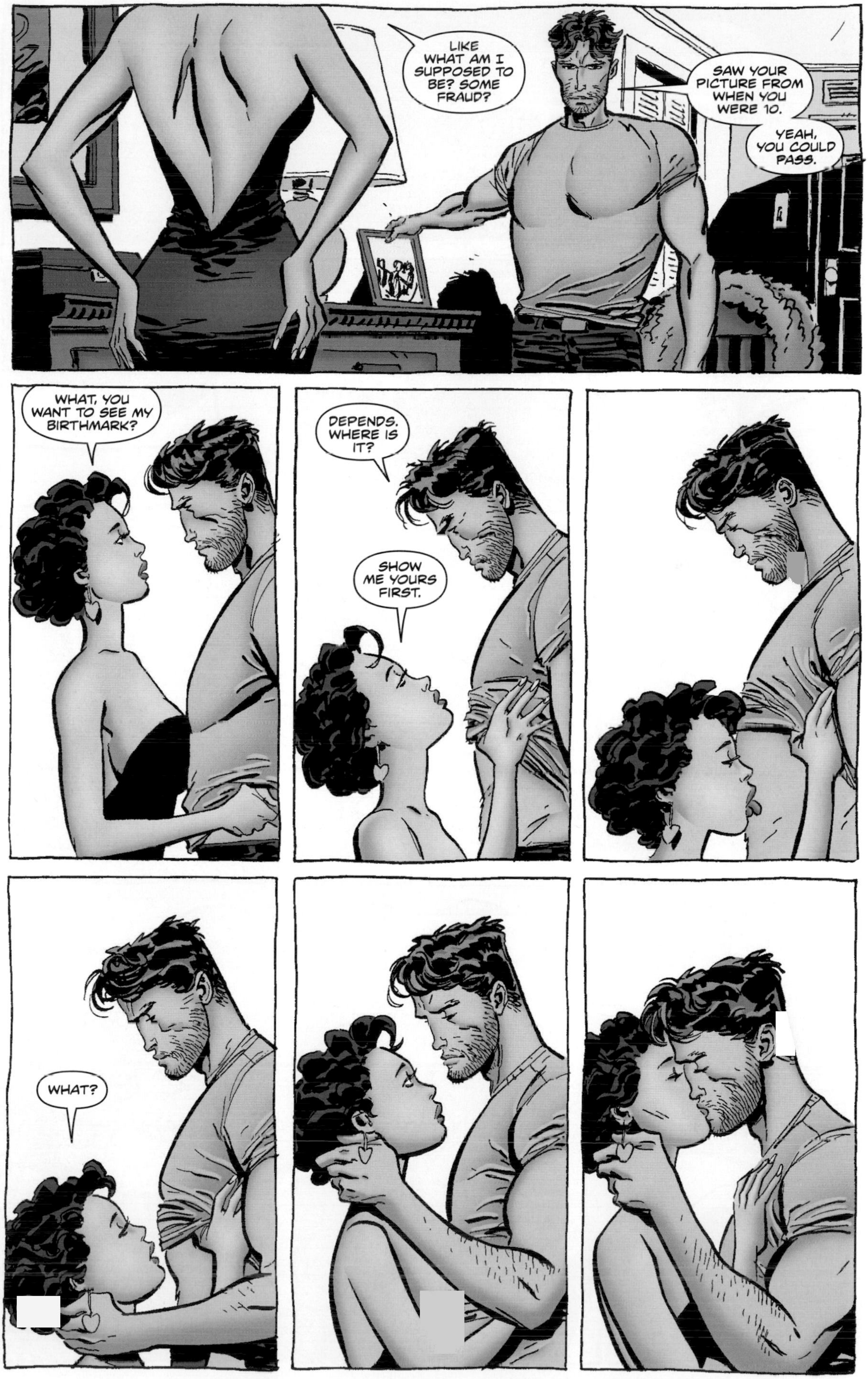
LIKE WHAT AM I SUPPOSED TO BE? SOME FRAUD?
SAW YOUR PICTURE FROM WHEN YOU WERE 10.
YEAH, YOU COULD PASS.
WHAT, YOU WANT TO SEE MY BIRTHMARK?
DEPENDS. WHERE IS IT?
SHOW ME YOURS FIRST.
WHAT?

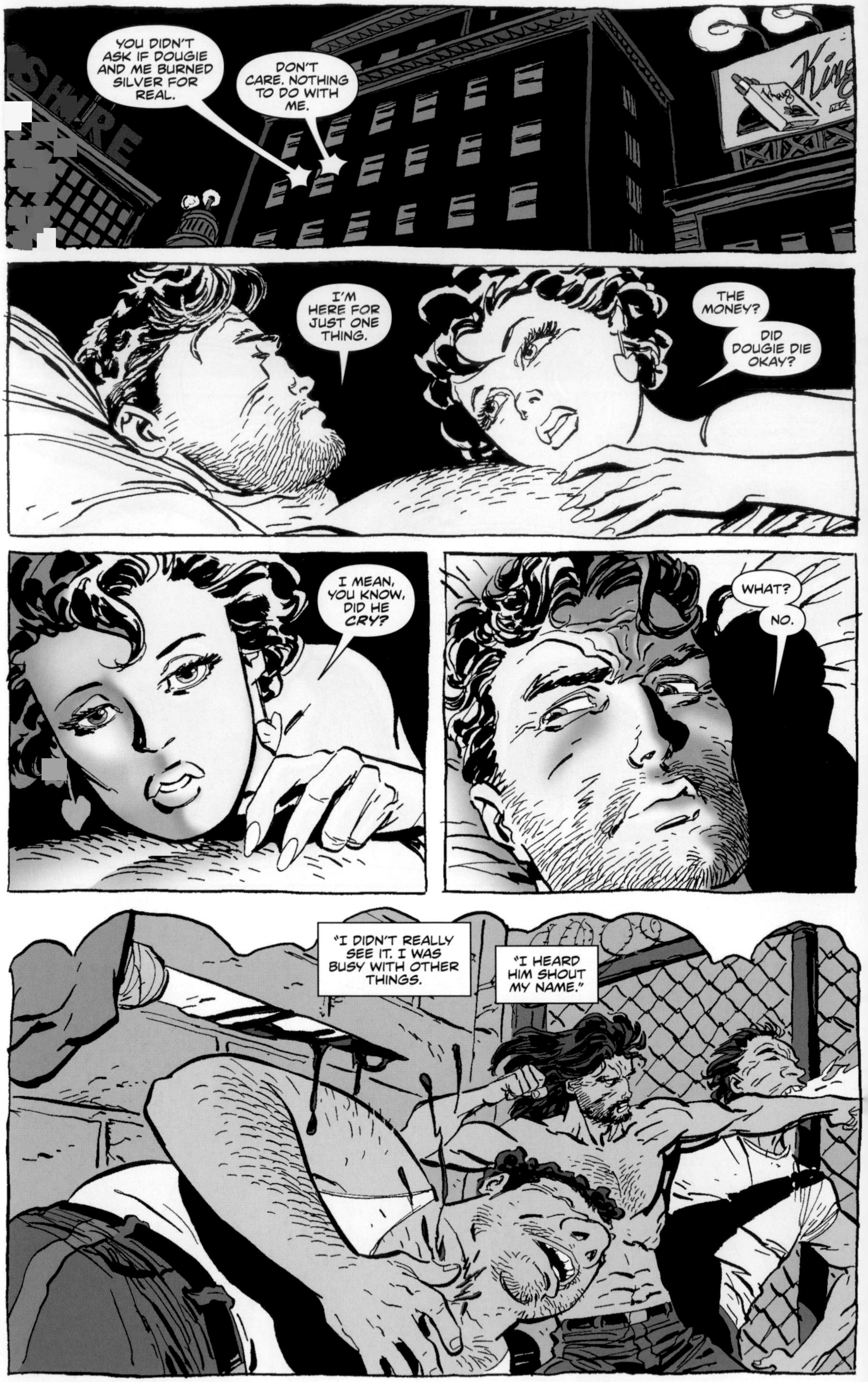
SHIRE
YOU DIDN'T ASK IF DOUGIE AND ME BURNED SILVER FOR REAL.
DON'T CARE. NOTHING TO DO WITH ME.
I'M HERE FOR JUST ONE THING.
THE MONEY?
DID DOUGIE DIE OKAY?
I MEAN, YOU KNOW, DID HE CRY?
WHAT?
NO.
"I DIDN'T REALLY SEE IT. I WAS BUSY WITH OTHER THINGS.
"I HEARD HIM SHOUT MY NAME."

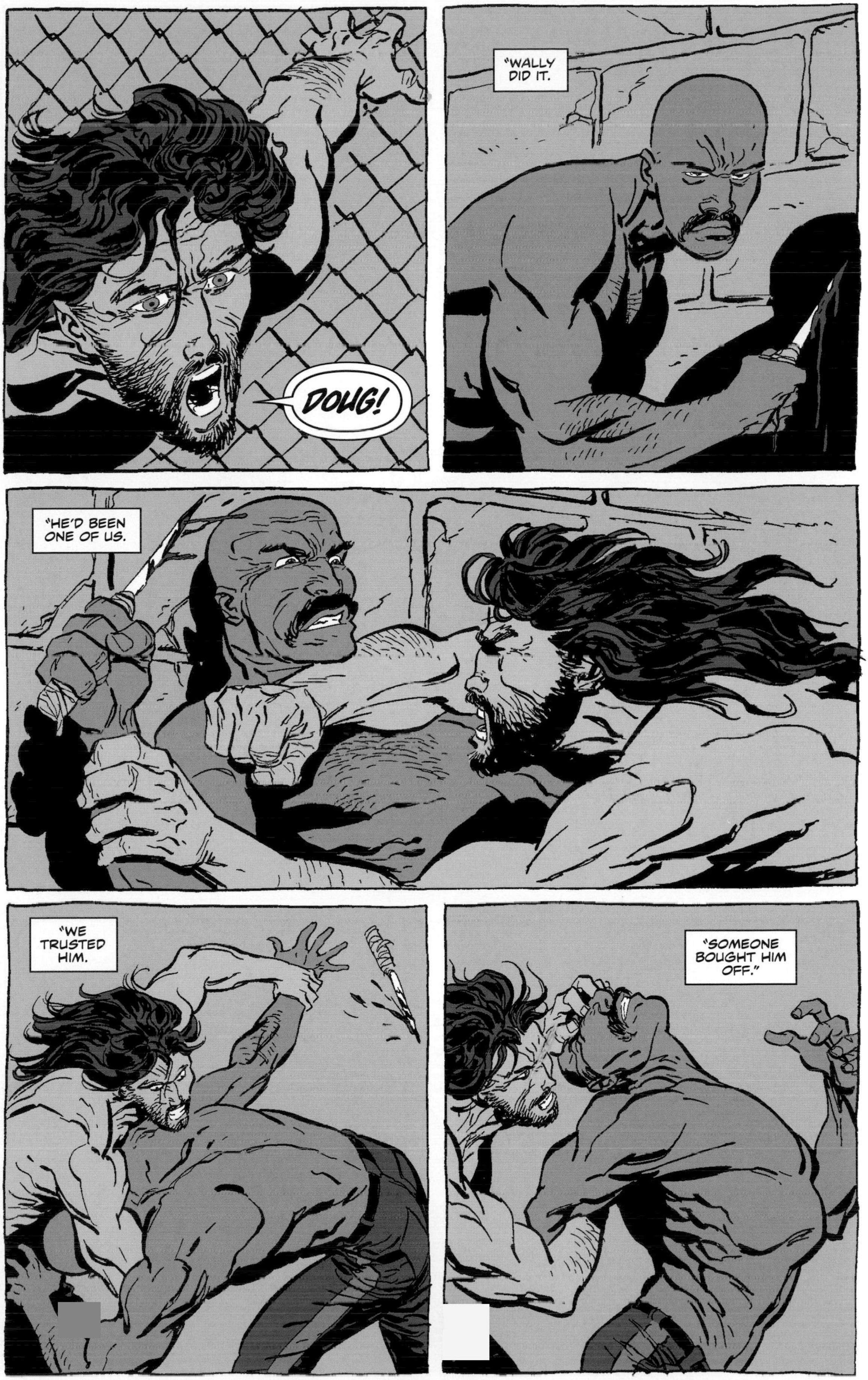
DOUG!
"WALLY DID IT.
"HE'D BEEN ONE OF US.
"WE TRUSTED HIM.
"SOMEONE BOUGHT HIM OFF."

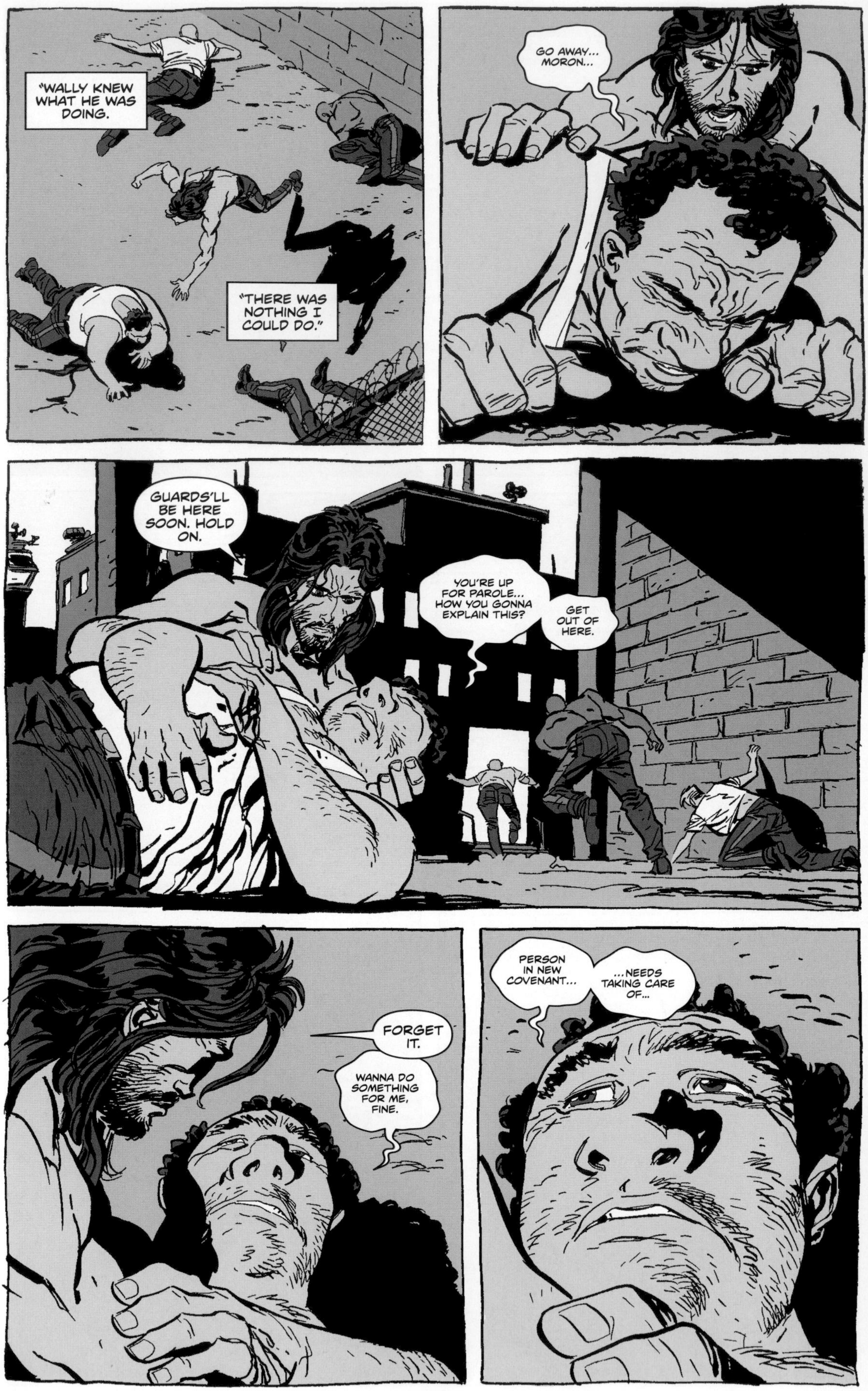
"WALLY KNEW WHAT HE WAS DOING.
"THERE WAS NOTHING I COULD DO."
GO AWAY... MORON...
GUARDS'LL BE HERE SOON. HOLD ON.
YOU'RE UP FOR PAROLE... HOW YOU GONNA EXPLAIN THIS?
GET OUT OF HERE.
FORGET IT.
WANNA DO SOMETHING FOR ME, FINE.
PERSON IN NEW COVENANT...
...NEEDS TAKING CARE OF...

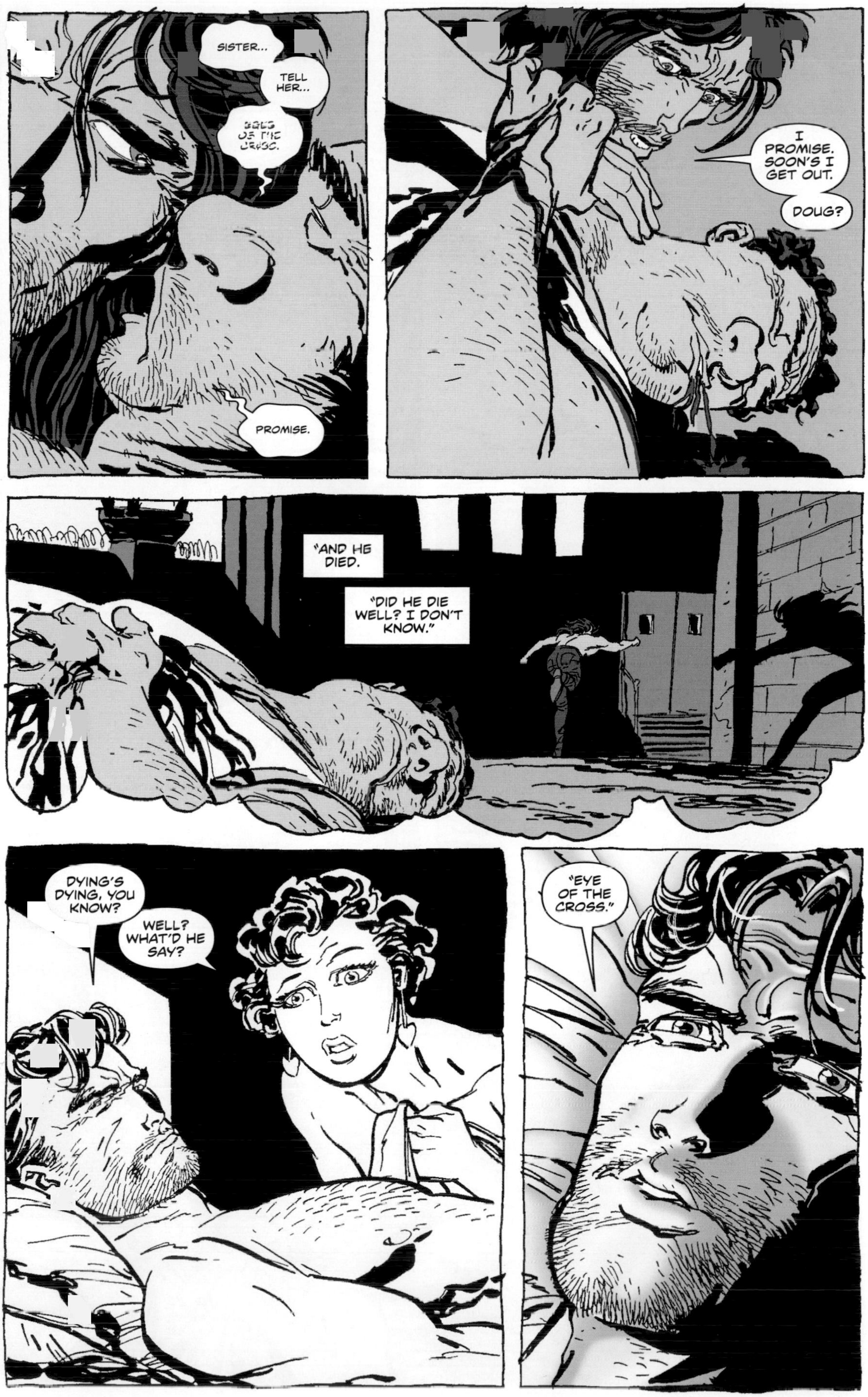
SISTER...
TELL HER...
PROMISE.
I PROMISE. SOON'S I GET OUT.
DOUG?
"AND HE DIED.
"DID HE DIE WELL? I DON'T KNOW."
DYING'S DYING, YOU KNOW?
WELL? WHAT'D HE SAY?
"EYE OF THE CROSS."

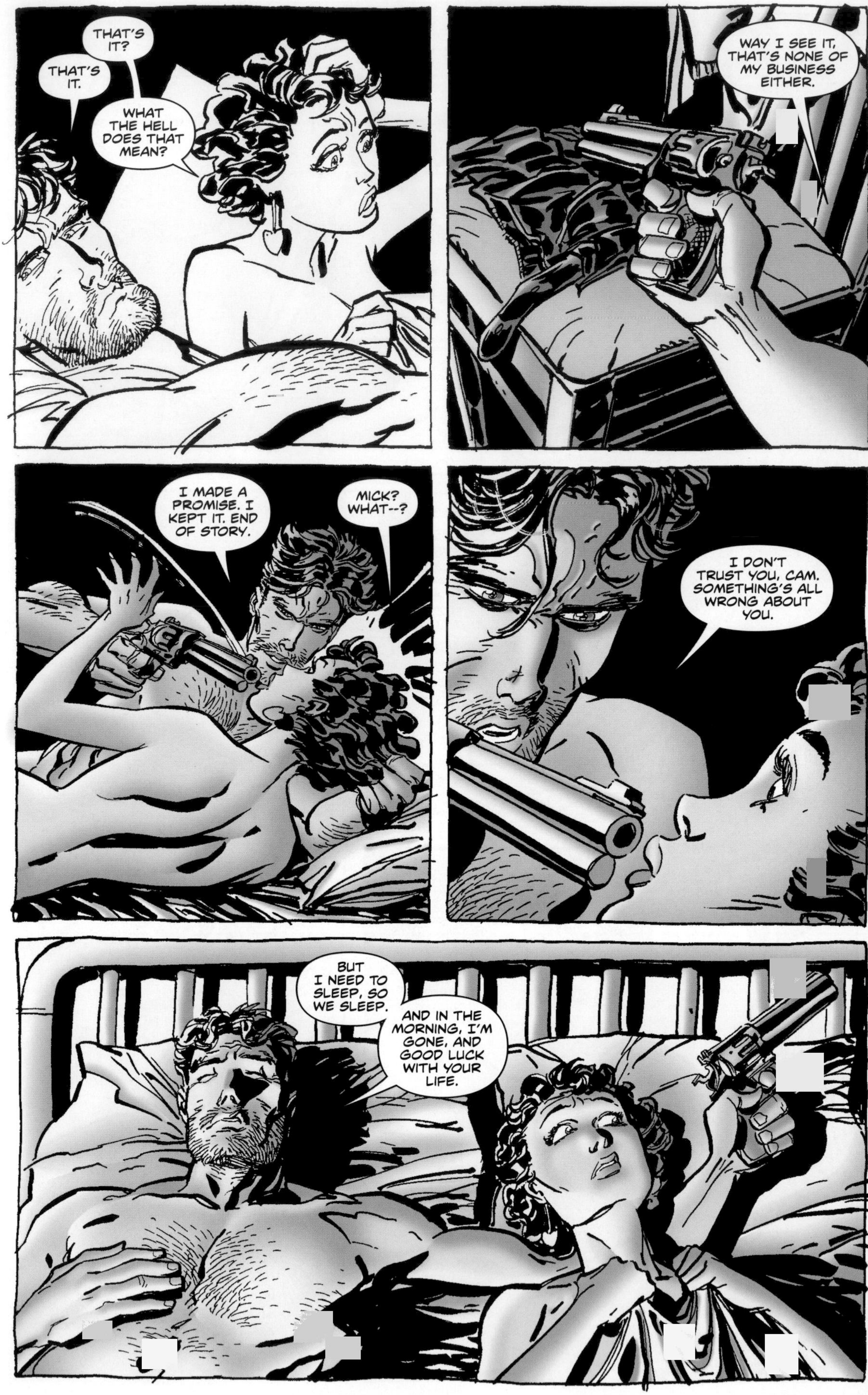
THAT'S IT?
THAT'S IT.
WHAT THE HELL DOES THAT MEAN?
WAY I SEE IT, THAT'S NONE OF MY BUSINESS EITHER.
I MADE A PROMISE. I KEPT IT. END OF STORY.
MICK? WHAT--?
I DON'T TRUST YOU, CAM. SOMETHING'S ALL WRONG ABOUT YOU.
BUT I NEED TO SLEEP, SO WE SLEEP.
AND IN THE MORNING, I'M GONE, AND GOOD LUCK WITH YOUR LIFE.

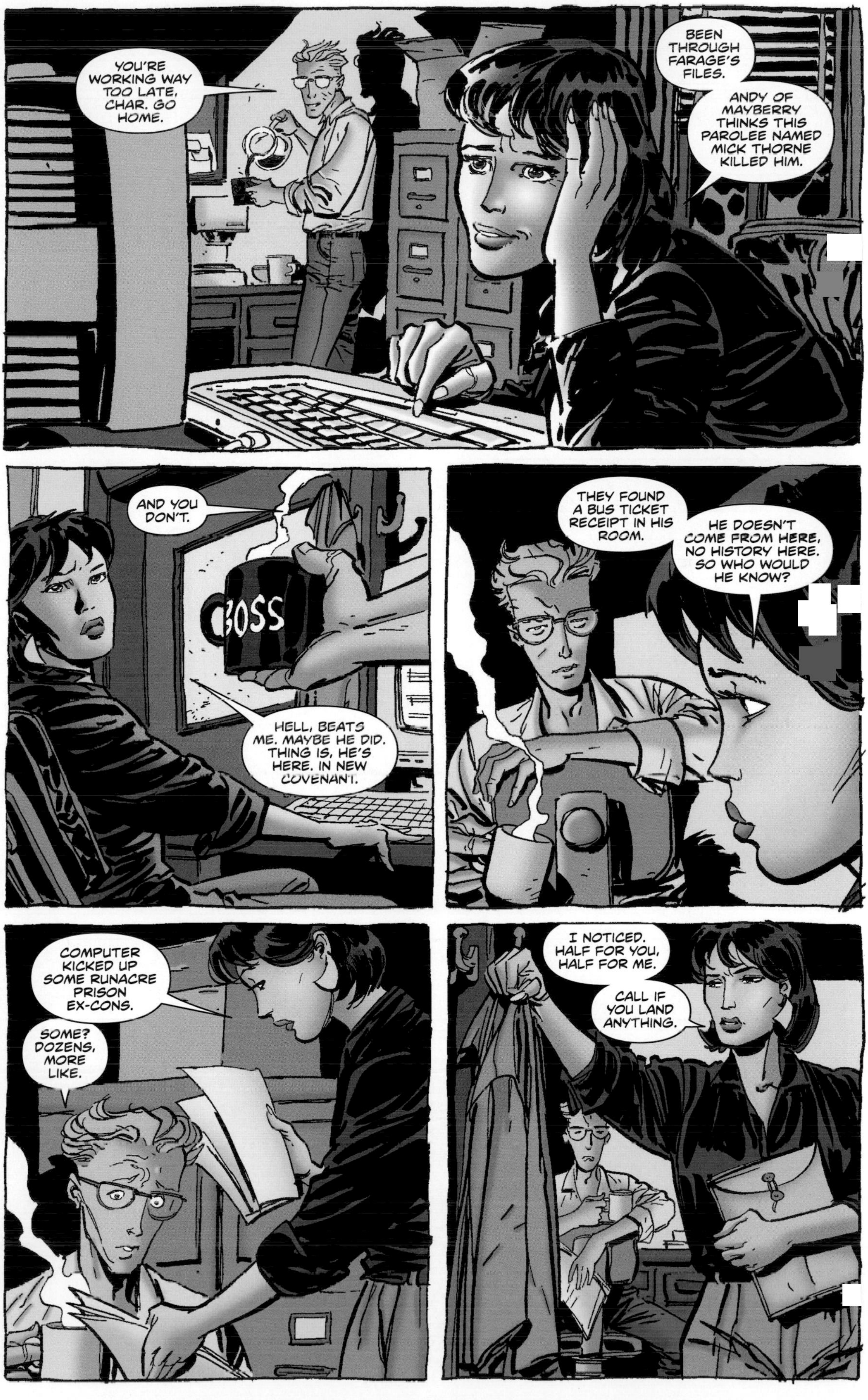
YOU'RE WORKING WAY TOO LATE, CHAR. GO HOME.
BEEN THROUGH FARAGE'S FILES.
ANDY OF MAYBERRY THINKS THIS PAROLEE NAMED MICK THORNE KILLED HIM.
AND YOU DON'T.
BOSS
HELL, BEATS ME. MAYBE HE DID. THING IS, HE'S HERE. IN NEW COVENANT.
THEY FOUND A BUS TICKET RECEIPT IN HIS ROOM.
HE DOESN'T COME FROM HERE, NO HISTORY HERE. SO WHO WOULD HE KNOW?
COMPUTER KICKED UP SOME RUNACRE PRISON EX-CONS.
SOME? DOZENS, MORE LIKE.
I NOTICED. HALF FOR YOU, HALF FOR ME.
CALL IF YOU LAND ANYTHING.

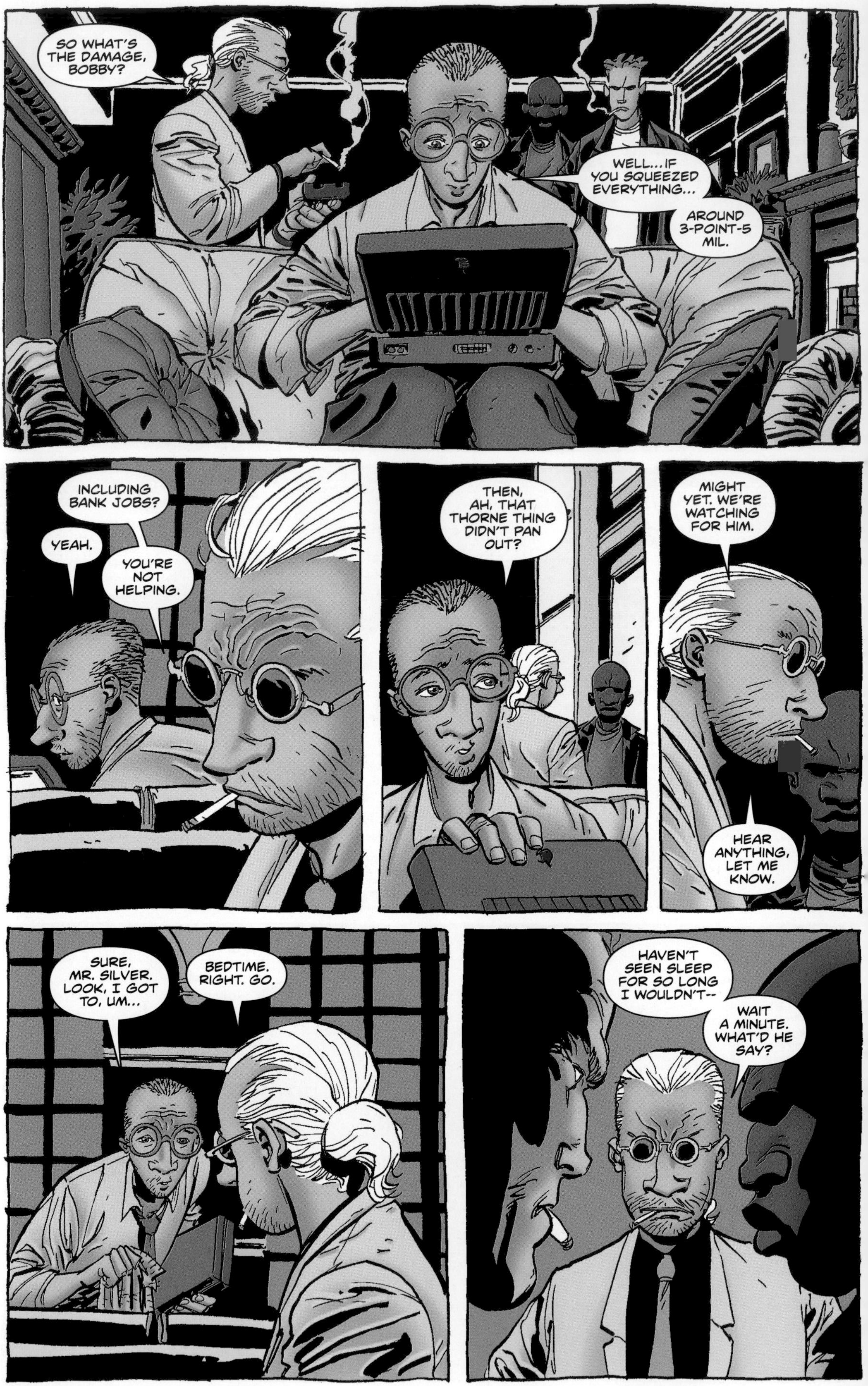
SO WHAT'S THE DAMAGE, BOBBY?
WELL...IF YOU SQUEEZED EVERYTHING...
AROUND 3-POINT-5 MIL.
INCLUDING BANK JOBS?
YEAH.
YOU'RE NOT HELPING.
THEN, AH, THAT THORNE THING DIDN'T PAN OUT?
MIGHT YET. WE'RE WATCHING FOR HIM.
HEAR ANYTHING, LET ME KNOW.
SURE, MR. SILVER. LOOK, I GOT TO, UM...
BEDTIME. RIGHT. GO.
HAVEN'T SEEN SLEEP FOR SO LONG I WOULDN'T--
WAIT A MINUTE. WHAT'D HE SAY?

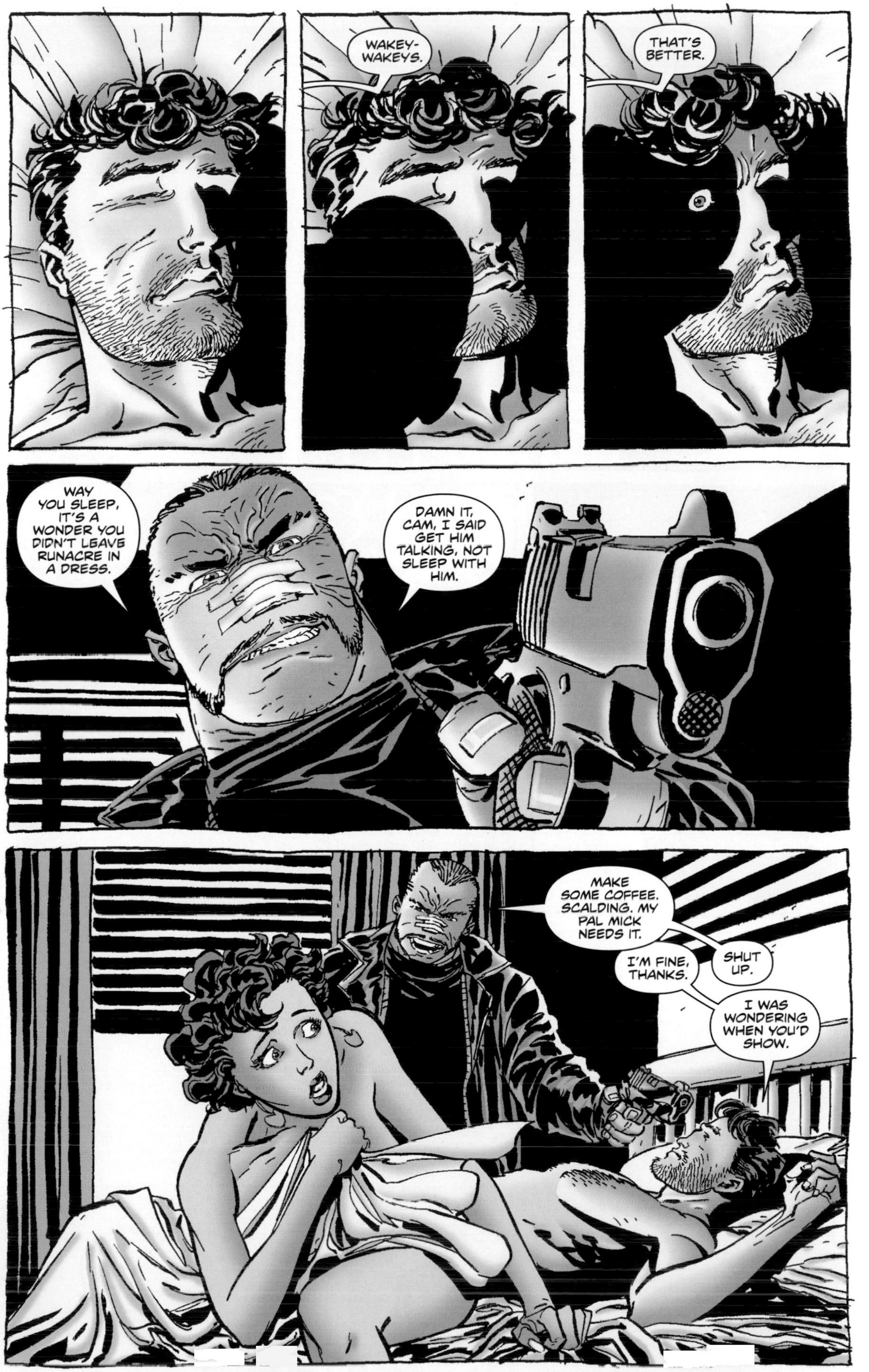
WAKEY-WAKEYS.
THAT'S BETTER.
WAY YOU SLEEP, IT'S A WONDER YOU DIDN'T LEAVE RUNACRE IN A DRESS.
DAMN IT, CAM, I SAID GET HIM TALKING, NOT SLEEP WITH HIM.
MAKE SOME COFFEE. SCALDING. MY PAL MICK NEEDS IT.
I'M FINE, THANKS.
SHUT UP.
I WAS WONDERING WHEN YOU'D SHOW.

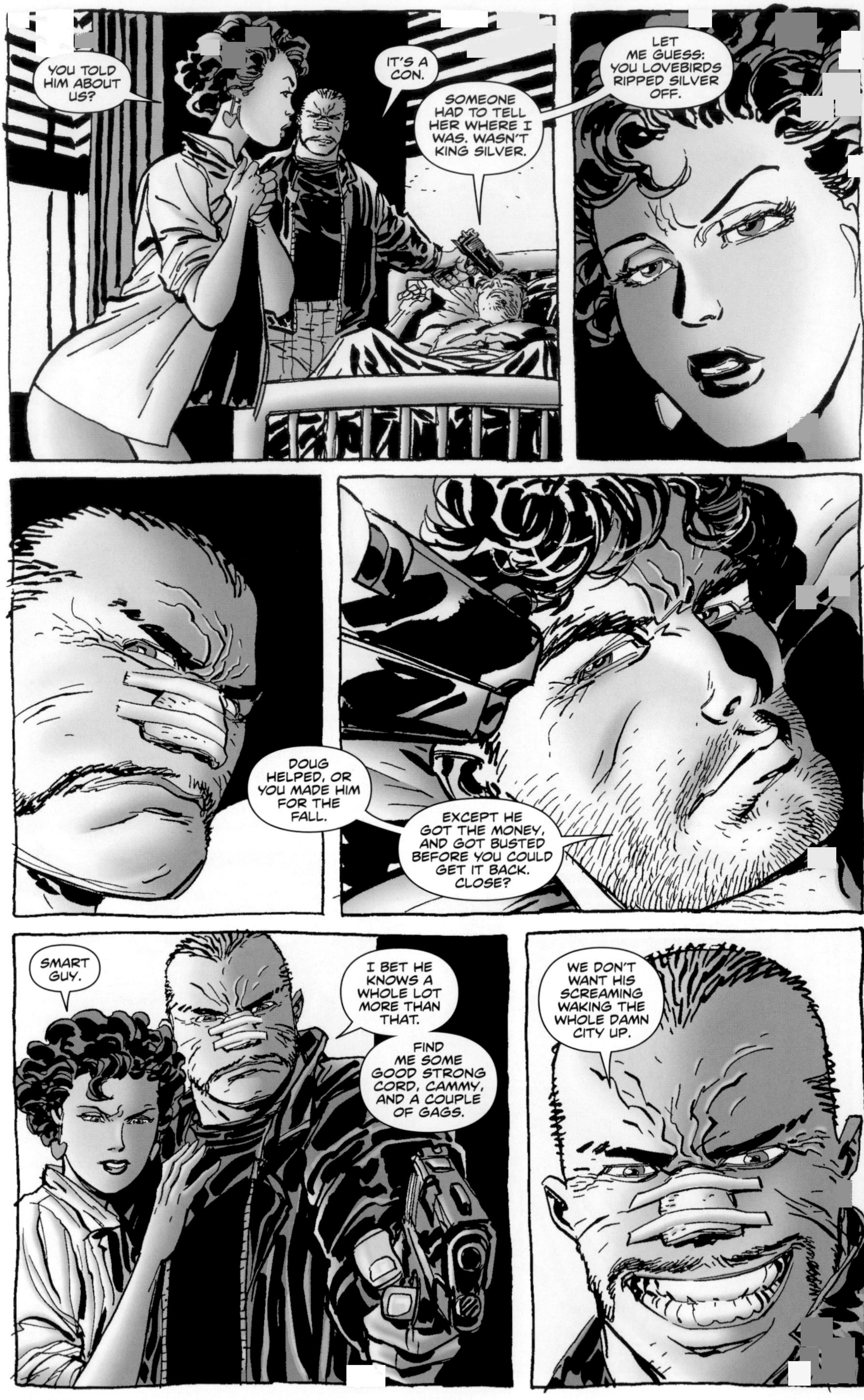
YOU TOLD HIM ABOUT US?
IT'S A CON.
SOMEONE HAD TO TELL HER WHERE I WAS. WASN'T KING SILVER.
LET ME GUESS: YOU LOVEBIRDS RIPPED SILVER OFF.
DOUG HELPED, OR YOU MADE HIM FOR THE FALL.
EXCEPT HE GOT THE MONEY, AND GOT BUSTED BEFORE YOU COULD GET IT BACK. CLOSE?
SMART GUY.
I BET HE KNOWS A WHOLE LOT MORE THAN THAT.
FIND ME SOME GOOD STRONG CORD, CAMMY, AND A COUPLE OF GAGS.
WE DON'T WANT HIS SCREAMING WAKING THE WHOLE DAMN CITY UP.

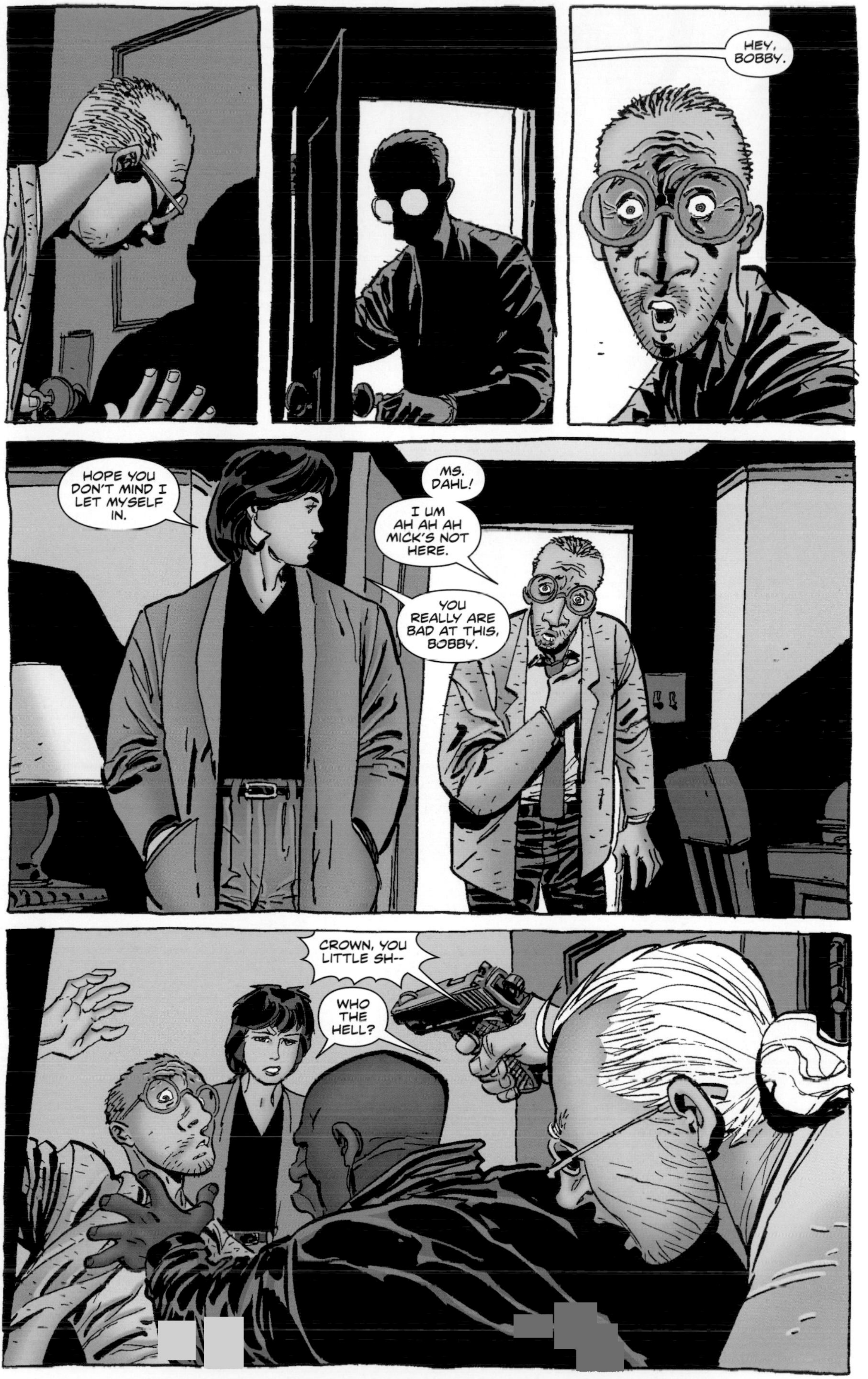
HEY, BOBBY.
HOPE YOU DON'T MIND I LET MYSELF IN.
MS. DAHL!
I UM AH AH AH MICK'S NOT HERE.
YOU REALLY ARE BAD AT THIS, BOBBY.
CROWN, YOU LITTLE SH--
WHO THE HELL?

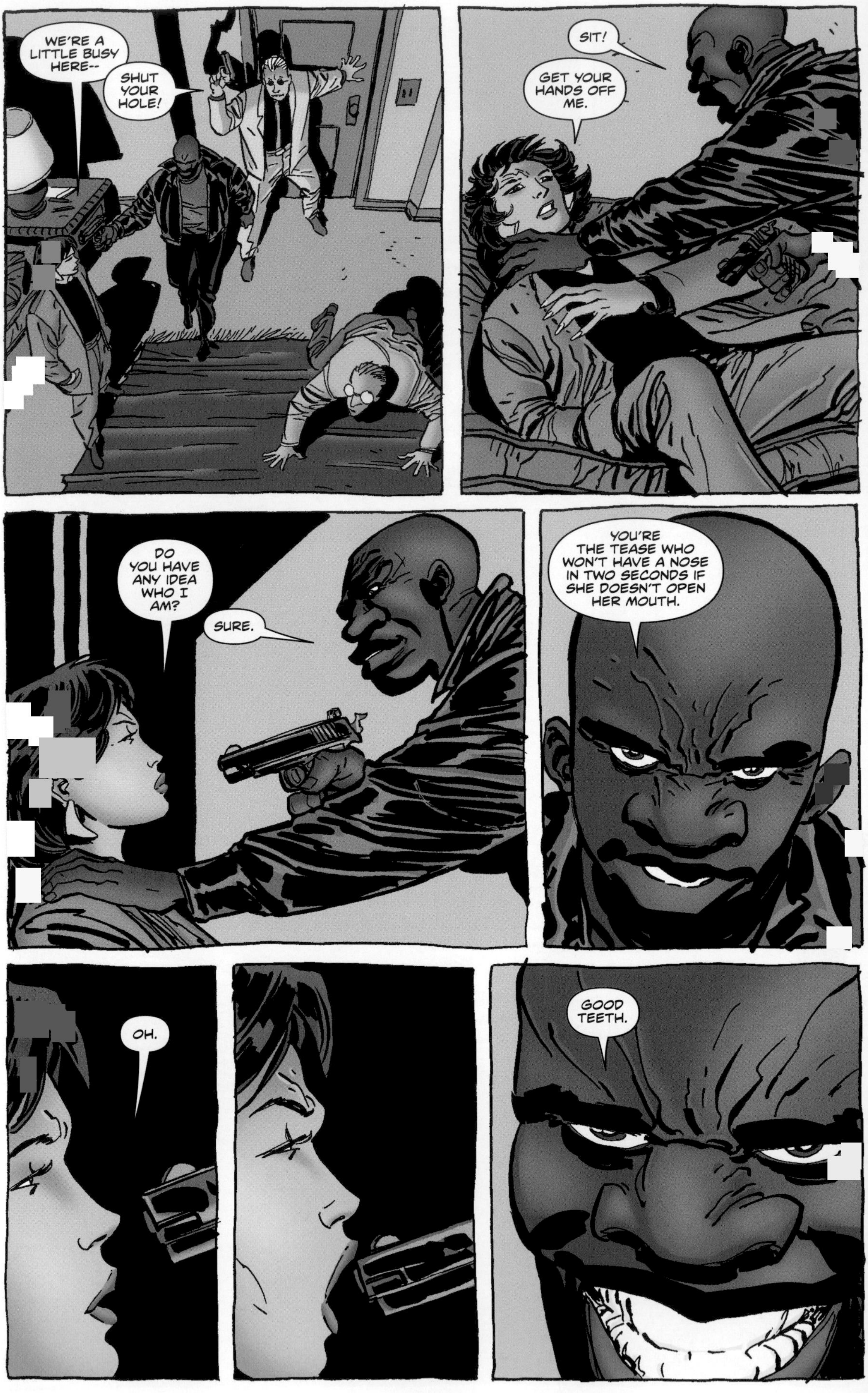
WE'RE A LITTLE BUSY HERE--
SHUT YOUR HOLE!
SIT!
GET YOUR HANDS OFF ME.
DO YOU HAVE ANY IDEA WHO I AM?
SURE.
YOU'RE THE TEASE WHO WON'T HAVE A NOSE IN TWO SECONDS IF SHE DOESN'T OPEN HER MOUTH.
OH.
GOOD TEETH.

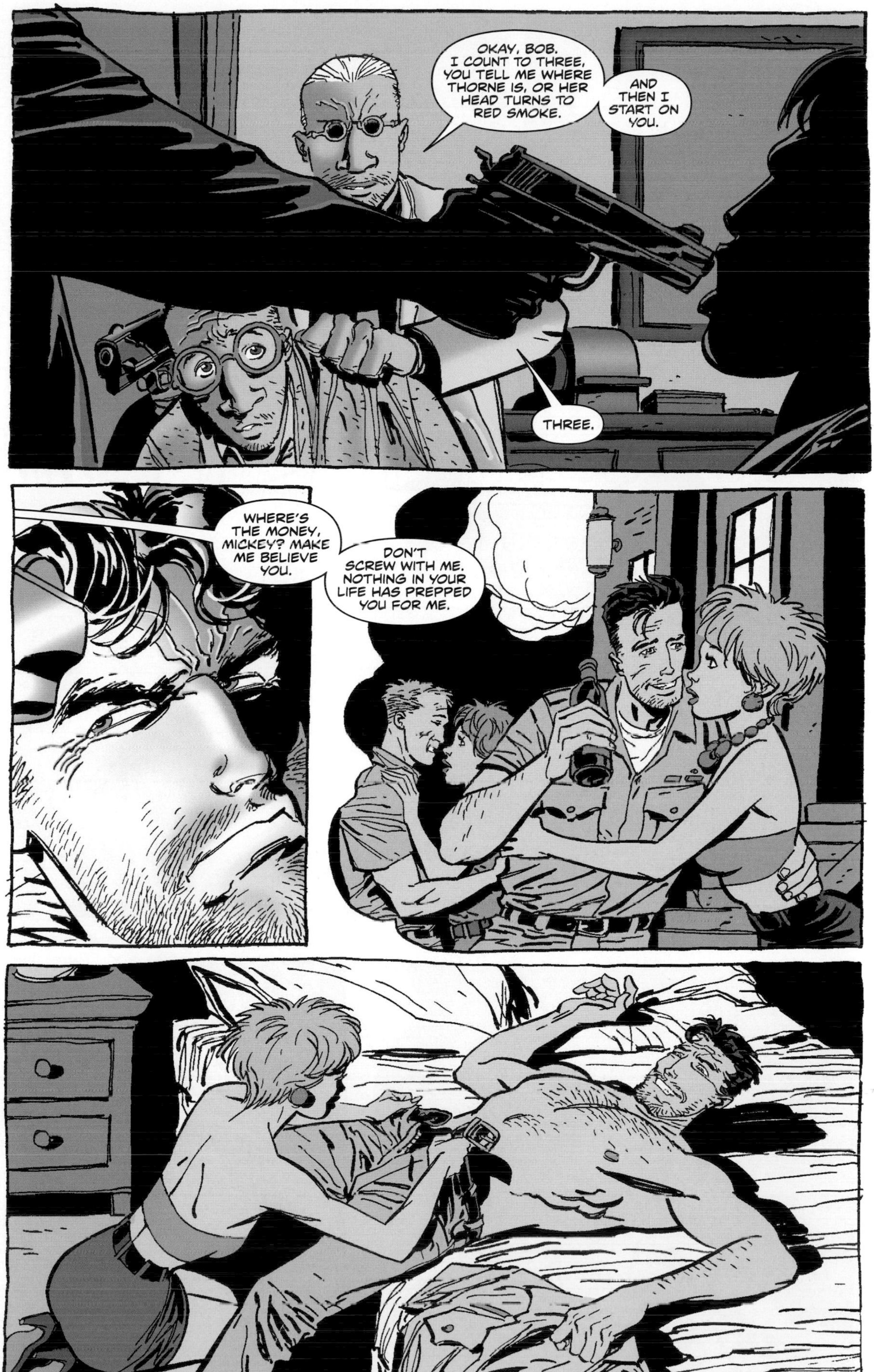
OKAY, BOB. I COUNT TO THREE, YOU TELL ME WHERE THORNE IS, OR HER HEAD TURNS TO RED SMOKE.
AND THEN I START ON YOU.
THREE.
WHERE'S THE MONEY, MICKEY? MAKE ME BELIEVE YOU.
DON'T SCREW WITH ME. NOTHING IN YOUR LIFE HAS PREPPED YOU FOR ME.

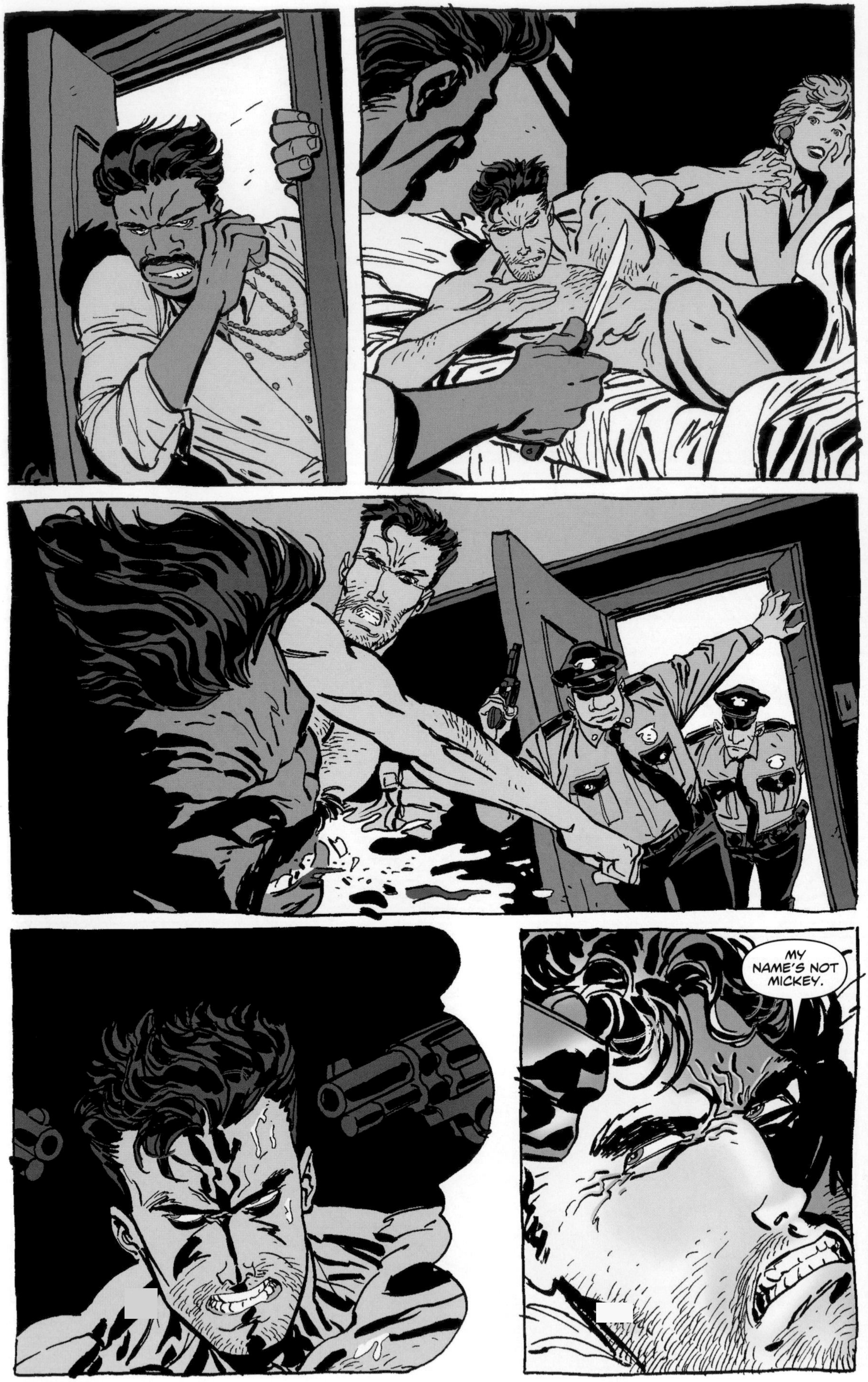
MY NAME'S NOT MICKEY.

DAMNED

"AFTER EIGHT YEARS,
MICK COULDN'T REMEMBER
WHEN HE WASN'T IN PRISON."

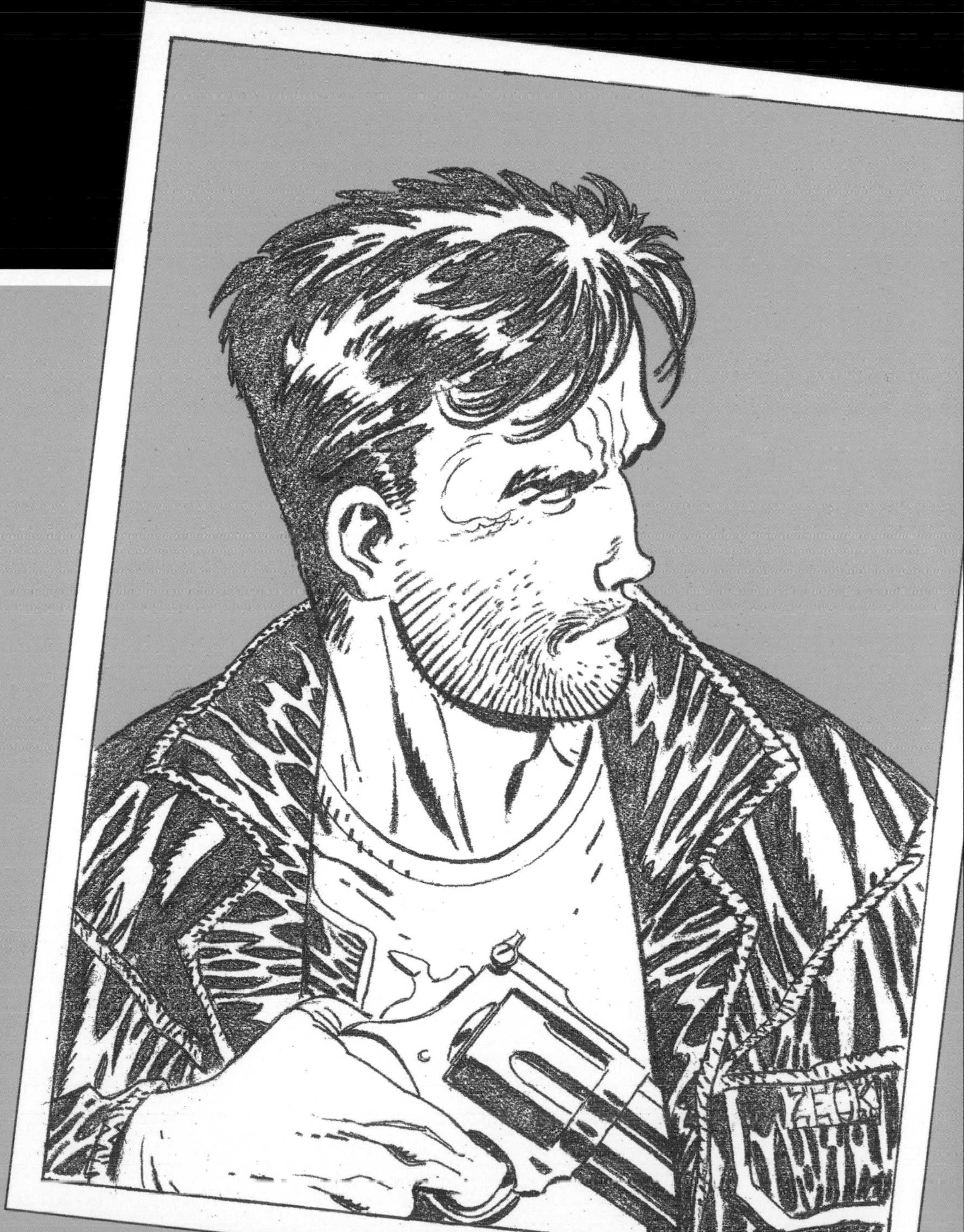
ZECK

CHAPTER FOUR

THE ONLY LINE
NO ONE CROSSES—

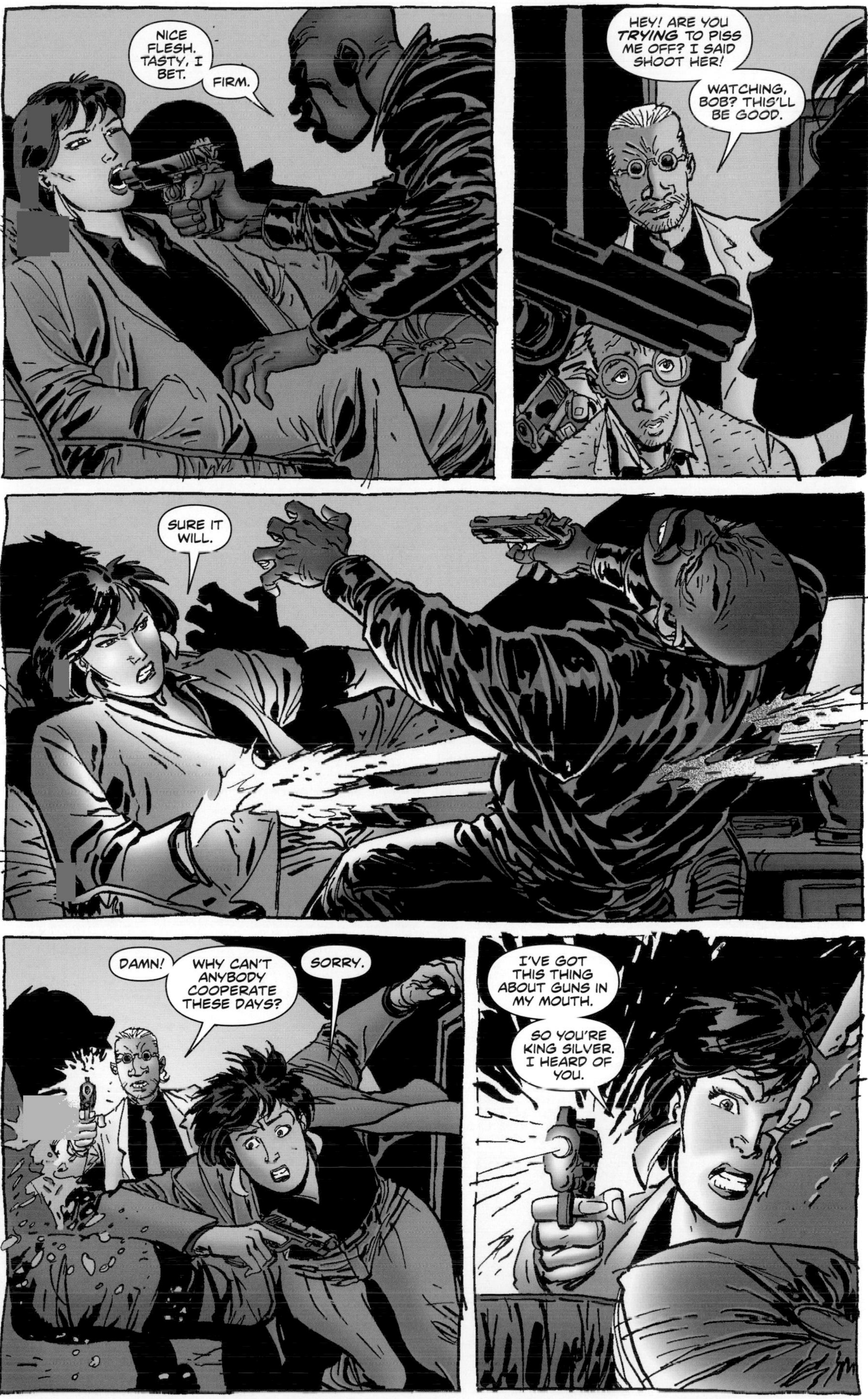
NICE FLESH. TASTY, I BET.
FIRM.
HEY! ARE YOU TRYING TO PISS ME OFF? I SAID SHOOT HER!
WATCHING, BOB? THIS'LL BE GOOD.
SURE IT WILL.
DAMN!
WHY CAN'T ANYBODY COOPERATE THESE DAYS?
SORRY.
I'VE GOT THIS THING ABOUT GUNS IN MY MOUTH.
SO YOU'RE KING SILVER. I HEARD OF YOU.

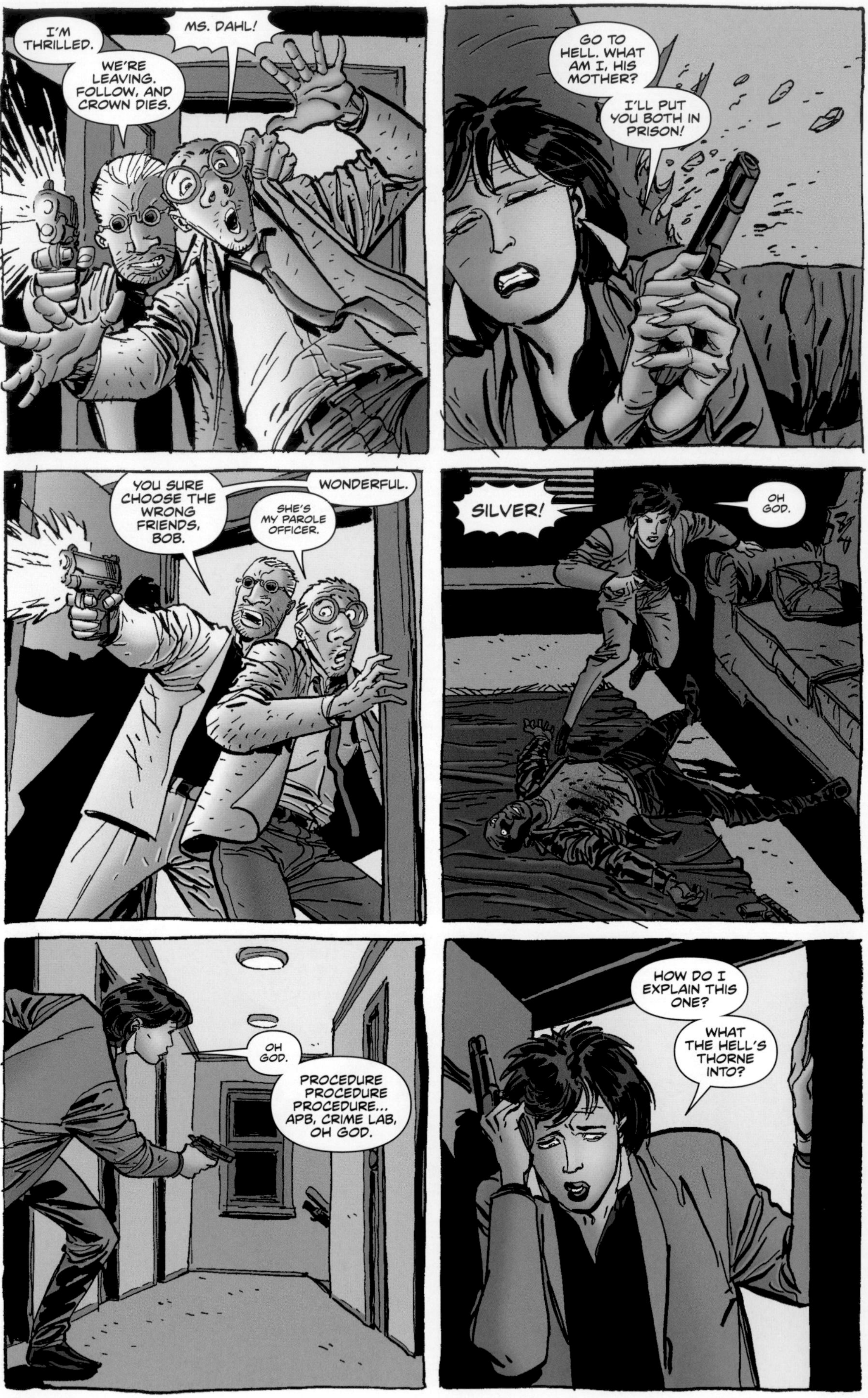
I'M THRILLED.
MS. DAHL!
WE'RE LEAVING. FOLLOW, AND CROWN DIES.
GO TO HELL. WHAT AM I, HIS MOTHER?
I'LL PUT YOU BOTH IN PRISON!
YOU SURE CHOOSE THE WRONG FRIENDS, BOB.
WONDERFUL.
SHE'S MY PAROLE OFFICER.
SILVER!
OH GOD.
OH GOD.
PROCEDURE PROCEDURE PROCEDURE... APB, CRIME LAB, OH GOD.
HOW DO I EXPLAIN THIS ONE?
WHAT THE HELL'S THORNE INTO?

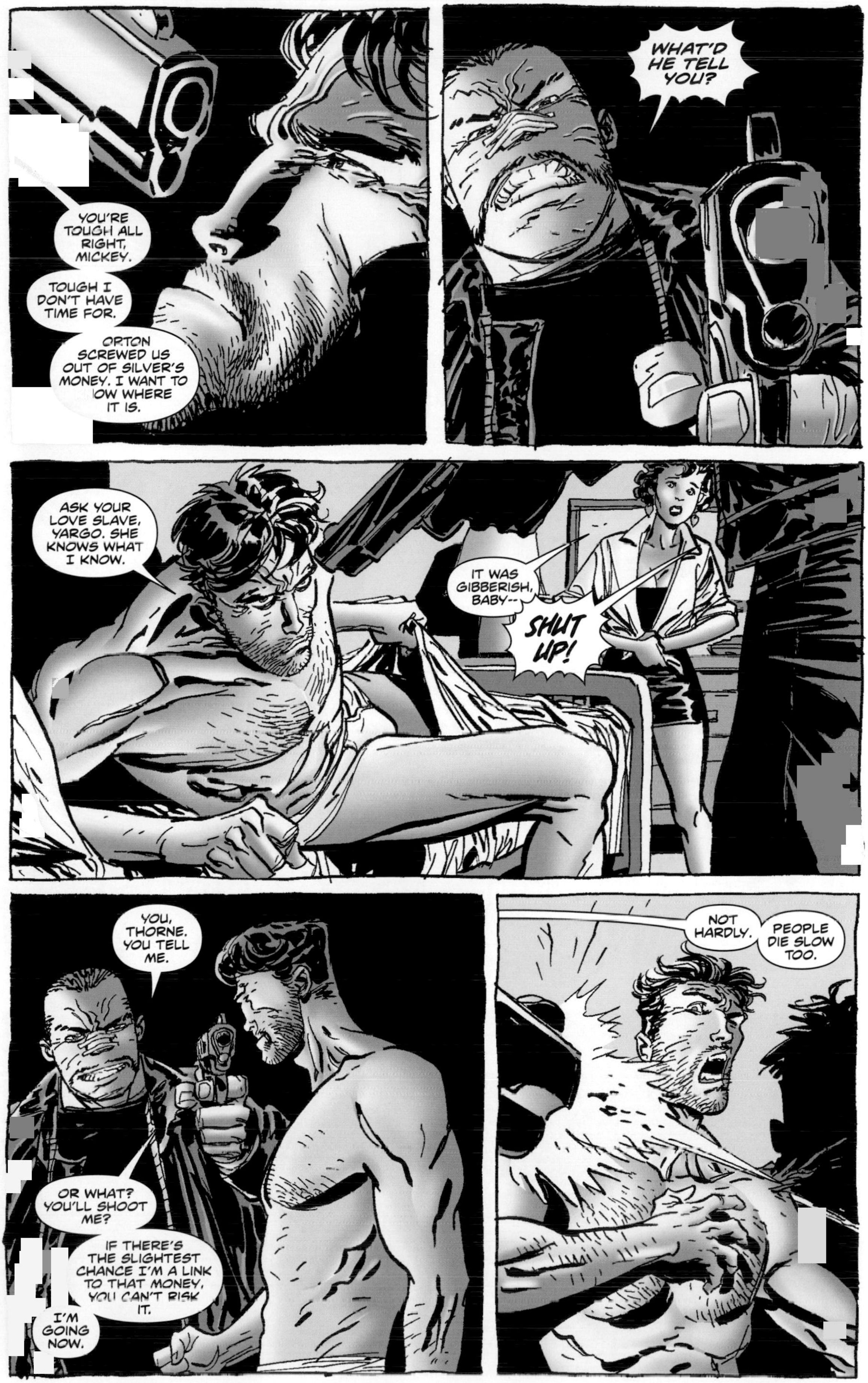
YOU'RE TOUGH ALL RIGHT, MICKEY.
TOUGH I DON'T HAVE TIME FOR.
ORTON SCREWED US OUT OF SILVER'S MONEY. I WANT TO KNOW WHERE IT IS.
WHAT'D HE TELL YOU?
ASK YOUR LOVE SLAVE, YARGO. SHE KNOWS WHAT I KNOW.
IT WAS GIBBERISH, BABY--
SHUT UP!
YOU, THORNE. YOU TELL ME.
OR WHAT? YOU'LL SHOOT ME?
IF THERE'S THE SLIGHTEST CHANCE I'M A LINK TO THAT MONEY, YOU CAN'T RISK IT.
I'M GOING NOW.
NOT HARDLY.
PEOPLE DIE SLOW TOO.

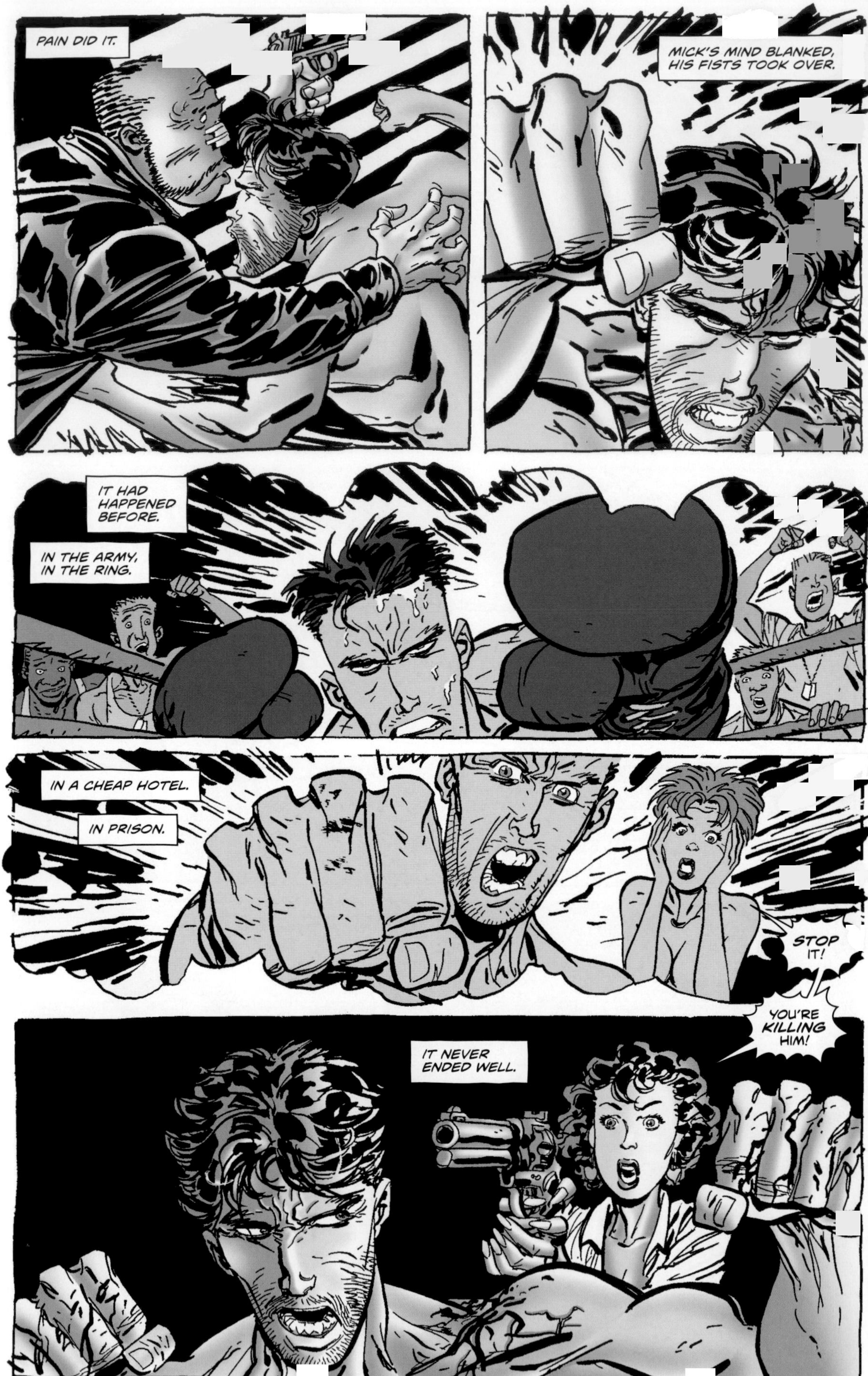
PAIN DID IT.
MICK'S MIND BLANKED, HIS FISTS TOOK OVER.
IT HAD HAPPENED BEFORE.
IN THE ARMY, IN THE RING.
IN A CHEAP HOTEL.
IN PRISON.
STOP IT!
YOU'RE KILLING HIM!
IT NEVER ENDED WELL.

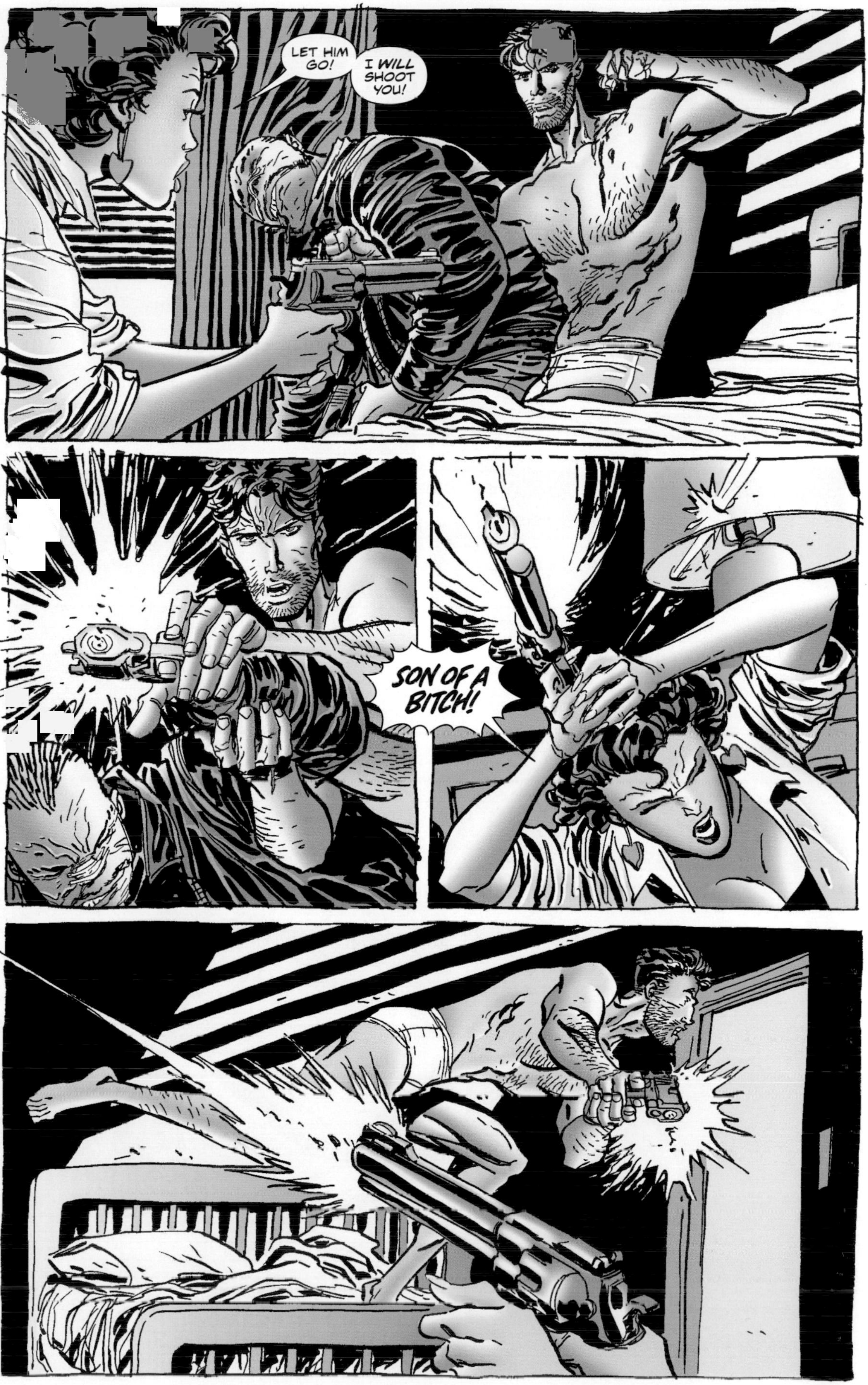
LET HIM GO!
I WILL SHOOT YOU!
SON OF A BITCH!

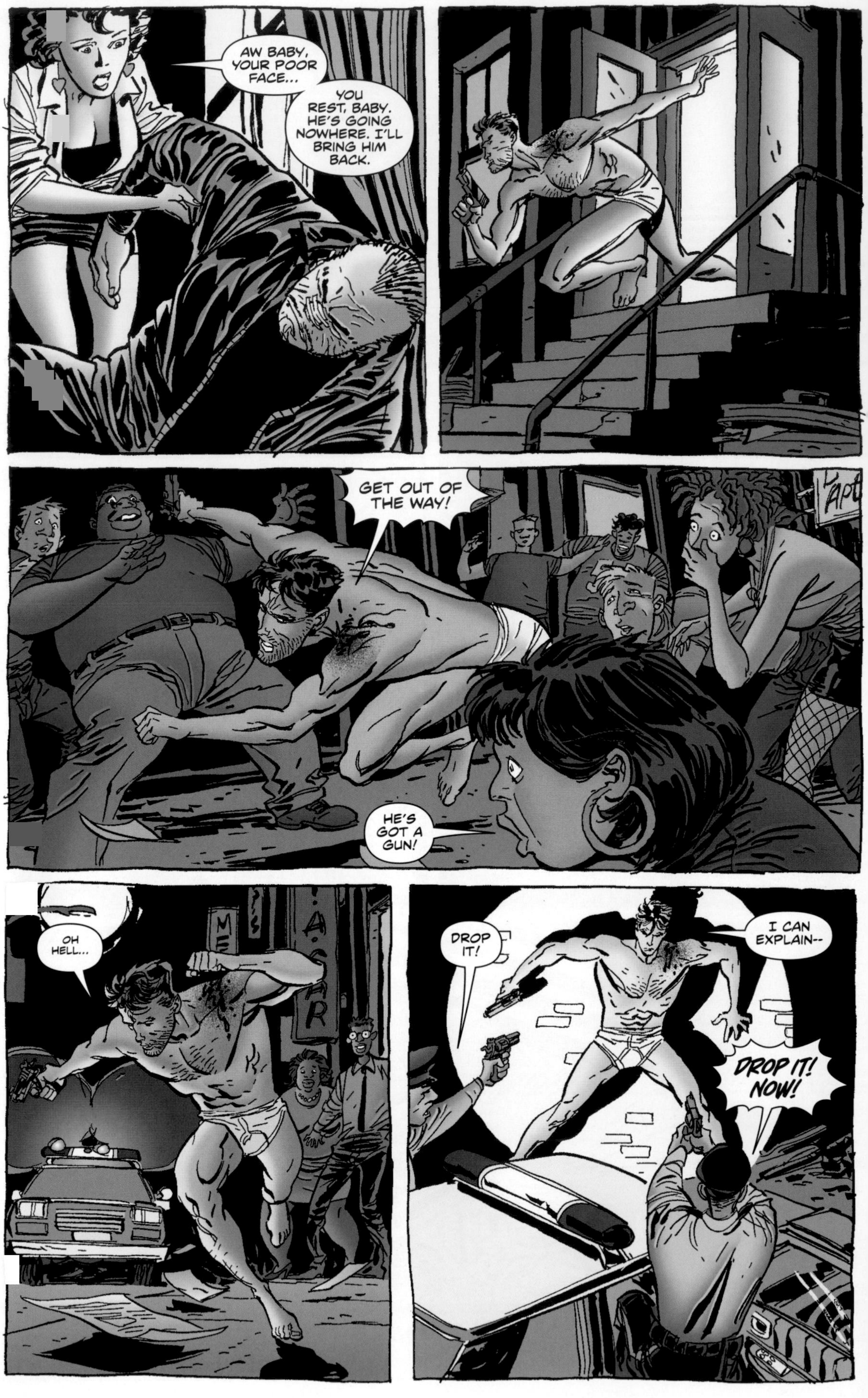
AW BABY, YOUR POOR FACE...
YOU REST, BABY. HE'S GOING NOWHERE. I'LL BRING HIM BACK.
GET OUT OF THE WAY!
HE'S GOT A GUN!
OH HELL...
DROP IT!
I CAN EXPLAIN--
DROP IT! NOW!

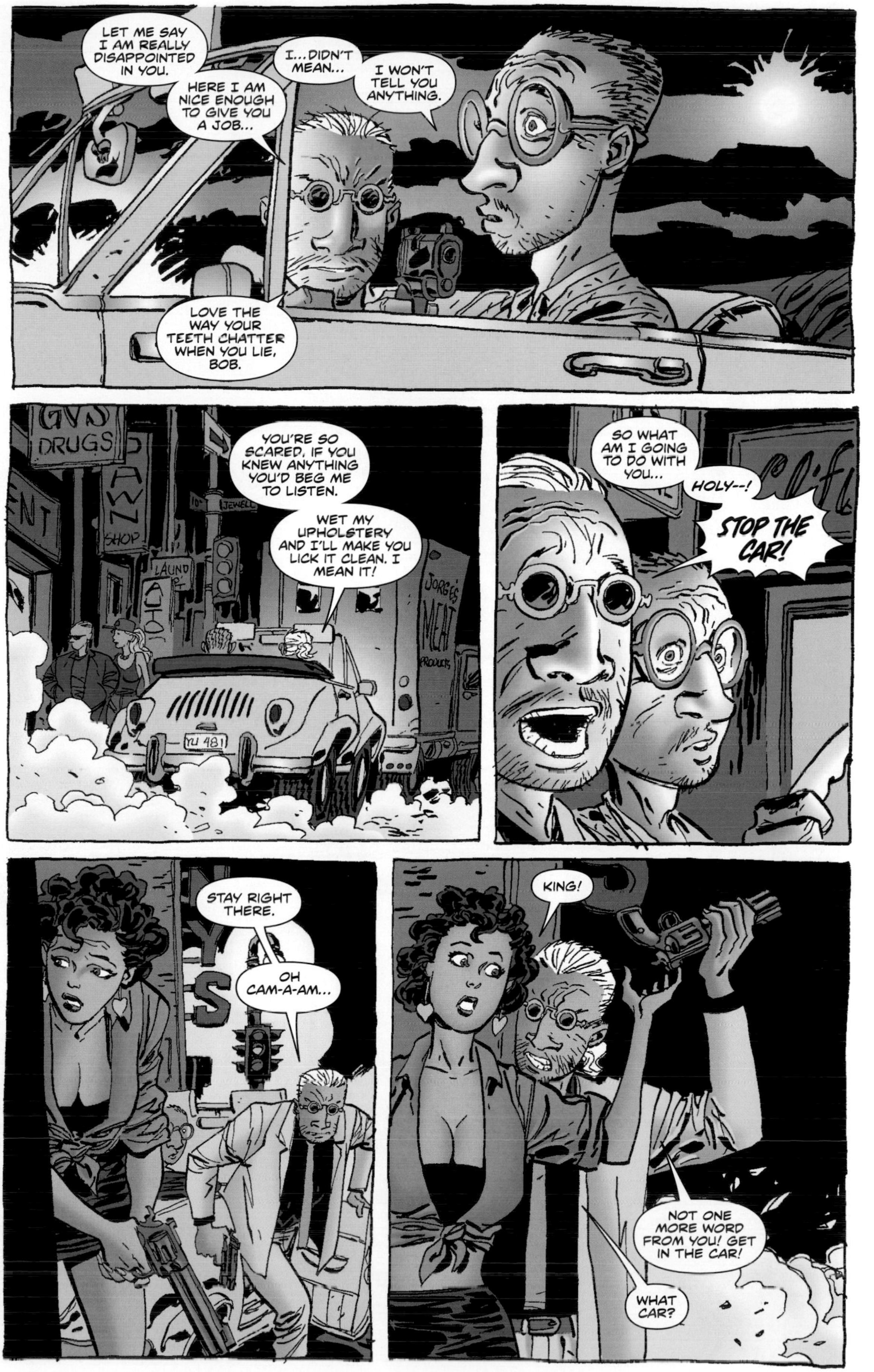
LET ME SAY I AM REALLY DISAPPOINTED IN YOU.
HERE I AM NICE ENOUGH TO GIVE YOU A JOB...
I...DIDN'T MEAN...
I WON'T TELL YOU ANYTHING.
LOVE THE WAY YOUR TEETH CHATTER WHEN YOU LIE, BOB.
YOU'RE SO SCARED, IF YOU KNEW ANYTHING YOU'D BEG ME TO LISTEN.
WET MY UPHOLSTERY AND I'LL MAKE YOU LICK IT CLEAN. I MEAN IT!
SO WHAT AM I GOING TO DO WITH YOU...
HOLY--!
STOP THE CAR!
STAY RIGHT THERE.
OH CAM-A-AM...
KING!
NOT ONE MORE WORD FROM YOU! GET IN THE CAR!
WHAT CAR?

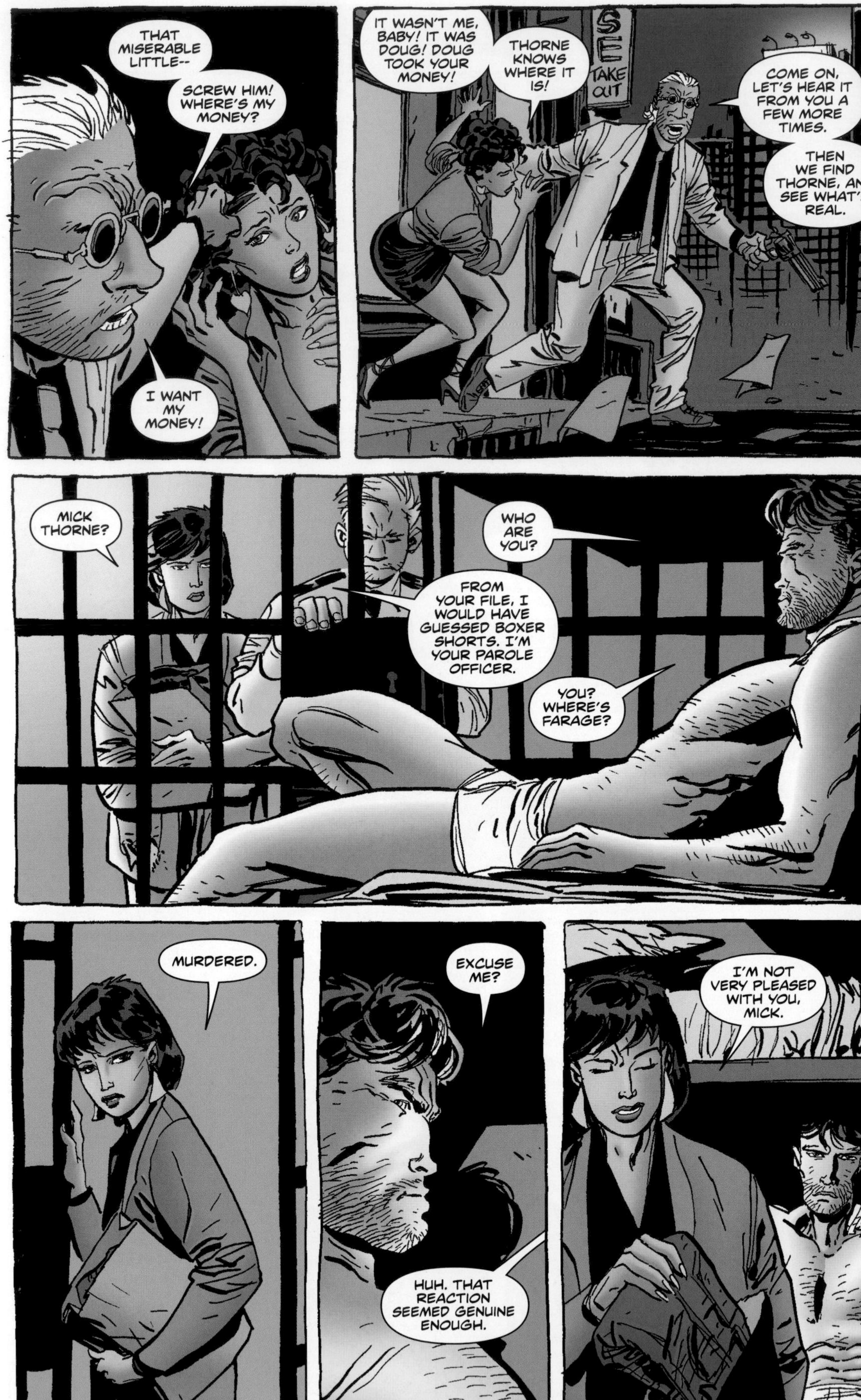
THAT MISERABLE LITTLE--
SCREW HIM! WHERE'S MY MONEY?
I WANT MY MONEY!
IT WASN'T ME, BABY! IT WAS DOUG! DOUG TOOK YOUR MONEY!
THORNE KNOWS WHERE IT IS!
SE
TAKE OUT
COME ON, LET'S HEAR IT FROM YOU A FEW MORE TIMES.
THEN WE FIND THORNE, AND SEE WHAT'S REAL.
MICK THORNE?
WHO ARE YOU?
FROM YOUR FILE, I WOULD HAVE GUESSED BOXER SHORTS. I'M YOUR PAROLE OFFICER.
YOU? WHERE'S FARAGE?
MURDERED.
EXCUSE ME?
HUH. THAT REACTION SEEMED GENUINE ENOUGH.
I'M NOT VERY PLEASED WITH YOU, MICK.

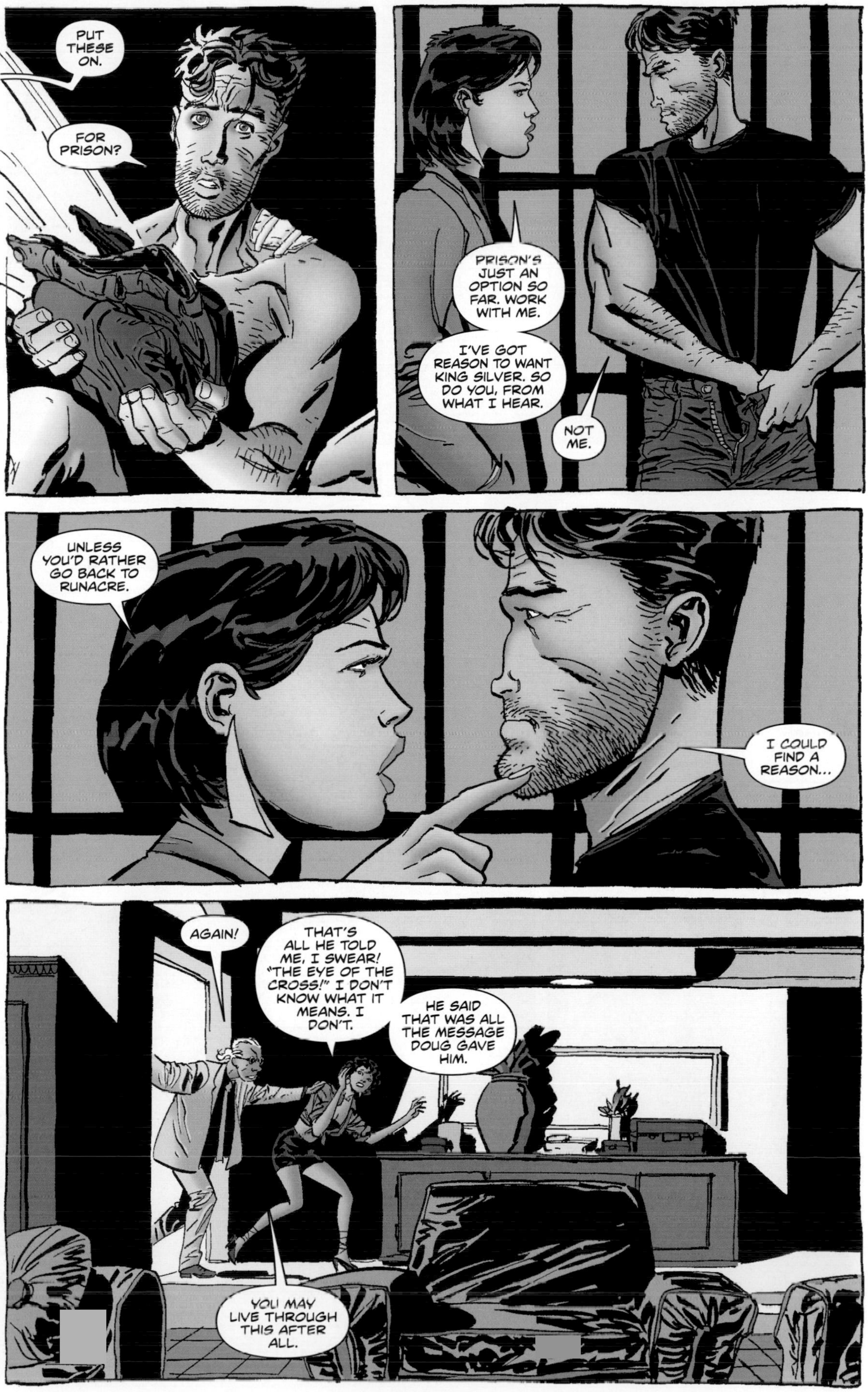
PUT THESE ON.
FOR PRISON?
PRISON'S JUST AN OPTION SO FAR. WORK WITH ME.
I'VE GOT REASON TO WANT KING SILVER. SO DO YOU, FROM WHAT I HEAR.
NOT ME.
UNLESS YOU'D RATHER GO BACK TO RUNACRE.
I COULD FIND A REASON...
AGAIN!
THAT'S ALL HE TOLD ME, I SWEAR! "THE EYE OF THE CROSS!" I DON'T KNOW WHAT IT MEANS. I DON'T.
HE SAID THAT WAS ALL THE MESSAGE DOUG GAVE HIM.
YOU MAY LIVE THROUGH THIS AFTER ALL.

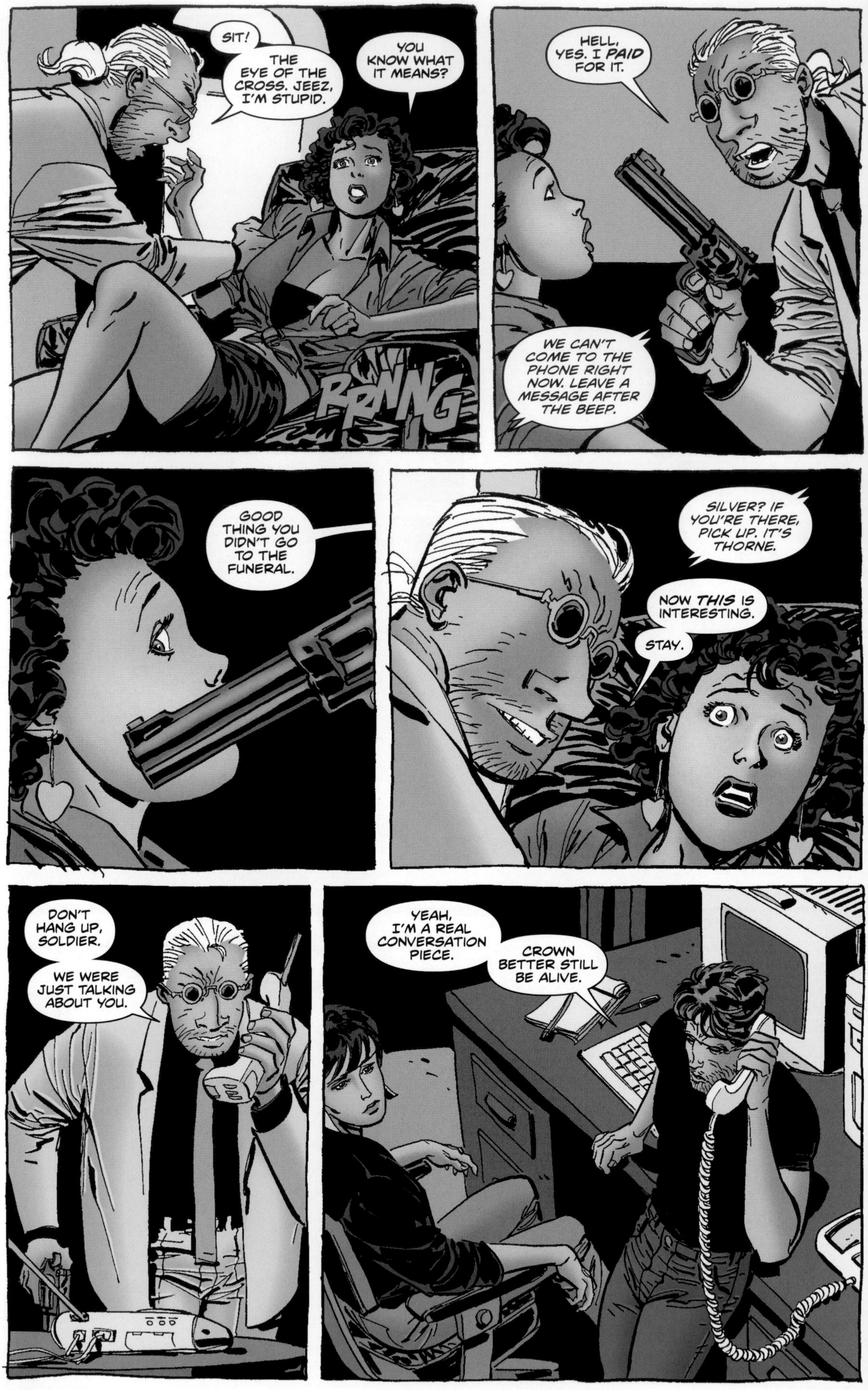
SIT!
THE EYE OF THE CROSS. JEEZ, I'M STUPID.
YOU KNOW WHAT IT MEANS?
RRNNG
HELL, YES. I PAID FOR IT.
WE CAN'T COME TO THE PHONE RIGHT NOW. LEAVE A MESSAGE AFTER THE BEEP.
GOOD THING YOU DIDN'T GO TO THE FUNERAL.
SILVER? IF YOU'RE THERE, PICK UP. IT'S THORNE.
NOW THIS IS INTERESTING.
STAY.
DON'T HANG UP, SOLDIER.
WE WERE JUST TALKING ABOUT YOU.
YEAH, I'M A REAL CONVERSATION PIECE.
CROWN BETTER STILL BE ALIVE.

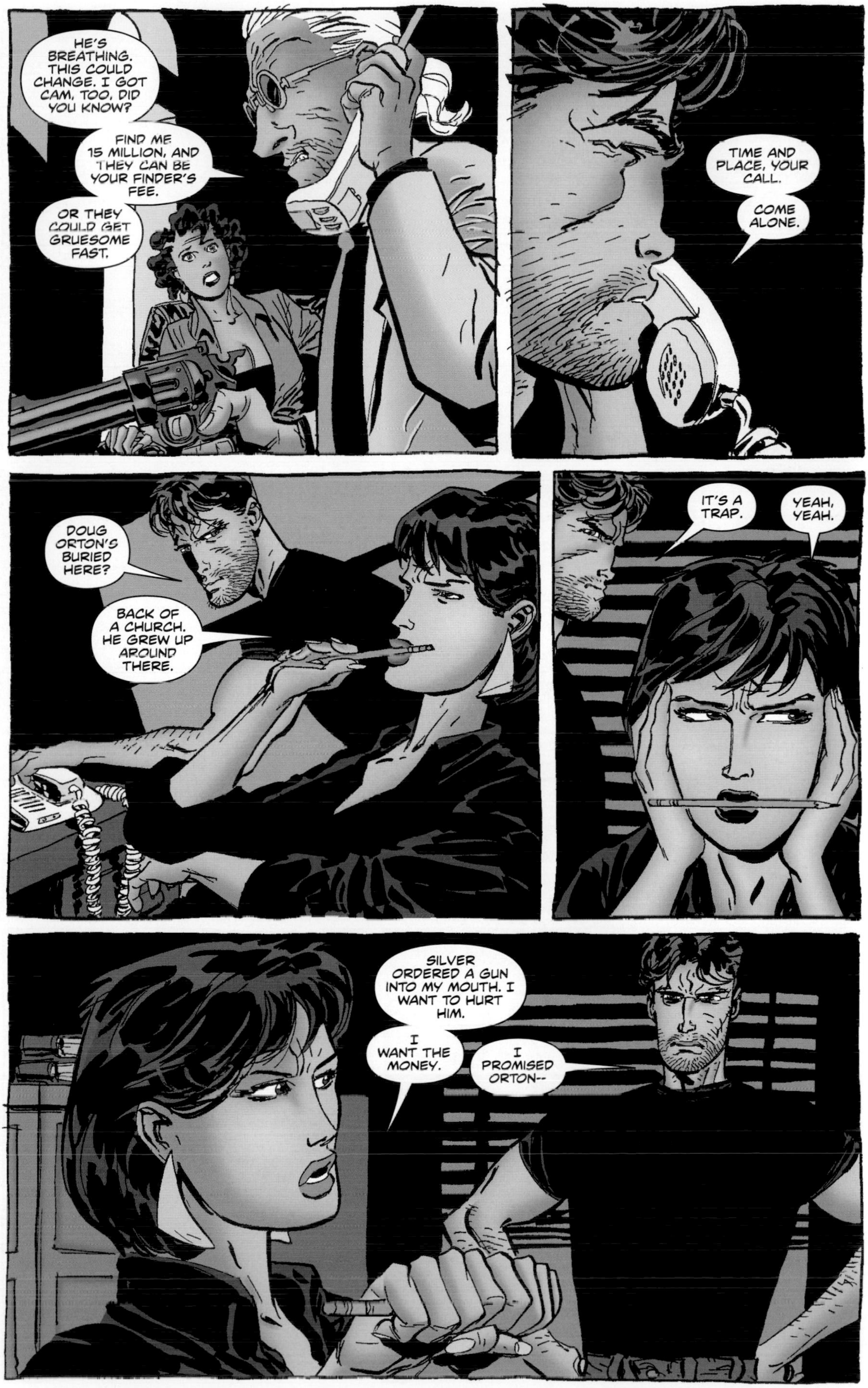
HE'S BREATHING. THIS COULD CHANGE. I GOT CAM, TOO, DID YOU KNOW?
FIND ME 15 MILLION, AND THEY CAN BE YOUR FINDER'S FEE.
OR THEY COULD GET GRUESOME FAST.
TIME AND PLACE, YOUR CALL.
COME ALONE.
DOUG ORTON'S BURIED HERE?
BACK OF A CHURCH. HE GREW UP AROUND THERE.
IT'S A TRAP.
YEAH, YEAH.
SILVER ORDERED A GUN INTO MY MOUTH. I WANT TO HURT HIM.
I WANT THE MONEY.
I PROMISED ORTON--

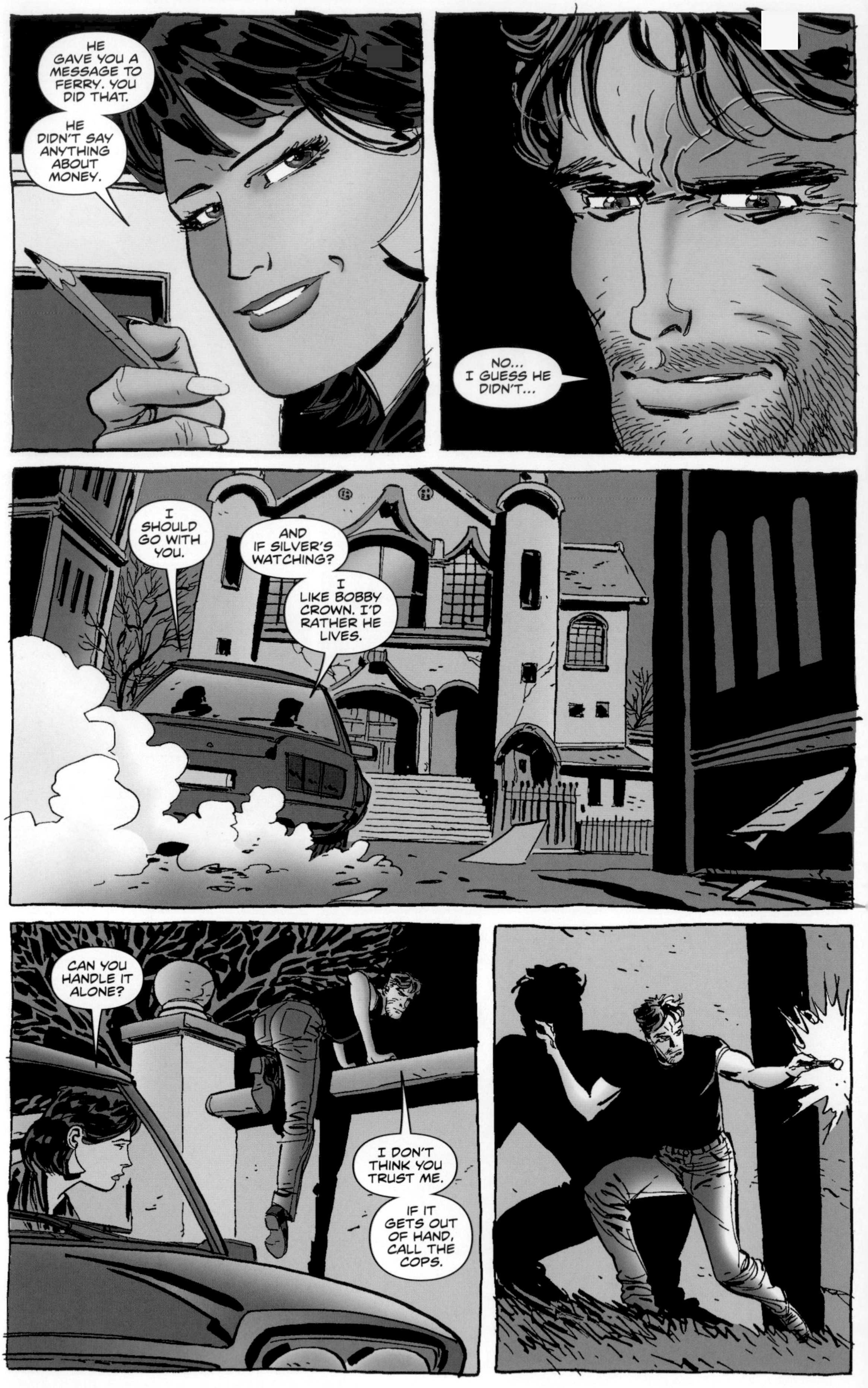
HE GAVE YOU A MESSAGE TO FERRY. YOU DID THAT.
HE DIDN'T SAY ANYTHING ABOUT MONEY.
NO... I GUESS HE DIDN'T...
I SHOULD GO WITH YOU.
AND IF SILVER'S WATCHING?
I LIKE BOBBY CROWN. I'D RATHER HE LIVES.
CAN YOU HANDLE IT ALONE?
I DON'T THINK YOU TRUST ME.
IF IT GETS OUT OF HAND, CALL THE COPS.

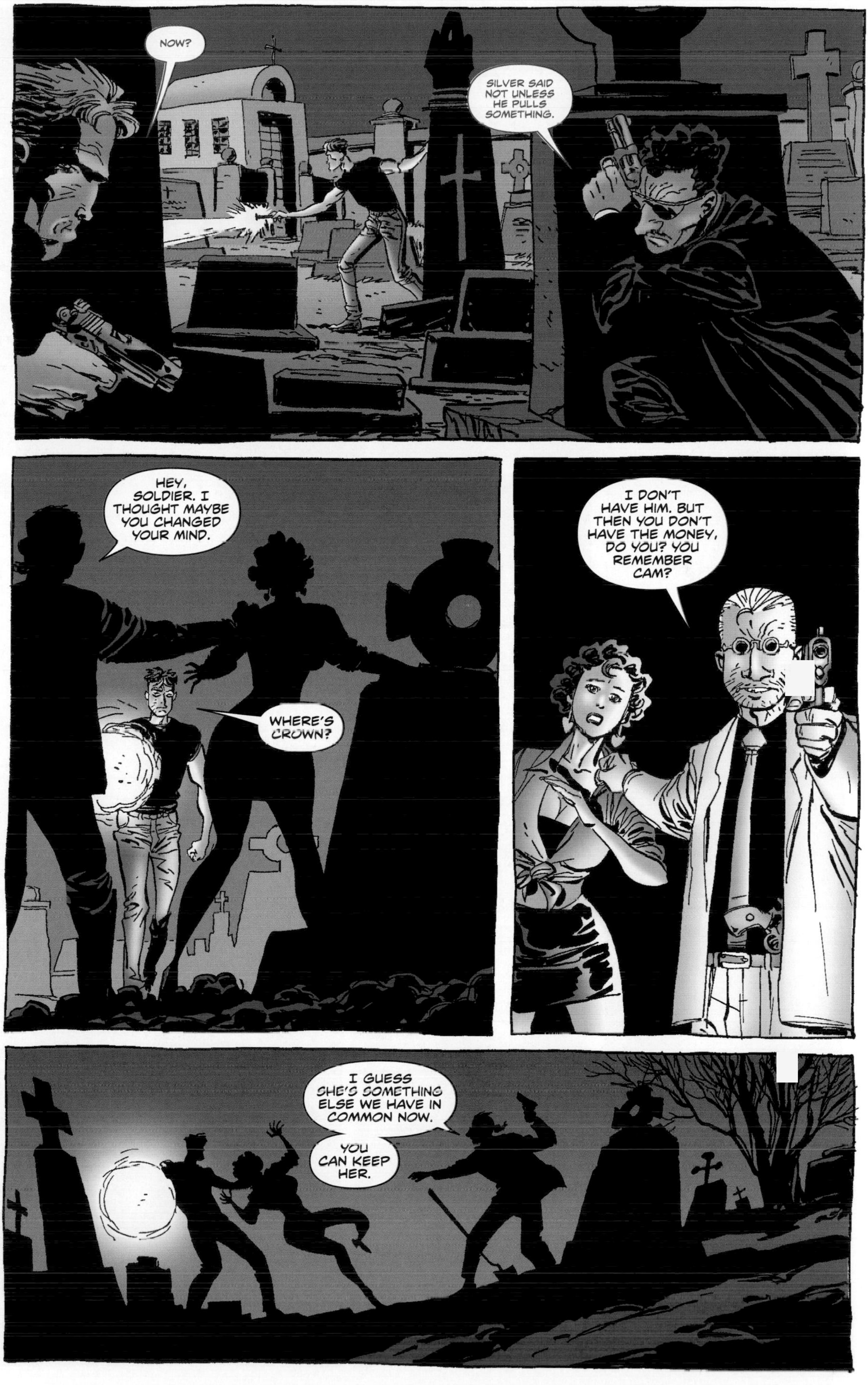
NOW?
SILVER SAID NOT UNLESS HE PULLS SOMETHING.
HEY, SOLDIER. I THOUGHT MAYBE YOU CHANGED YOUR MIND.
WHERE'S CROWN?
I DON'T HAVE HIM. BUT THEN YOU DON'T HAVE THE MONEY, DO YOU? YOU REMEMBER CAM?
I GUESS SHE'S SOMETHING ELSE WE HAVE IN COMMON NOW.
YOU CAN KEEP HER.

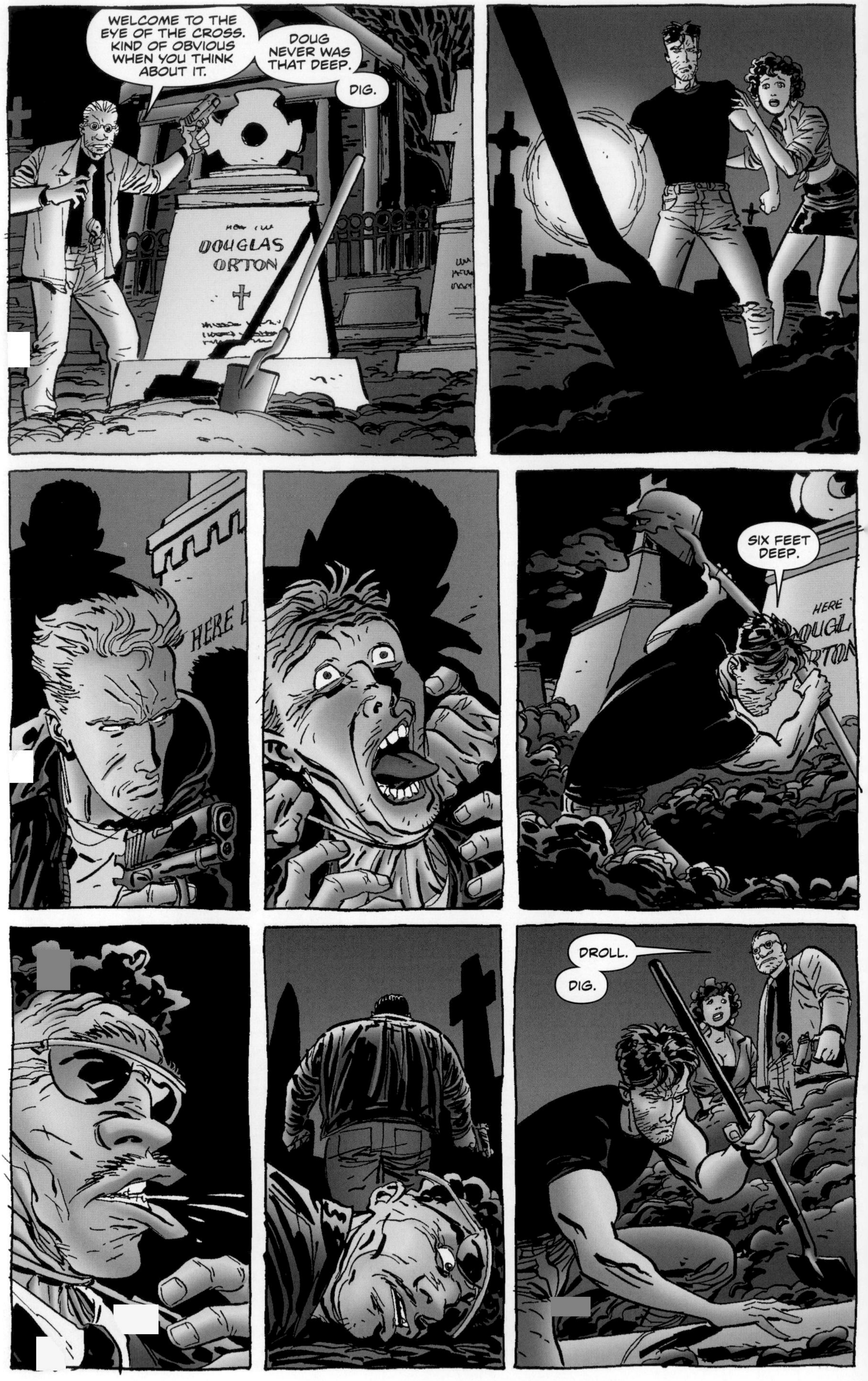
WELCOME TO THE EYE OF THE CROSS. KIND OF OBVIOUS WHEN YOU THINK ABOUT IT.
DOUG NEVER WAS THAT DEEP.
DIG.
DOUGLAS ORTON
SIX FEET DEEP.
DROLL.
DIG.

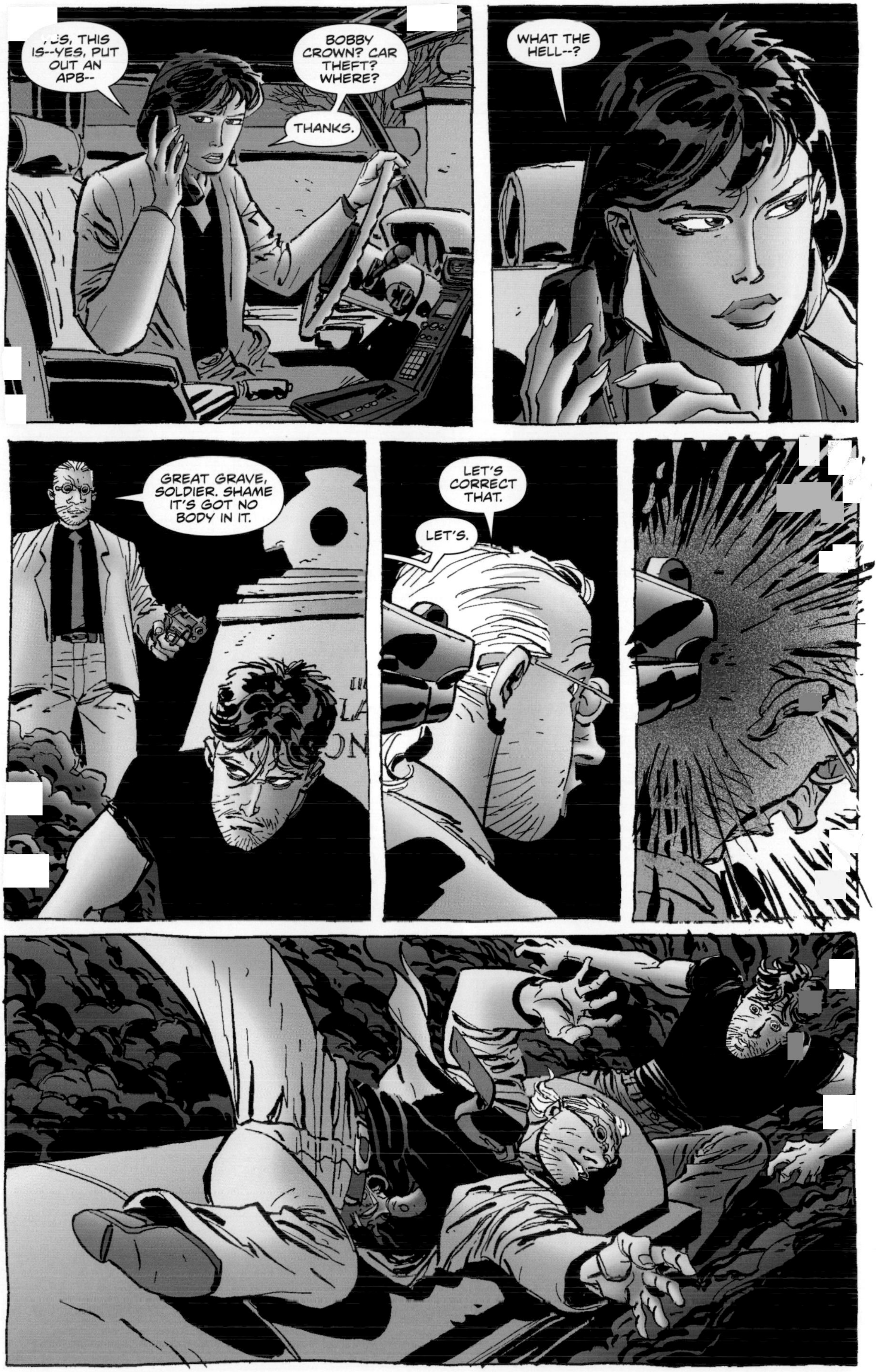
YES, THIS IS--YES, PUT OUT AN APB--
BOBBY CROWN? CAR THEFT? WHERE?
THANKS.
WHAT THE HELL--?
GREAT GRAVE, SOLDIER. SHAME IT'S GOT NO BODY IN IT.
LET'S CORRECT THAT.
LET'S.

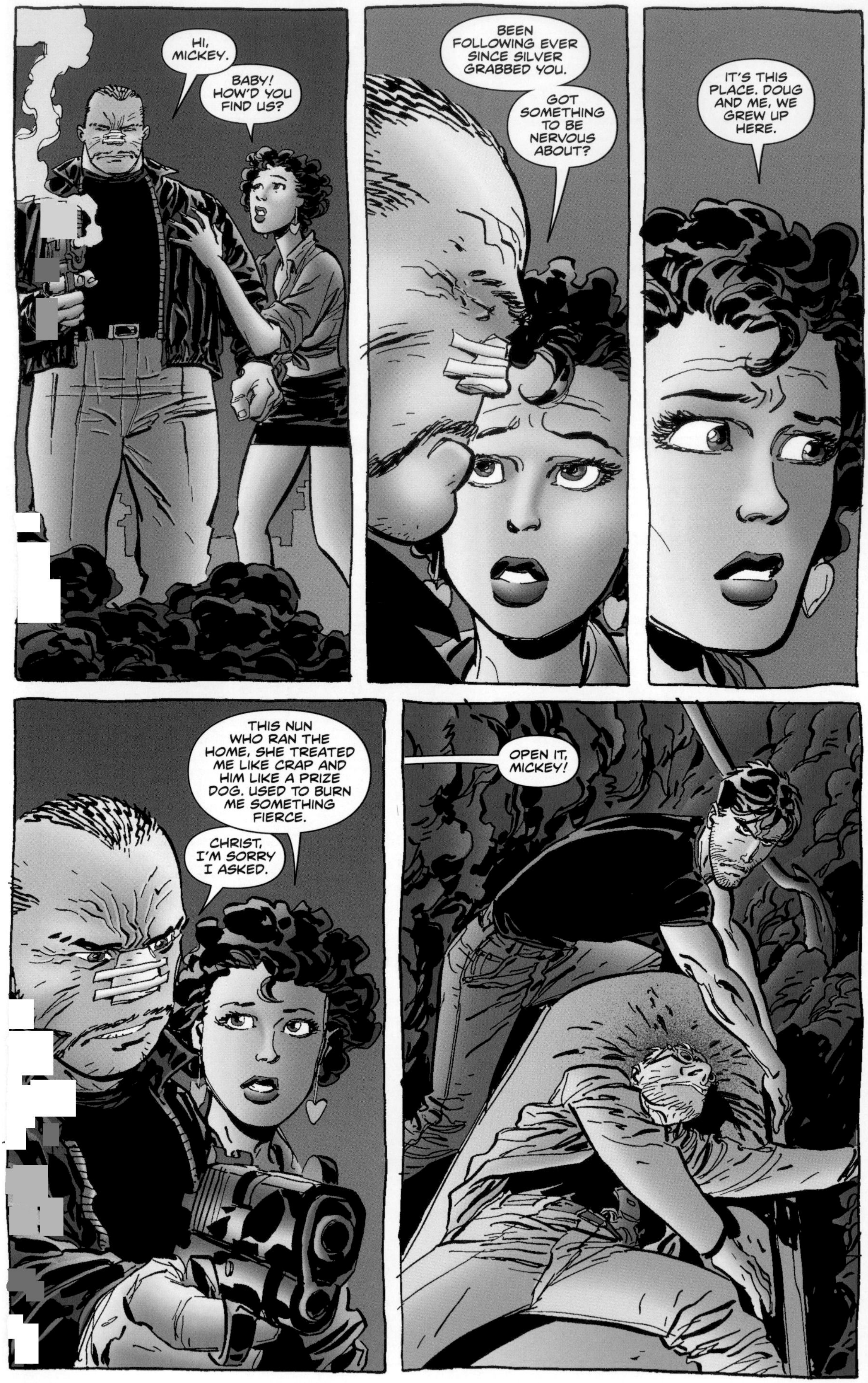
HI, MICKEY.
BABY! HOW'D YOU FIND US?
BEEN FOLLOWING EVER SINCE SILVER GRABBED YOU.
GOT SOMETHING TO BE NERVOUS ABOUT?
IT'S THIS PLACE. DOUG AND ME, WE GREW UP HERE.
THIS NUN WHO RAN THE HOME, SHE TREATED ME LIKE CRAP AND HIM LIKE A PRIZE DOG. USED TO BURN ME SOMETHING FIERCE.
CHRIST, I'M SORRY I ASKED.
OPEN IT, MICKEY!

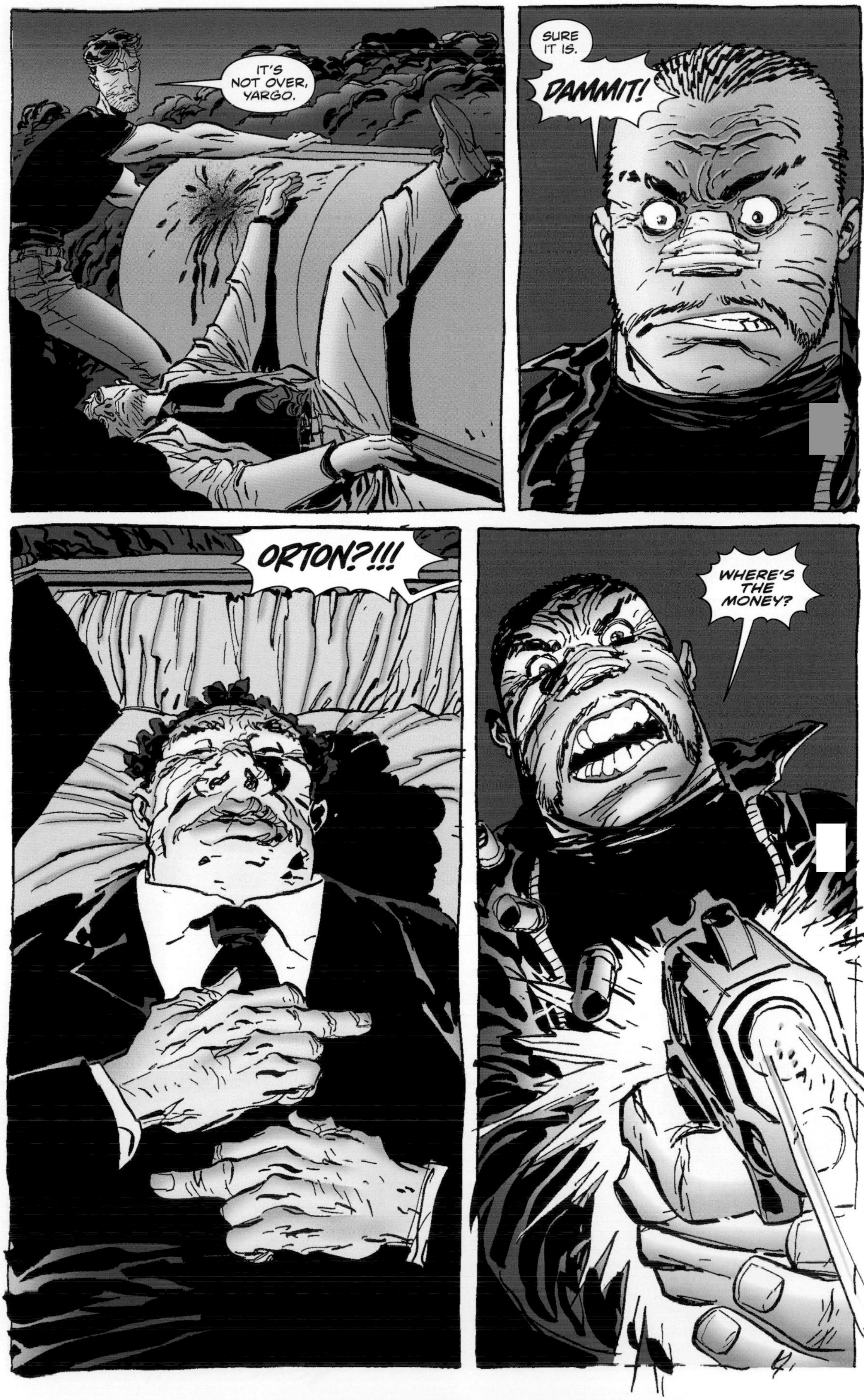
IT'S NOT OVER, YARGO.
SURE IT IS.
DAMMIT!
ORTON?!!!
WHERE'S THE MONEY?

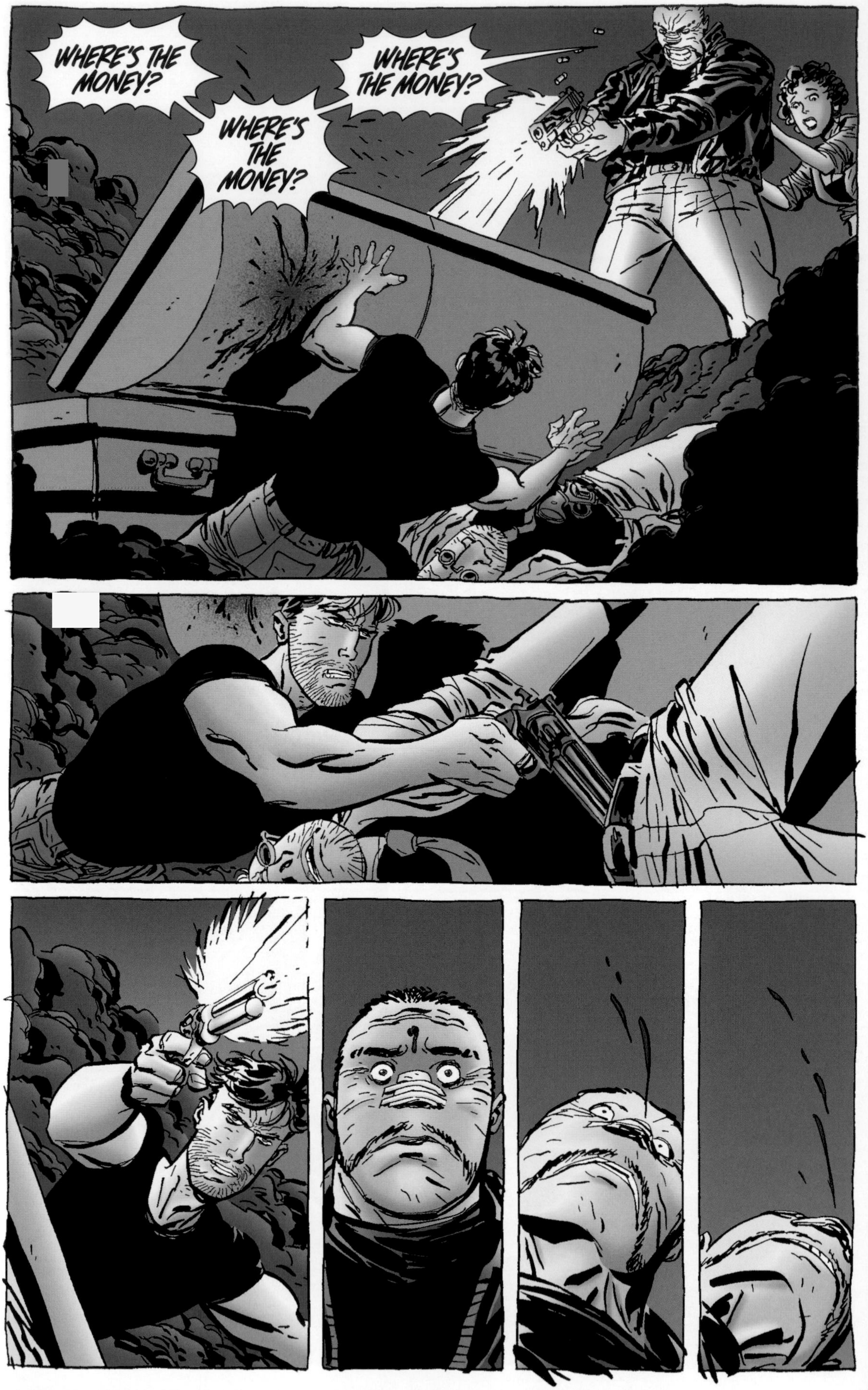
WHERE'S THE MONEY?
WHERE'S THE MONEY?
WHERE'S THE MONEY?

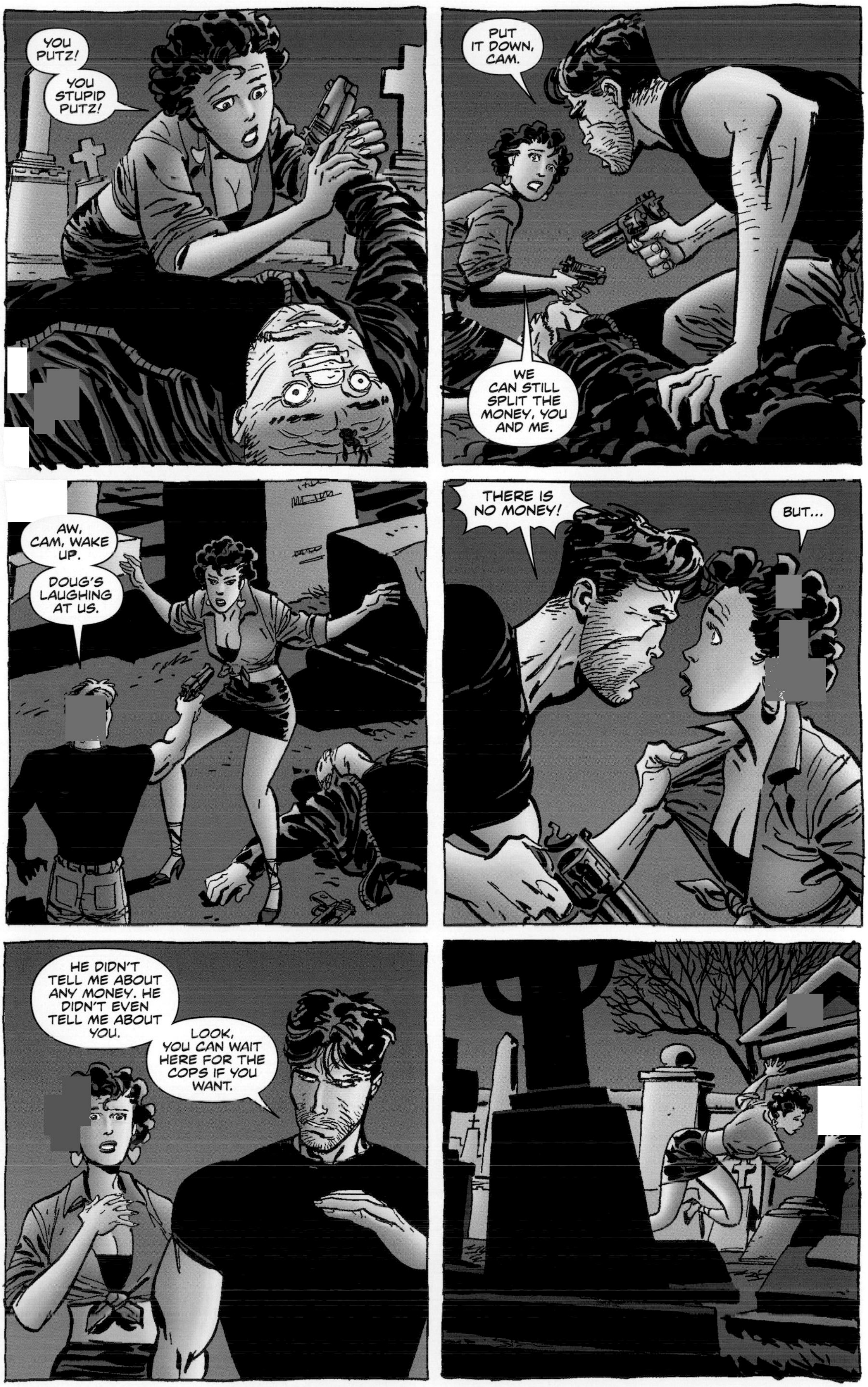
YOU PUTZ!
YOU STUPID PUTZ!
PUT IT DOWN, CAM.
WE CAN STILL SPLIT THE MONEY, YOU AND ME.
AW, CAM, WAKE UP.
DOUG'S LAUGHING AT US.
THERE IS NO MONEY!
BUT...
HE DIDN'T TELL ME ABOUT ANY MONEY. HE DIDN'T EVEN TELL ME ABOUT YOU.
LOOK, YOU CAN WAIT HERE FOR THE COPS IF YOU WANT.

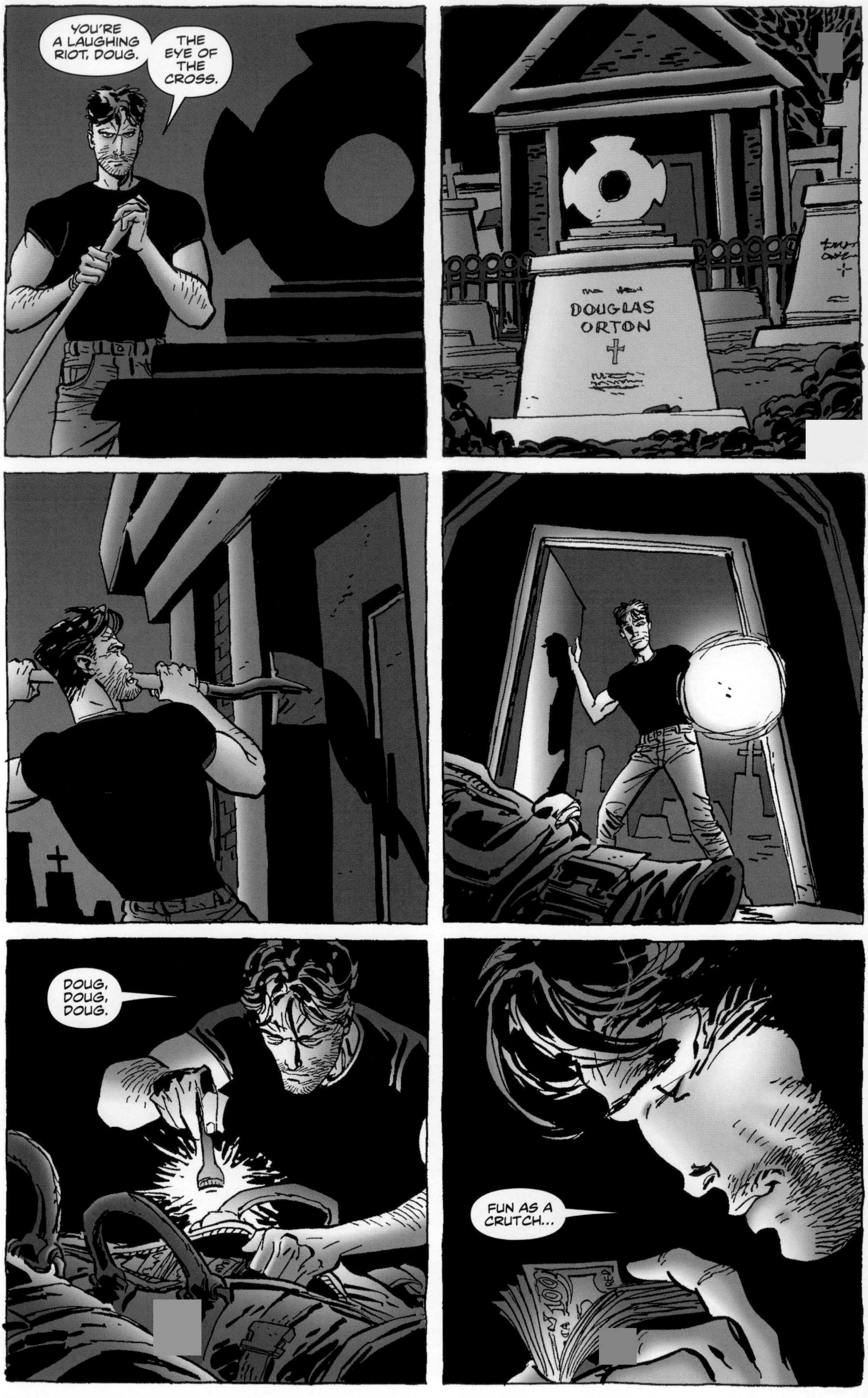
YOU'RE A LAUGHING RIOT, DOUG.
THE EYE OF THE CROSS.
DOUGLAS ORTON
DOUG, DOUG, DOUG.
FUN AS A CRUTCH...

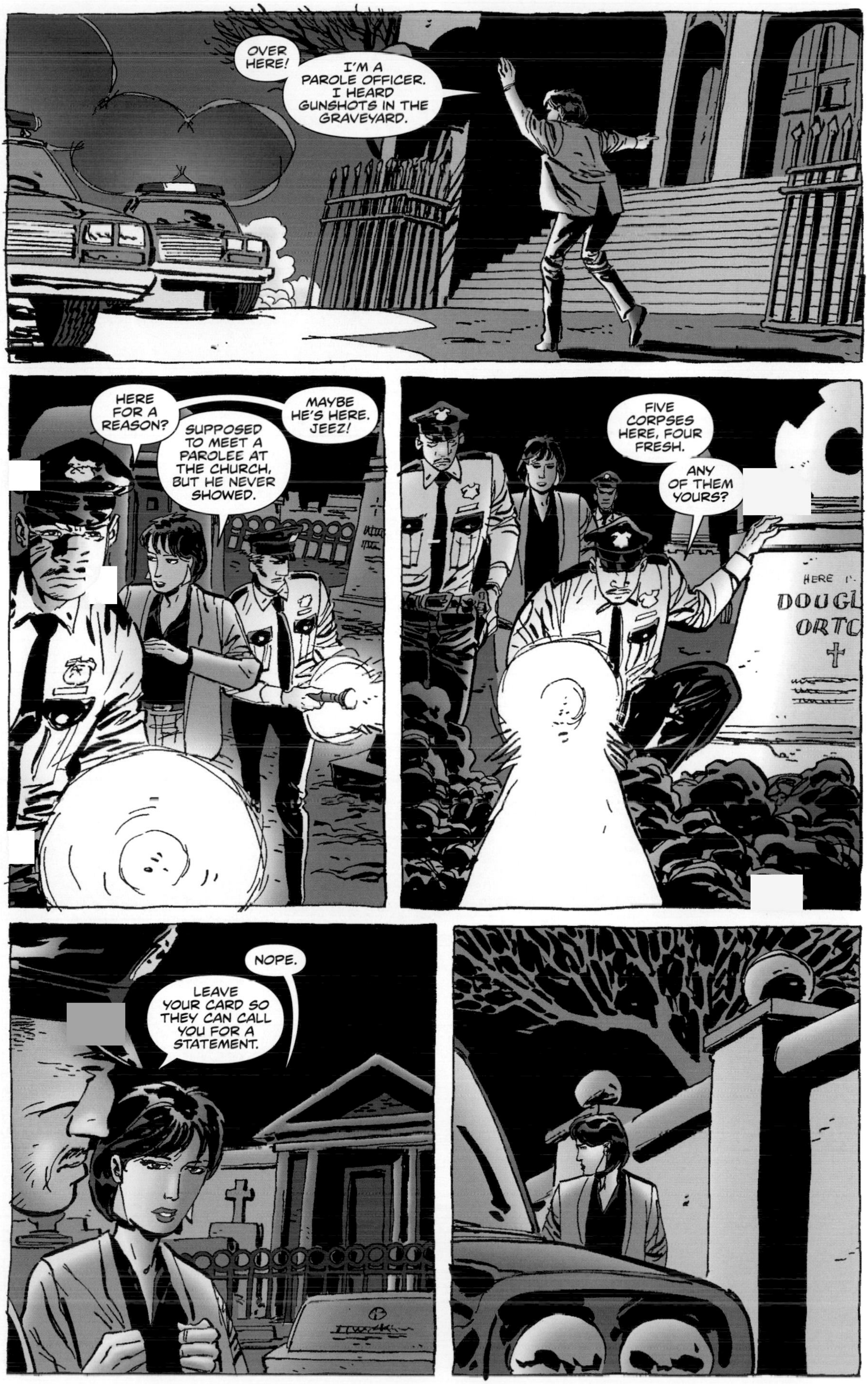
OVER HERE!
I'M A PAROLE OFFICER. I HEARD GUNSHOTS IN THE GRAVEYARD.
HERE FOR A REASON?
SUPPOSED TO MEET A PAROLEE AT THE CHURCH, BUT HE NEVER SHOWED.
MAYBE HE'S HERE. JEEZ!
FIVE CORPSES HERE, FOUR FRESH.
ANY OF THEM YOURS?
HERE I
DOUGL
ORTC
LEAVE YOUR CARD SO THEY CAN CALL YOU FOR A STATEMENT.
NOPE.

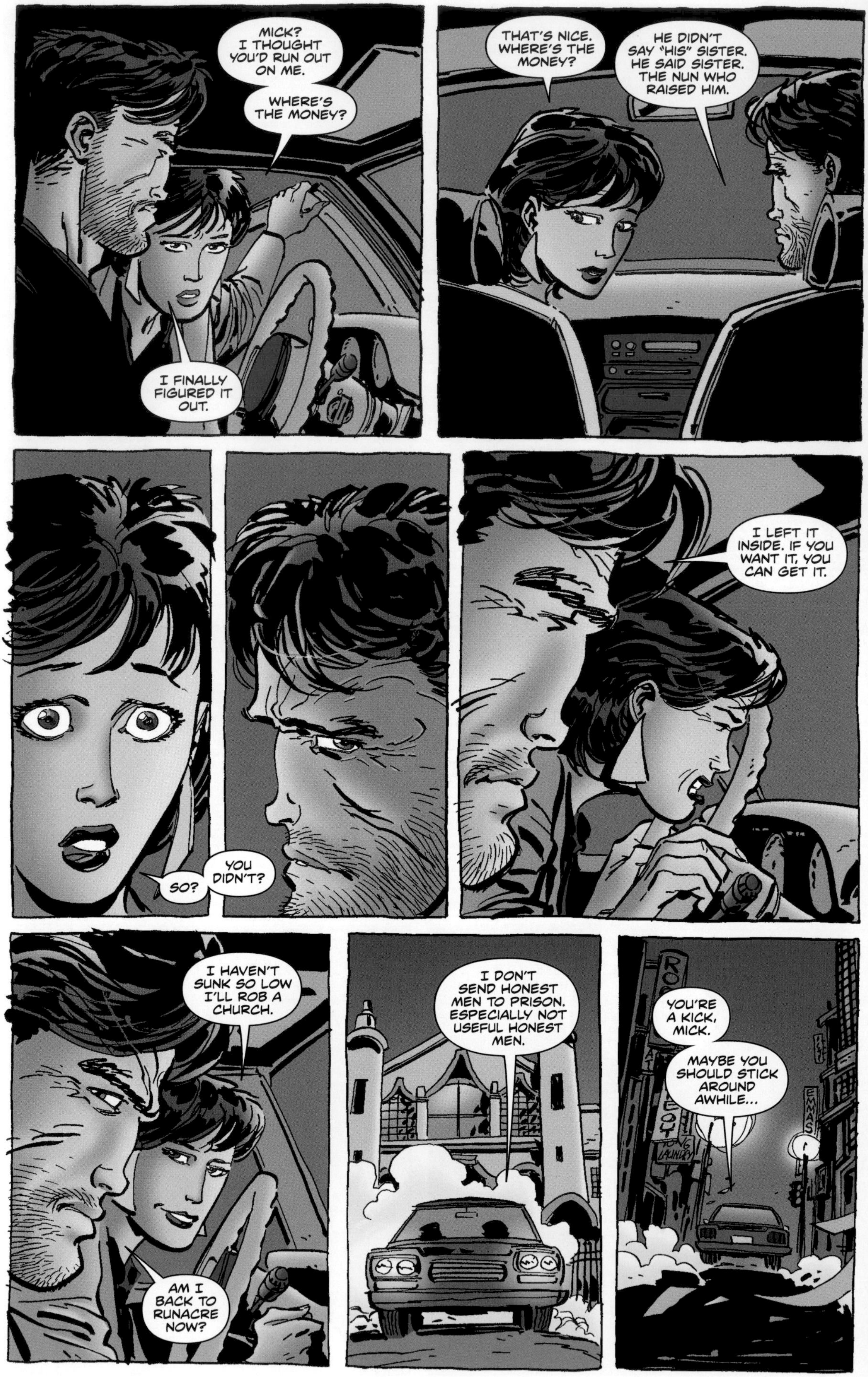
MICK? I THOUGHT YOU'D RUN OUT ON ME.
WHERE'S THE MONEY?
I FINALLY FIGURED IT OUT.
THAT'S NICE. WHERE'S THE MONEY?
HE DIDN'T SAY "HIS" SISTER. HE SAID SISTER. THE NUN WHO RAISED HIM.
SO?
YOU DIDN'T?
I LEFT IT INSIDE. IF YOU WANT IT, YOU CAN GET IT.
I HAVEN'T SUNK SO LOW I'LL ROB A CHURCH.
AM I BACK TO RUNACRE NOW?
I DON'T SEND HONEST MEN TO PRISON. ESPECIALLY NOT USEFUL HONEST MEN.
YOU'RE A KICK, MICK.
MAYBE YOU SHOULD STICK AROUND AWHILE...

DAMNED

EPILOGUE

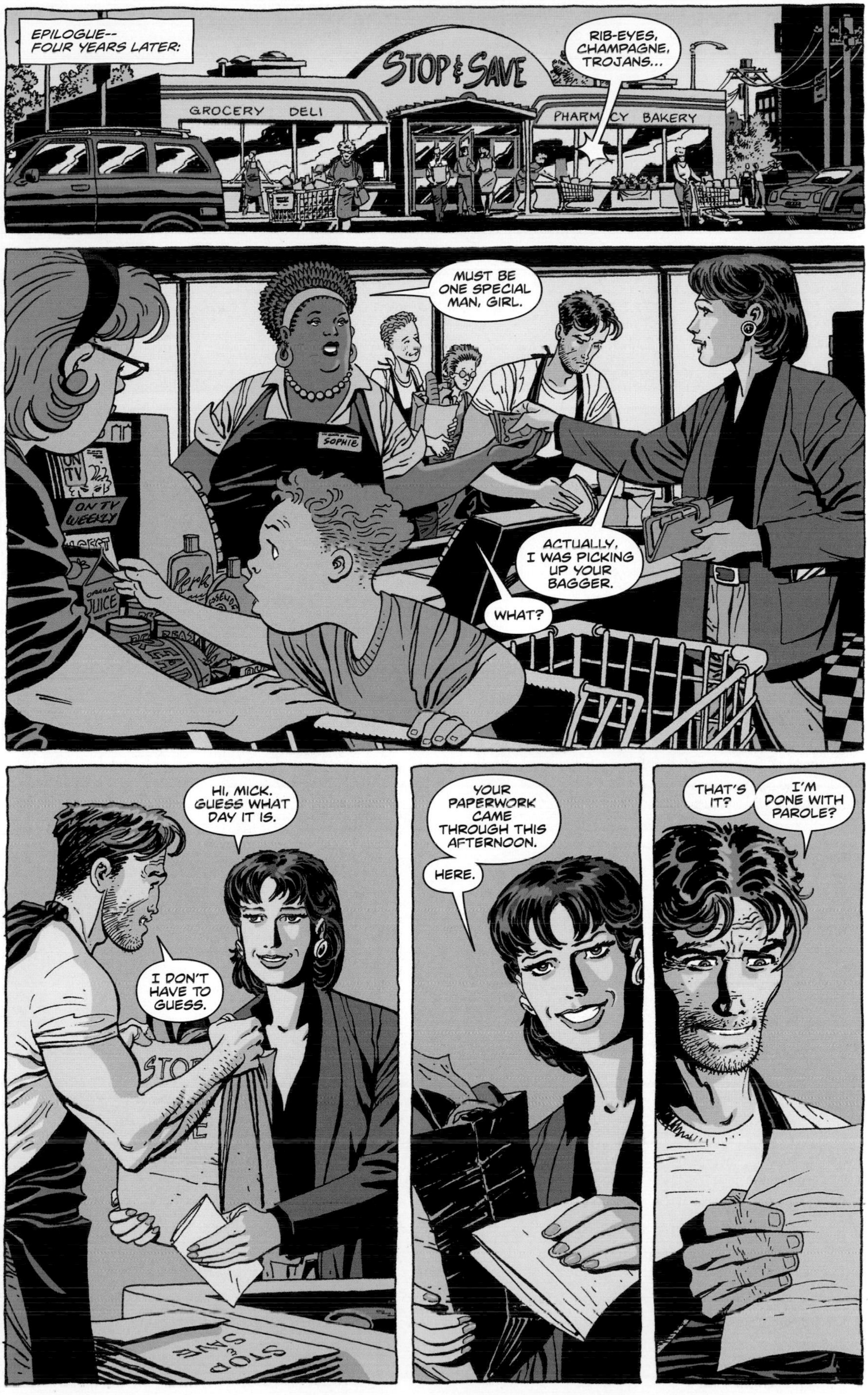
EPILOGUE--
FOUR YEARS LATER:
STOP & SAVE
GROCERY DELI
PHARMACY BAKERY
RIB-EYES, CHAMPAGNE, TROJANS...
MUST BE ONE SPECIAL MAN, GIRL.
SOPHIE
ACTUALLY, I WAS PICKING UP YOUR BAGGER.
WHAT?
HI, MICK. GUESS WHAT DAY IT IS.
I DON'T HAVE TO GUESS.
YOUR PAPERWORK CAME THROUGH THIS AFTERNOON.
HERE.
THAT'S IT?
I'M DONE WITH PAROLE?

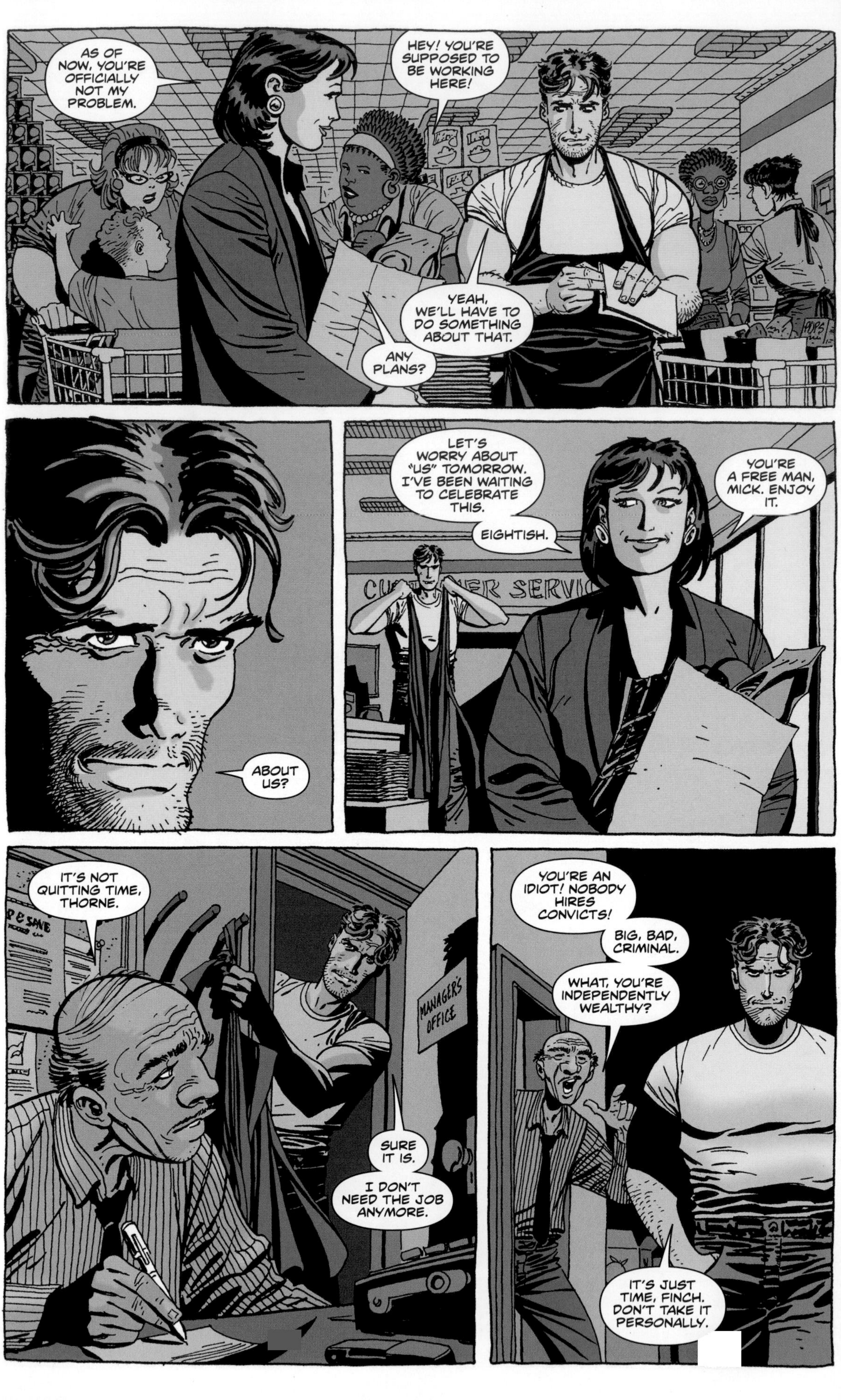
AS OF NOW, YOU'RE OFFICIALLY NOT MY PROBLEM.
HEY! YOU'RE SUPPOSED TO BE WORKING HERE!
YEAH, WE'LL HAVE TO DO SOMETHING ABOUT THAT.
ANY PLANS?
ABOUT US?
LET'S WORRY ABOUT "US" TOMORROW. I'VE BEEN WAITING TO CELEBRATE THIS.
YOU'RE A FREE MAN, MICK. ENJOY IT.
EIGHTISH.
IT'S NOT QUITTING TIME, THORNE.
MANAGER'S OFFICE
SURE IT IS.
I DON'T NEED THE JOB ANYMORE.
YOU'RE AN IDIOT! NOBODY HIRES CONVICTS!
BIG, BAD, CRIMINAL.
WHAT, YOU'RE INDEPENDENTLY WEALTHY?
IT'S JUST TIME, FINCH. DON'T TAKE IT PERSONALLY.

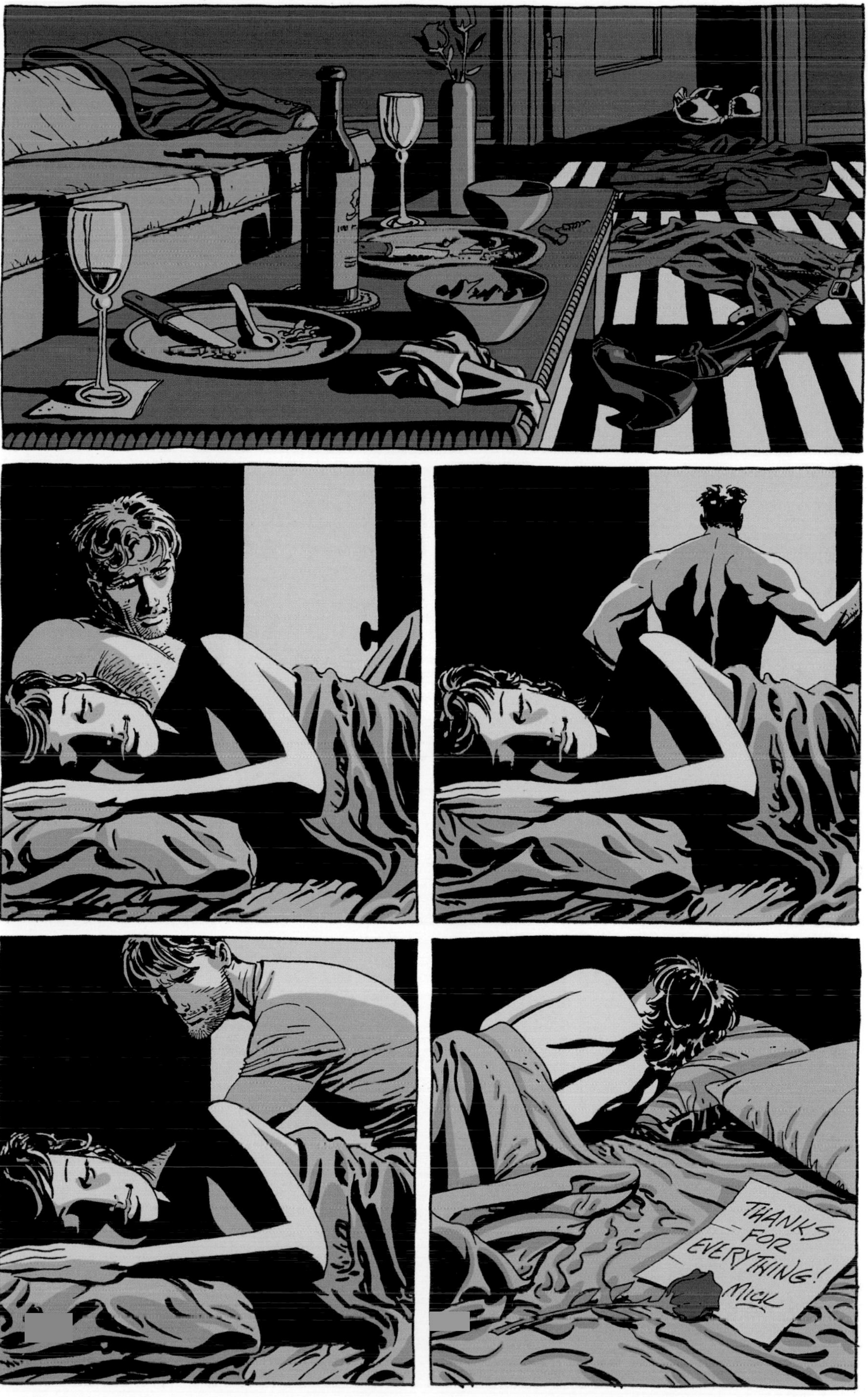
THANKS FOR EVERYTHING!
MICK

IN FOUR YEARS, MICK THORNE HADN'T MENTIONED THAT NIGHT.

HE'D BEEN PATIENT.

LUCKY.

3rd DISTRIC RENEWAL

YOUR TAX DO WORKING FO

DETOUR
NO THRU TRAFFIC

CTION SITE

CAM ORTON WAS LONG GONE.

CHARLOTTE NEVER BROUGHT UP THE MONEY.

NO ONE CONNECTED HIM TO ANYTHING.

SISTER CECILIA EMMACULAT
BELOVED SERVANT OF GOD

NO ONE HAD THOUGHT TO SPEAK TO THE NUN.

HERE LIES
DOUGLAS ORTON

ONLY HE KNEW WHAT SHE'D SAID THAT NIGHT.

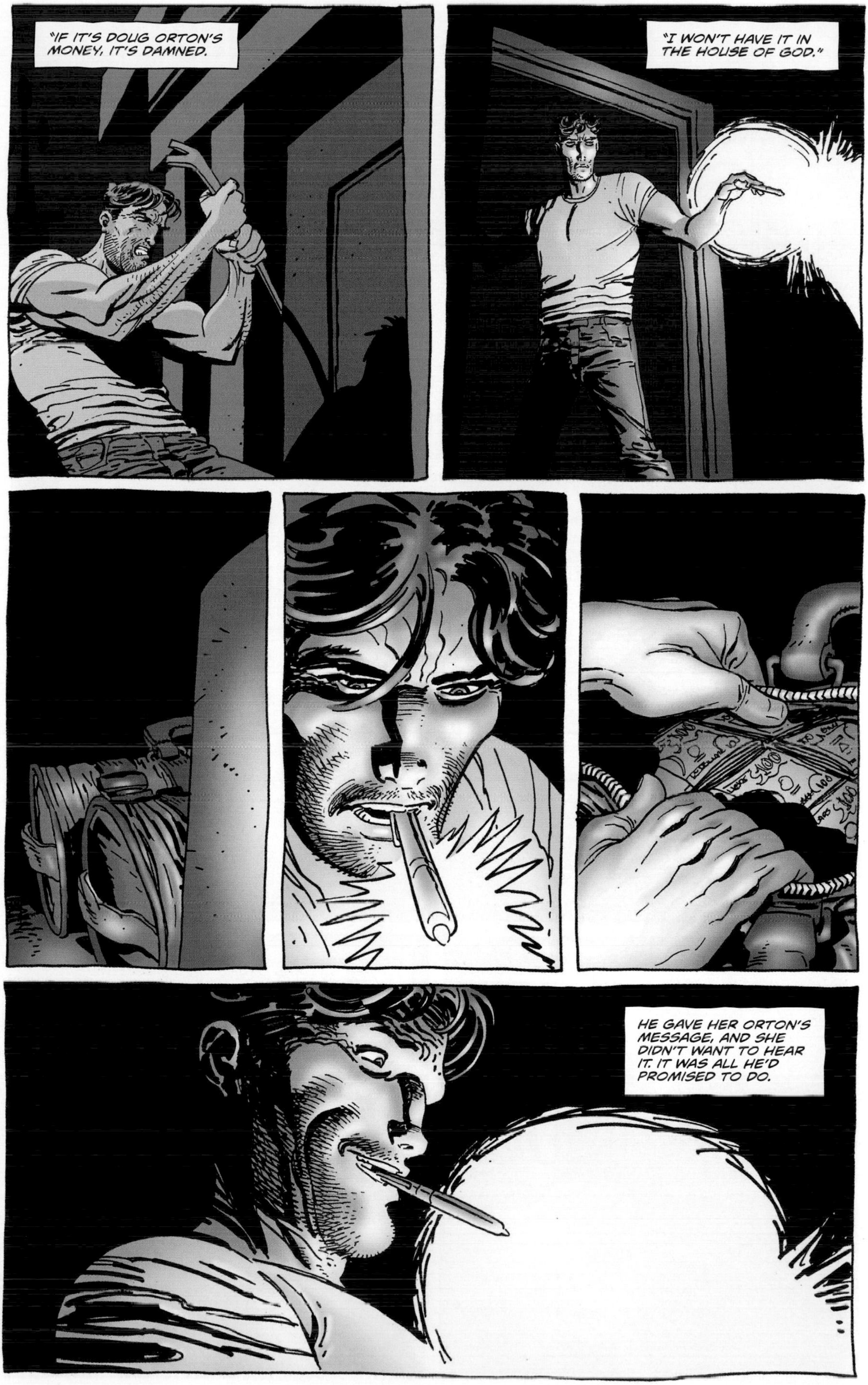
"IF IT'S DOUG ORTON'S MONEY, IT'S DAMNED.
"I WON'T HAVE IT IN THE HOUSE OF GOD."
HE GAVE HER ORTON'S MESSAGE, AND SHE DIDN'T WANT TO HEAR IT. IT WAS ALL HE'D PROMISED TO DO.

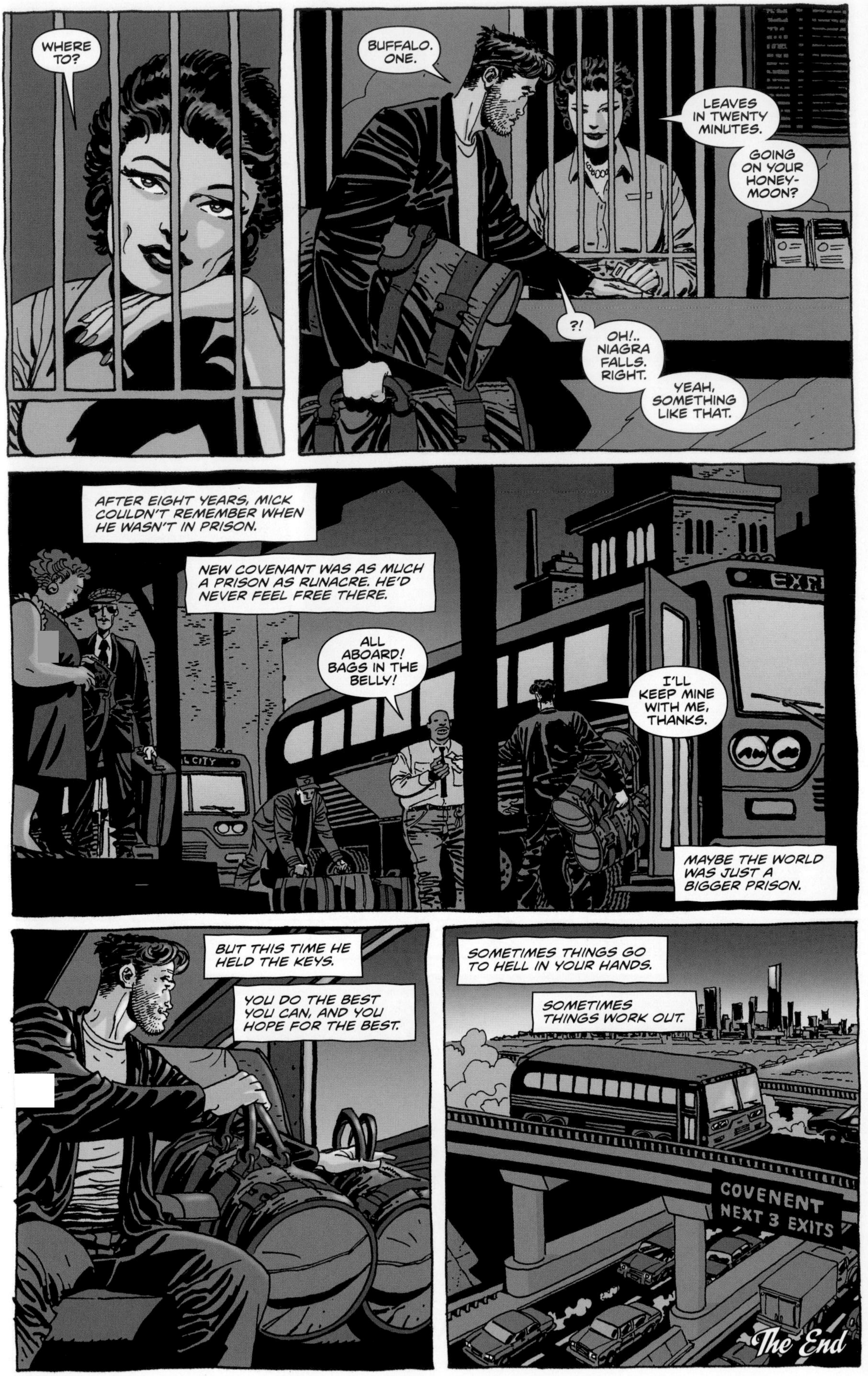
WHERE TO?
BUFFALO. ONE.
LEAVES IN TWENTY MINUTES.
GOING ON YOUR HONEY-MOON?
?!
OH!.. NIAGRA FALLS. RIGHT.
YEAH, SOMETHING LIKE THAT.
AFTER EIGHT YEARS, MICK COULDN'T REMEMBER WHEN HE WASN'T IN PRISON.
NEW COVENANT WAS AS MUCH A PRISON AS RUNACRE. HE'D NEVER FEEL FREE THERE.
ALL ABOARD! BAGS IN THE BELLY!
I'LL KEEP MINE WITH ME, THANKS.
MAYBE THE WORLD WAS JUST A BIGGER PRISON.
BUT THIS TIME HE HELD THE KEYS.
YOU DO THE BEST YOU CAN, AND YOU HOPE FOR THE BEST.
SOMETIMES THINGS GO TO HELL IN YOUR HANDS.
SOMETIMES THINGS WORK OUT.
COVENENT NEXT 3 EXITS
The End

ANATOMY OF A COVER
BY MIKE ZECK

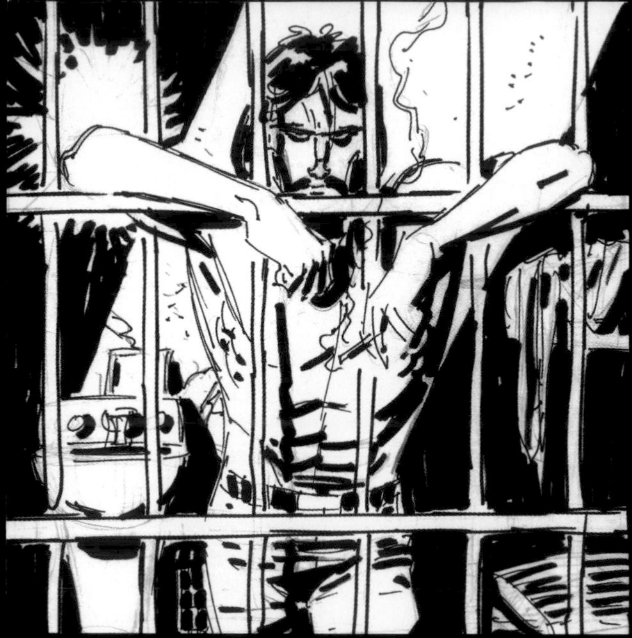
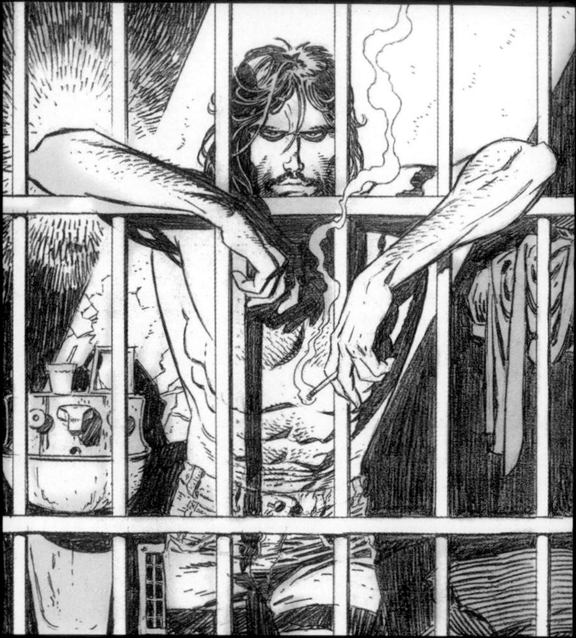
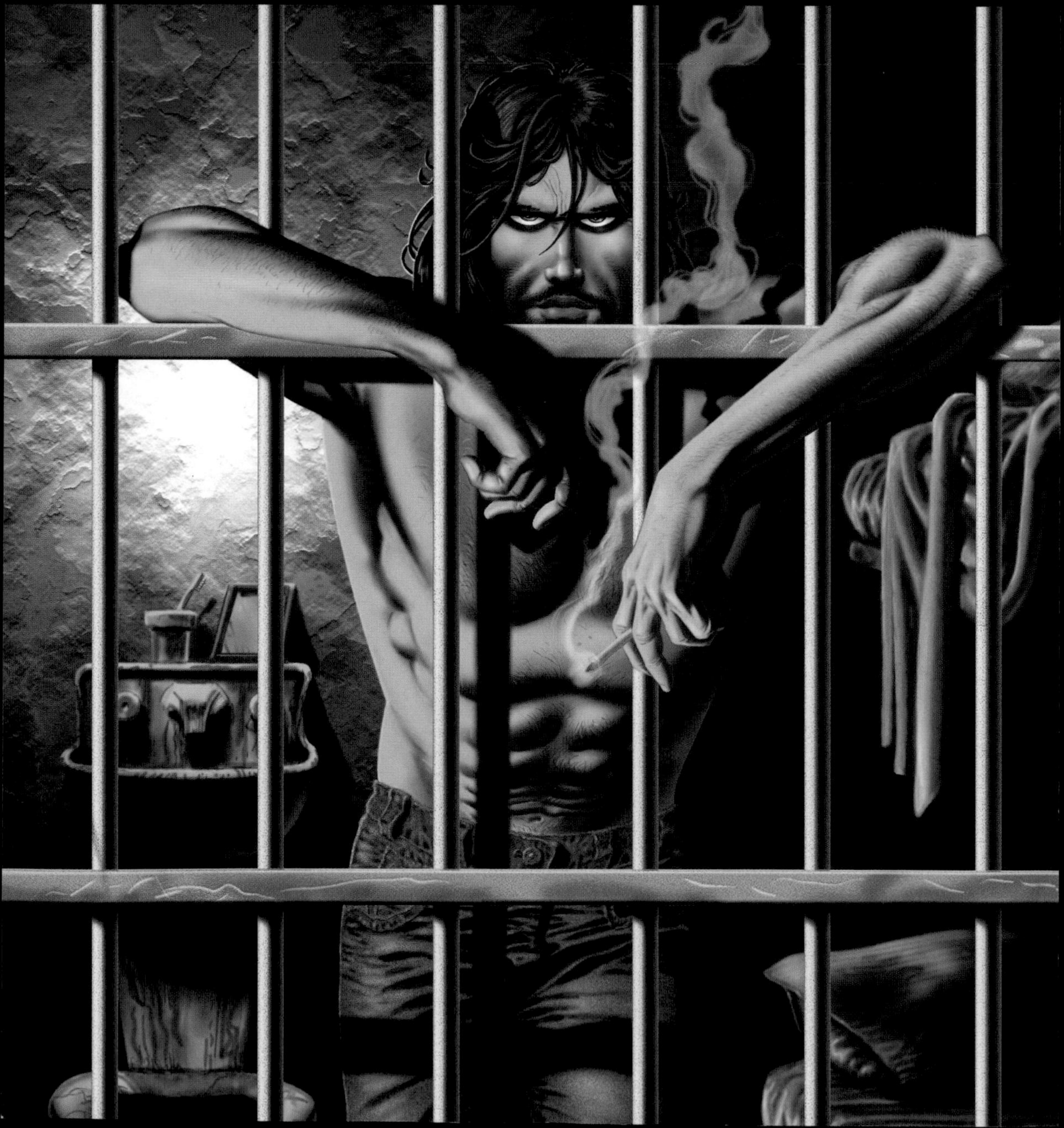

ISSUE ONE

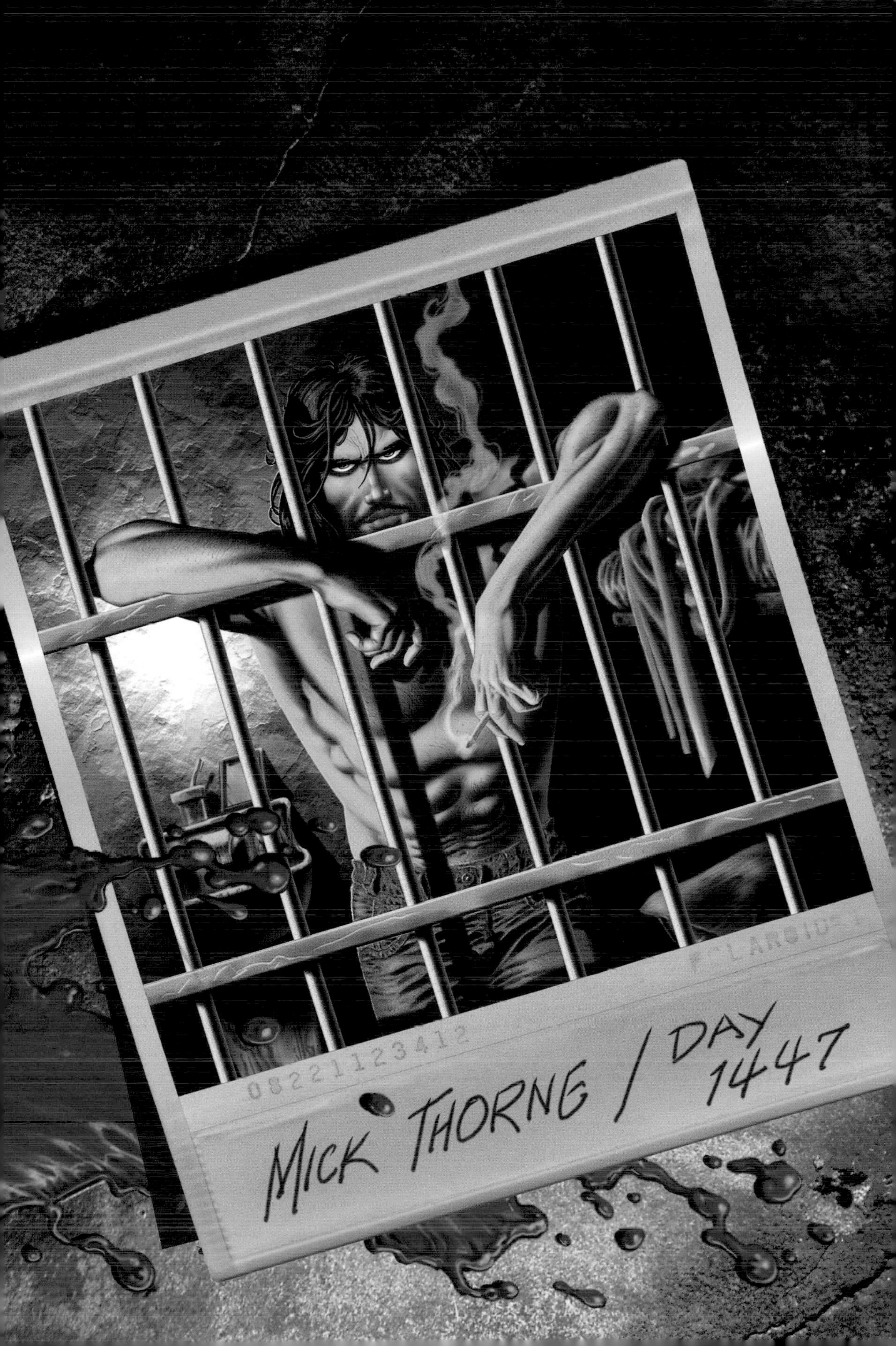
POLAROID
08221123412
MICK THORNE / DAY 1447

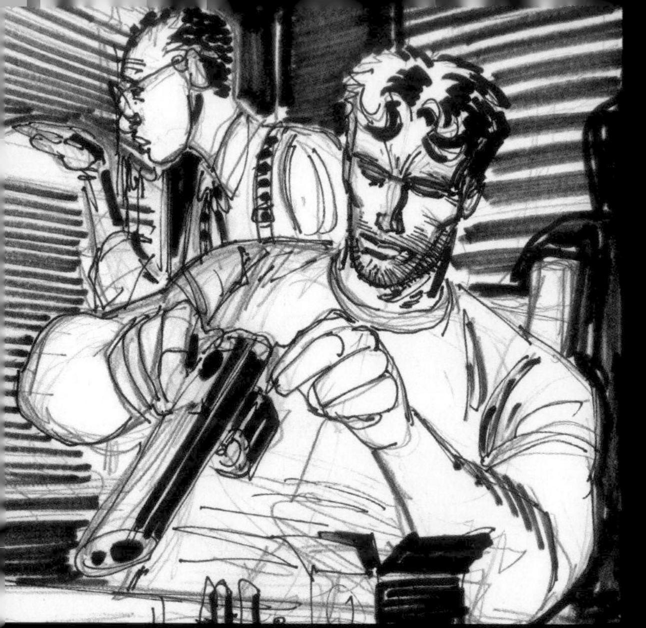
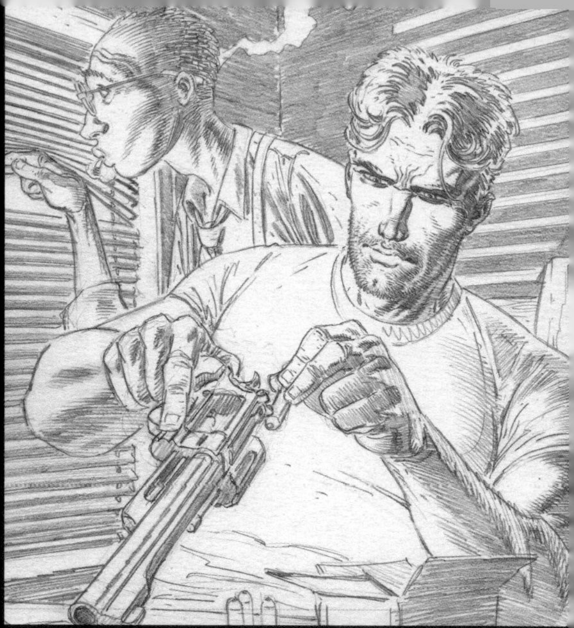
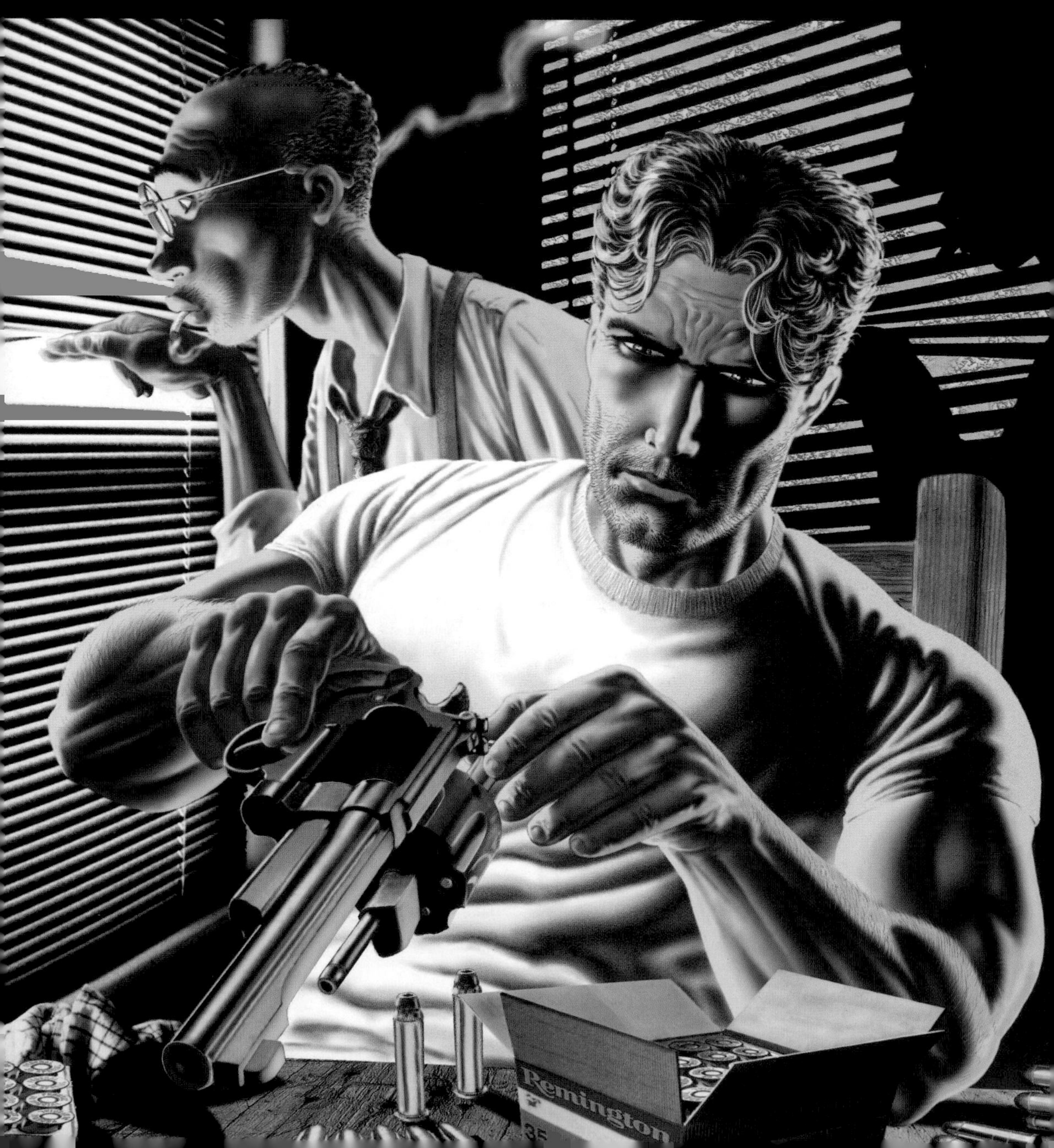
Remington
35

ISSUE TWO

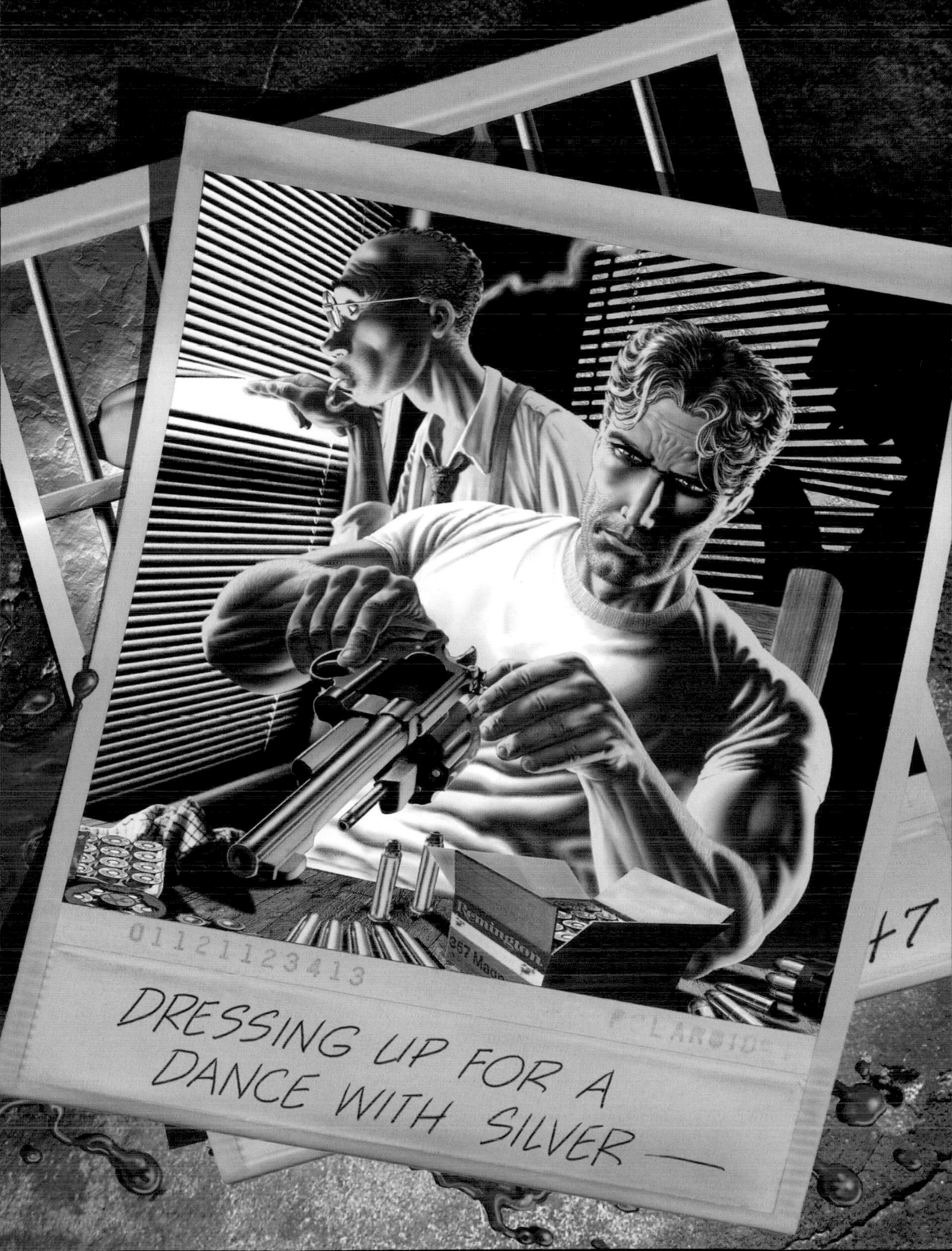
Remington
357 Mag
01121123413
DRESSING UP FOR A
DANCE WITH SILVER —

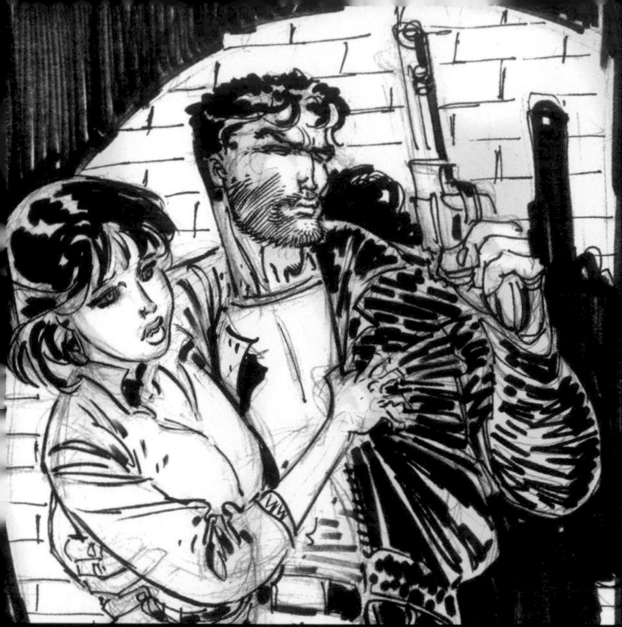
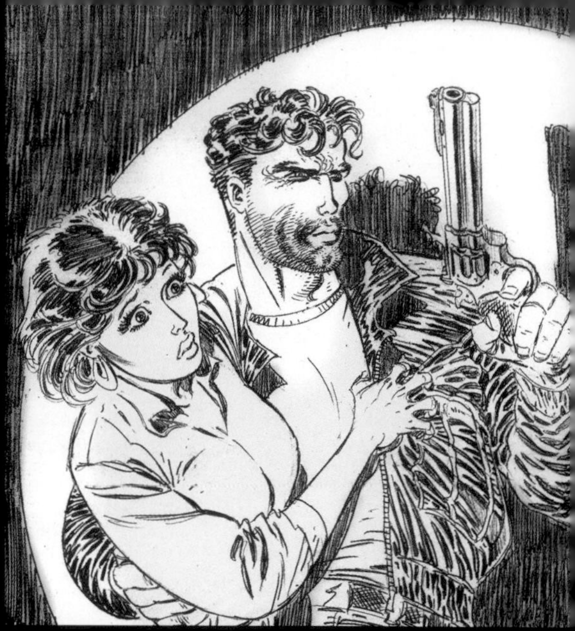
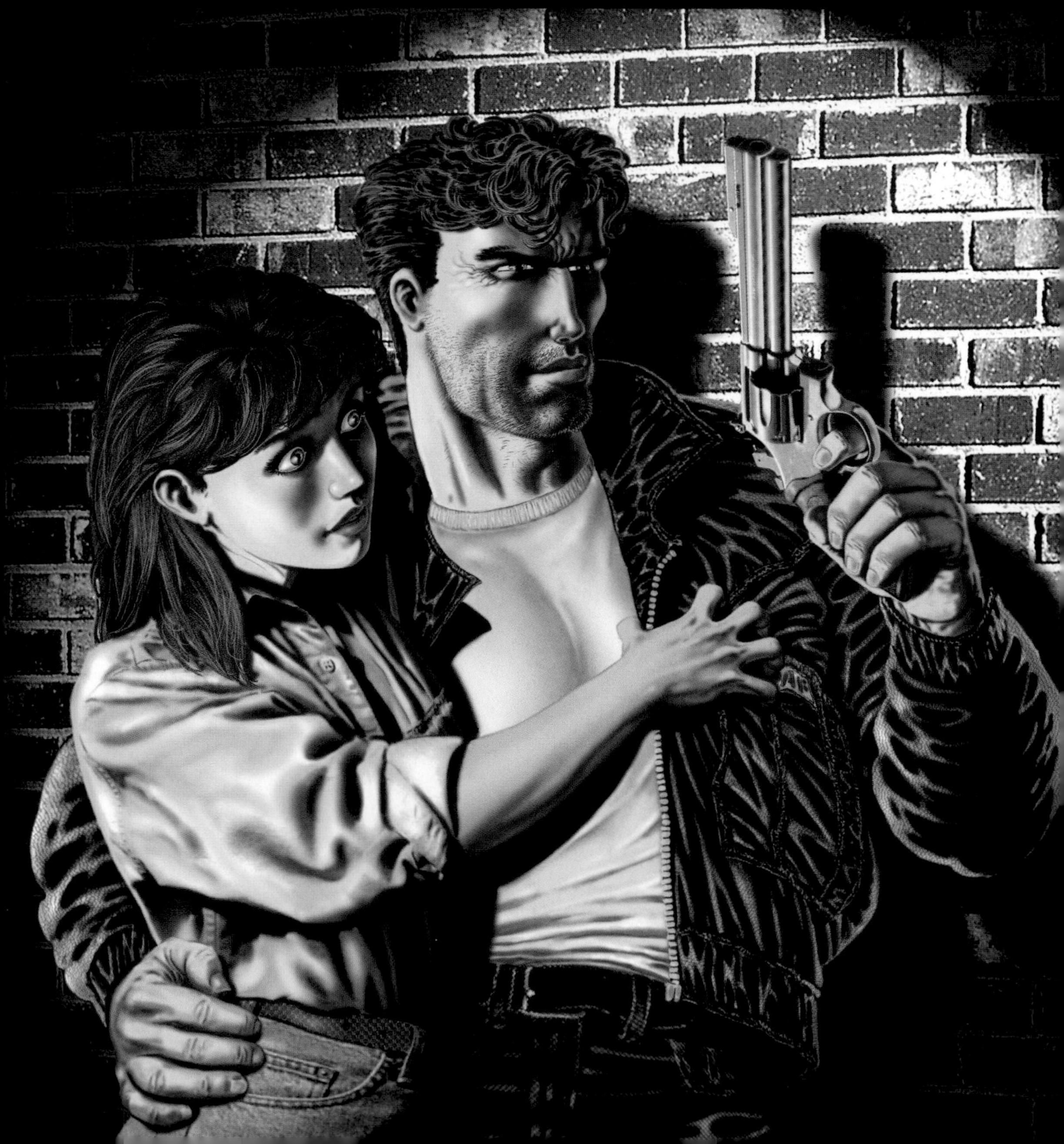

ISSUE THREE

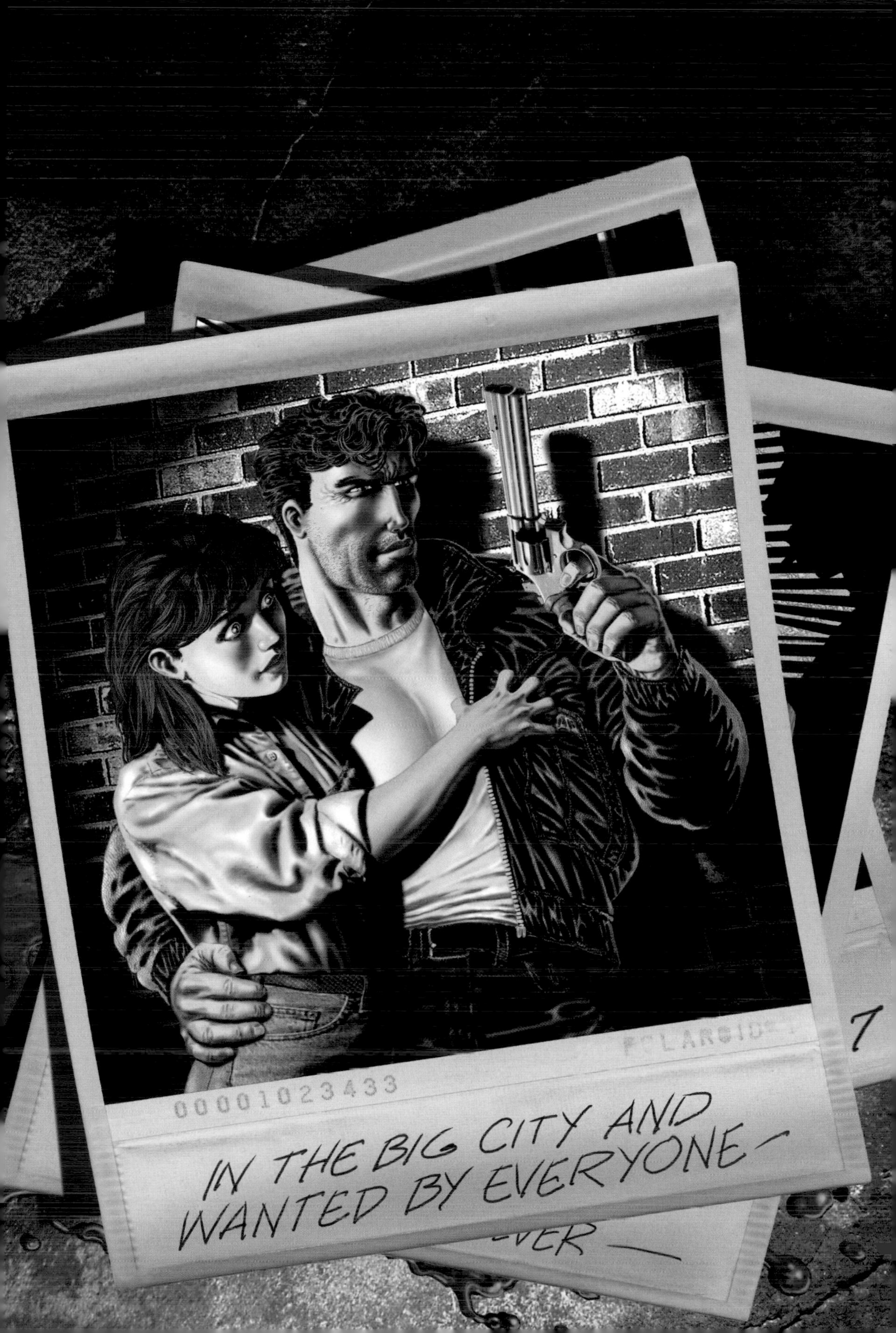
00001023433
IN THE BIG CITY AND
WANTED BY EVERYONE—

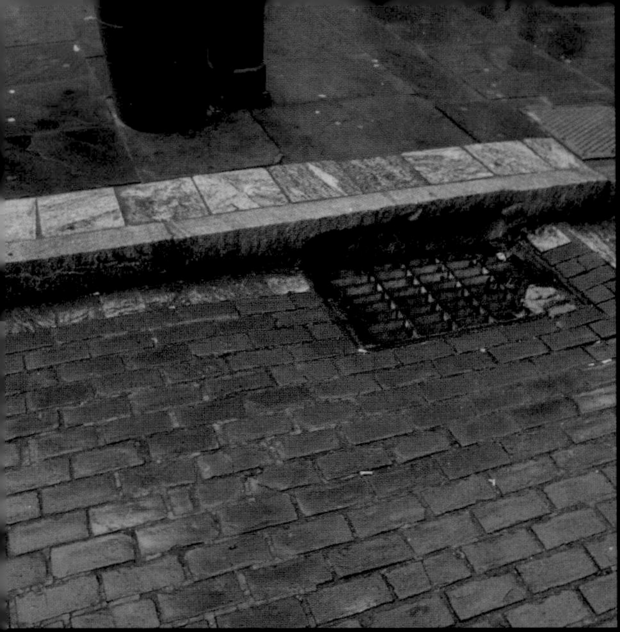
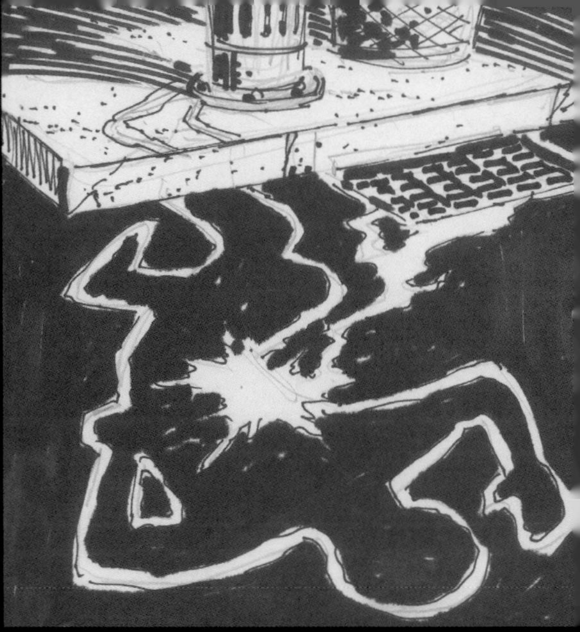
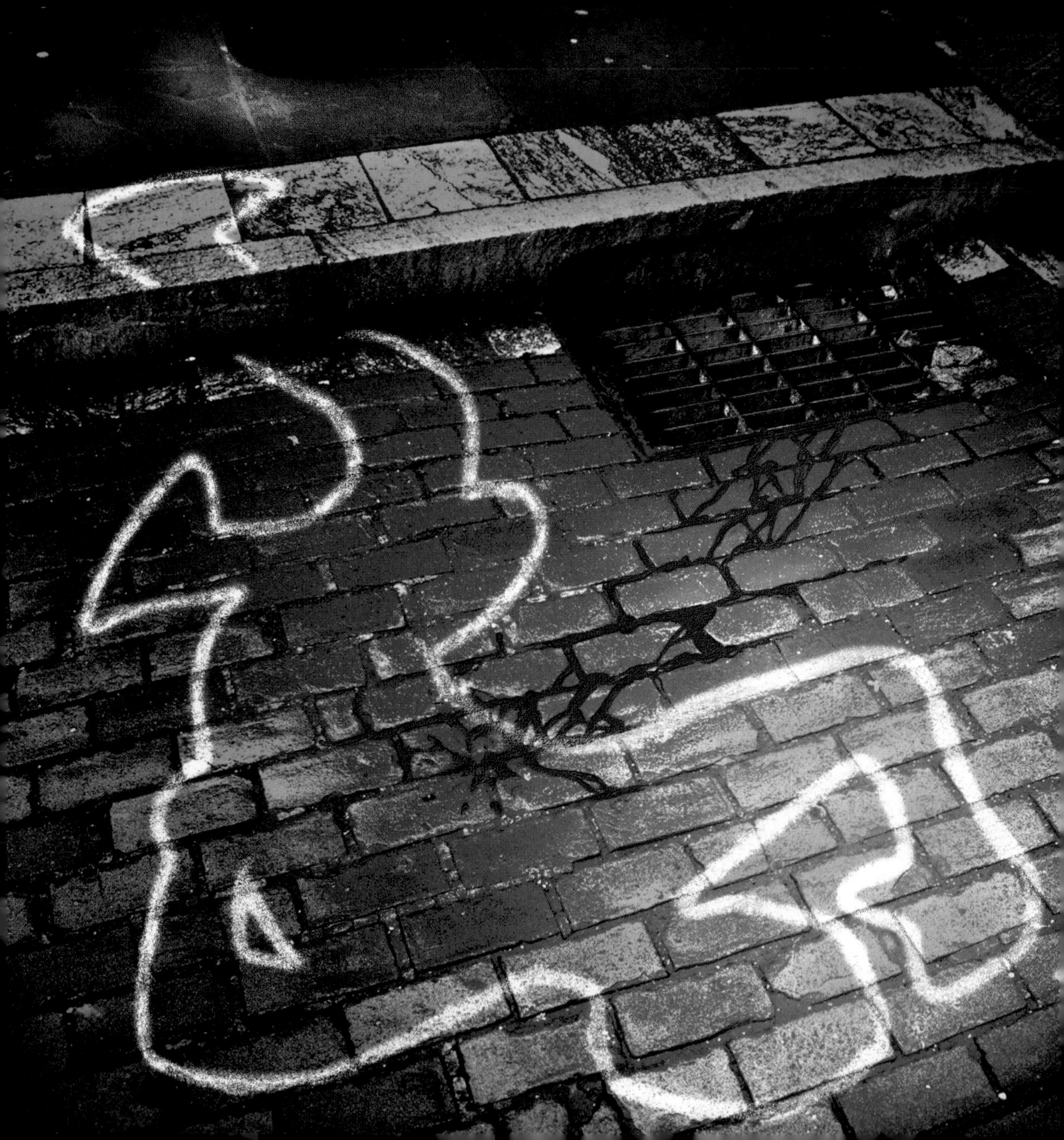

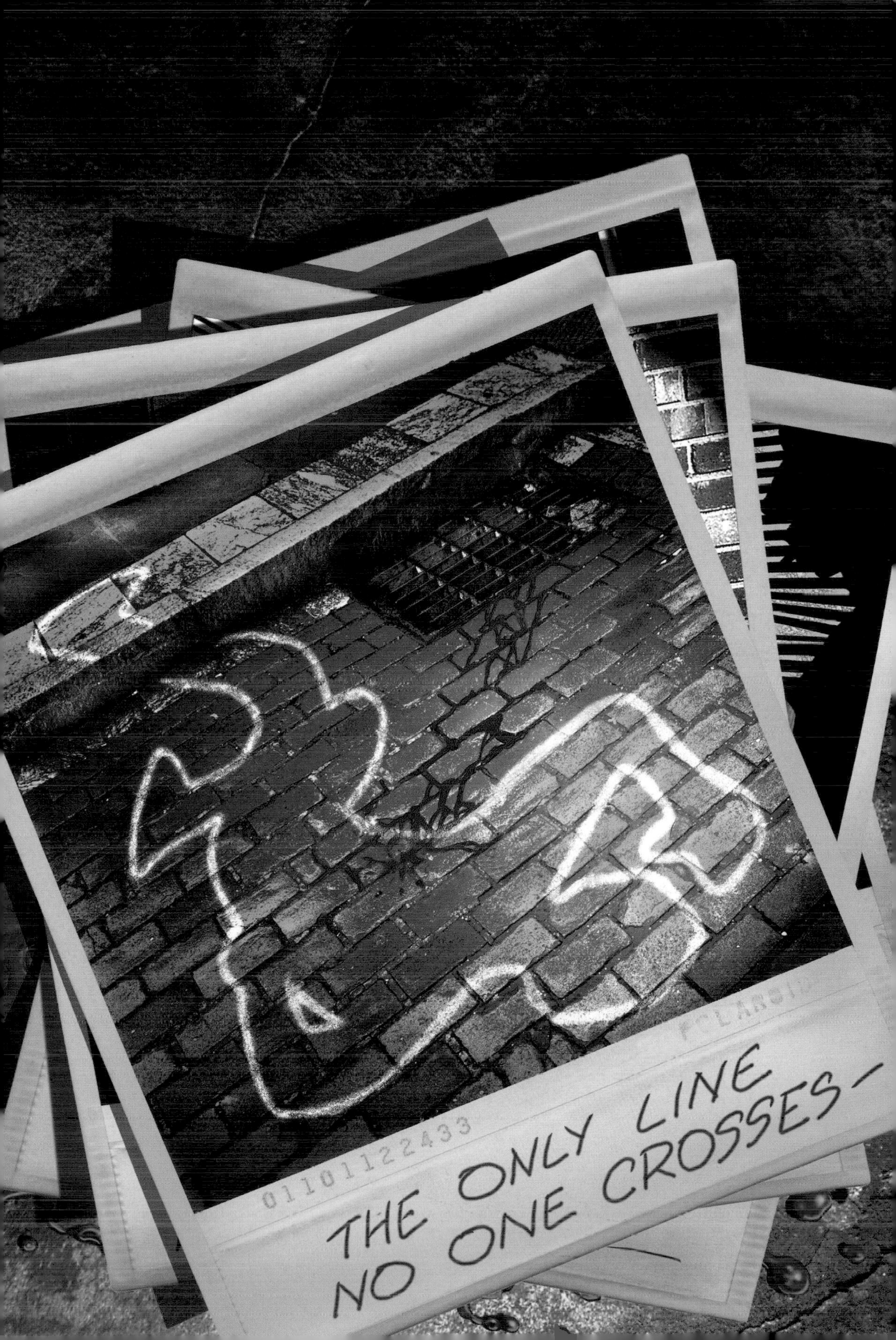
POLAROID
01101122433
THE ONLY LINE
NO ONE CROSSES-

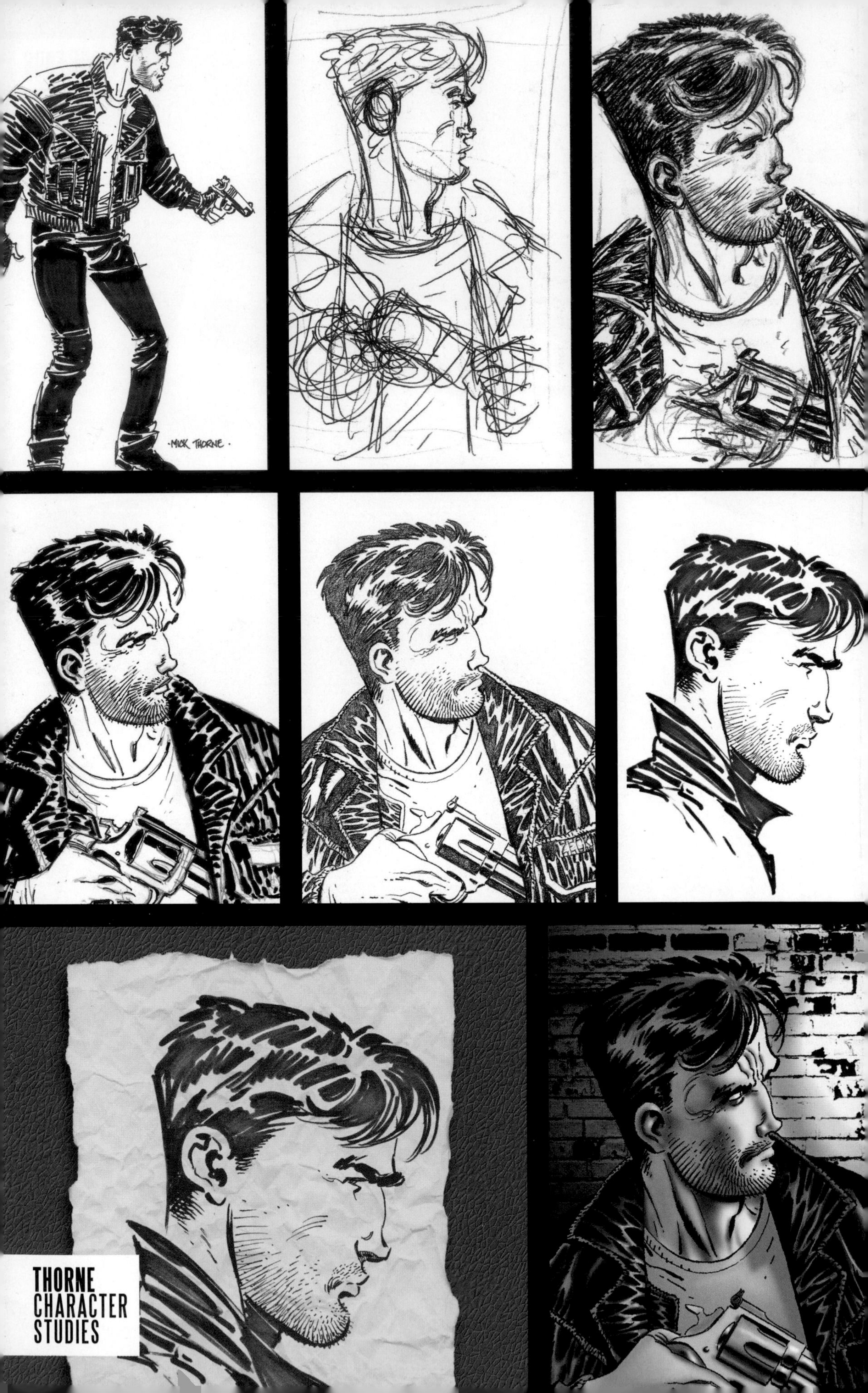
·MICK THORNE·

THORNE
CHARACTER
STUDIES